A Memory of Nightshade

A MEMORY OF NIGHTSHADE

THE
SCENTED COURT
· BOOK 2 ·

A.L. KNORR

Books by A.L. Knorr

Elemental Origins Series

Born of Water

Born of Fire

Born of Earth

Born of Æther

Born of Air

The Elementals

The Siren's Curse

Salt & Stone

Salt & the Sovereign

Salt & the Sisters

Earth Magic Rises

Bones of the Witch

Ashes of the Wise

Heart of the Fae

Arcturus Academy

Firecracker

Fire Trap

Fire Games

Legends of Fire

Source Fire

Rings of the Inconquo

Born of Metal

Metal Guardian

Metal Angel

Mermaid's Return

Returning

Falling

Surfacing

Elemental Novellas

Pyro, A Fire Novella

Heat, A Fire Novella

The Kacy Chronicles

Descendant

Ascendant

Combatant

Transcendent

The Scented Court

A Blossom at Midnight

A Memory of Nightshade

A Daughter of Winter

A Prince of Autumn

To learn more visit www.alknorrbooks.com.

ISBN 5x8 Paperback 978-1-989338-39-1

ISBN 5.5x8.5 Hardcover 978-1-989338-41-4

ISBN 6x9 Large Print Hardcover 978-1-989338-45-2

Part One

Prologue

Sasha stared at the distant smudges of green and brown. He stood with booted feet lodged in two feet of snow, the other Silverfae seated behind him, dozens of them, mostly male, eating and talking in low tones about the conditions of the road, and the way they'd been rounded up and told on very short notice that they'd been selected to make the journey to Solana for the Midwinter Festival.

They'd been told it was time for the Silverfae to branch out. Time to rebuild the network they'd had many decades ago. And Prince Ruskin, Queen Sylifke's only son, was the perfect representative to send, but he needed a beautiful entourage to accompany him. No prince could make an impact without a large group of supporters.

Those chosen had to look more Silverfae than simply fae, which meant only those with the palest eyes, and the whitest hair were asked to go. It also meant only those who were tall, healthy, nicely muscled, and with a beautiful bone structure. They were to enchant the Scented Court with their exotic presence, they were to enthrall the citizens of Solana and Ivryndians visiting from other kingdoms. They were to set the stage for alliances, trade agreements and open roads between Silverfall and the other nations of Ivryndi. They were to bring back wagonloads—transitioning into sleighs at the border—full of Solanan perfumes and cosmetics, beautifully scented products to enhance the ice-white hair and porcelain skin of the Silverfae elite.

They had been warned they would have to endure some difficulties. The weather for example would be uncomfortably warm. They would sweat. They might have to change or even bathe multiple times per day. There would be irritating insects, which could also be noisy at night. These flying critters were special to the court and even allowed indoors. The latter was whispered in horror. The food would be too rich, too varied, poorly combined and poorly prepared. The courtiers would be shallow and would not understand Silverfae culture or etiquette. They would have their own strange ways of behaving, which might involve unusual rituals, ridiculous ceremonies and trumpery.

By the time Prince Ruskin's entourage had been fully informed and were ready to leave, Sasha was very confused, but too embarrassed to ask someone to clarify whether this trip was a privilege or a punishment, an honor or a castigation.

Due to actions his father—Elvio, Queen Sylifke's ex-sorcerer—had taken when Sasha was too young to remember, Sasha was a member of an undesirable family.

These same actions had forever bent Elvio like a tree growing on an intolerably windy slope, prematurely aged and deformed. Yet Sasha had still been chosen for this mission, not because he had the right build and features, but because the purpose of the trip was only partly to do with alliances.

What the other Silverfae did not know, was that Prince Ruskin was looking for someone. Someone who had been poorly described in a poem. A poem that Sasha was only allowed to read part of—and he was certainly not allowed to understand the significance of this person.

Sasha, promised by his father to Queen Sylifke as payment for his mistakes, had been raised alongside Prince Ruskin at the Court of Silverfall. They'd had the same fencing master, the same tutors, the same elocution training and language classes. They were even friendly once, when they were young boys. But those memories were so faded and Sasha and Ruskin were so clearly no longer friends that it left Sasha wondering whether those memories were merely tricks of his mind.

It had all changed when Sasha hit a major growth spurt at the age of fourteen. In the course of a year he'd gained six inches over Ruskin. Where the boys had once been well matched, now Sasha was undeniably advantaged over the shorter, stockier prince. Though Ruskin was older by a mere seven months, Sasha's voice had changed first, he was able to grow facial hair first; he'd put muscle on faster and was beautifully proportioned, with the long limbs the Silverfae admired. The females had taken obvious notice of him at court, even the daughters of the richest nobles and most powerful aristocracy.

By the age of fifteen, Ruskin—a previously decent lad with nice manners and gracious speech—had become hostile toward Sasha. He still took every opportunity to lord his royal heritage, never letting Sasha forget that Elvio had betrayed Queen Sylifke, shaming himself and his kin. Yes, Sasha was permitted to live at court to pay off the debt, but Sasha had traitor's blood running through his veins, he had a deceiver's name, and a turncoat's genes. Sasha came to dread his classes, because in every session Ruskin was there, abusing him, calling him ugly names, cheating to beat him—while the instructors and masters looked the other way. Ruskin was the prince, Sasha an indentured servant with no one to advocate for him. His only friend had been Rialta.

Rialta.

Surely the other reason he was chosen for this mission.

The big white direwolf bounded through the snow on the mountainside, then stuck her face deep in the powdery stuff and froze, still as marble, listening for prey. She exploded high into the air in a powerful and graceful leap, sending her snout straight down upon her prey. She did this at least a dozen times before she was full.

Sasha was the only fauna fae in the Silverfall Court, despised as much as he was admired, a source of disgust as much as fascination. What kind of fae has a bond with an animal? No one could deny the benefits of being magically bonded with a creature like Rialta. She made every hunt successful, she lifted the heart of anyone who set eyes upon her, she delighted the young Silverfae and shared her body heat with Sasha on bitterly cold nights… which was all of them. Yet somehow, she was also sneered at, a target of derision, and Sasha considered inferior because of his strange magical union with a "smelly overgrown dog."

This too was Prince Ruskin's doing. His trail of sycophants and flatterers—without a drop of genuine love between them—scorned whoever he scorned. Whom he ridiculed, they ridiculed more viciously. Whom he derided, they disparaged even more bitterly.

One benefit of this journey to Solana was the chance for a bit of air, time away from court and its snide residents. In Solana, the Silverfae would be on their best behavior, and one of their imperatives was to give an impression of unity and decency among themselves. Sasha looked forward to not being the brunt of open gibes, and for Rialta to be valued the way familiars should be. After all, Solana had a whole retinue of fauna fae. Sasha was desperately curious about them. But he had to wait patiently to reach the famous palace, lit with etherlights and smelling of roses, so he could see them for himself.

Smiling, Sasha watched Rialta bound through the snow, happy. *They* were happy, and traveling felt good. They had no other friends, but they didn't need anyone aside from each other. Sasha believed he was lucky, blessed, and this blessing was a secret treasure that he carried within his heart, protected like a rare jewel. No one could take it away from him.

Heavy cloud cover blocked out most of the light, but where a few errant shafts pushed through and touched the covered hillside and white-dusted trees, the snow sparkled. It took Sasha's breath away. Beyond this frozen hillside, somewhere far ahead where the brown and green smudges waited, was their destination: a land without snow. They would see the green of leaves, and the rusty brown of iron-rich soils, they would see flowers. No one had prepared Sasha for the feeling of anticipation. Even the bad stuff would be easy to bear to get to see the earth uncovered and smelling like something other than frozen minerals and falling snow. Sasha's whole body swept with goosebumps. Solana's winter was balmier than Silverfall's warmest summer.

"Wolfboy! Eat or starve. We move in ten minutes."

Grudgingly, Sasha returned to the circle of courtiers. Someone passed him a plate of the worst cuts of cheese, the driest and hardest jerky, and stalest crusts of bread. A chunk of dirty snow floated in his tea.

He sat without a word of complaint and swallowed it all down.

Chapter One:

Jessamine

The reins slipped through Jess's fingers as she pulled her mare to a stop in front of the cottage she had grown up in. She stared at it. Had it always been so small?

Just ahead of her, Regalis dismounted. He took the bridles of both horses with an encouraging smile. "Welcome home, Jessamine."

They hadn't talked much on the journey but somehow that had been okay. It had been comfortable, even companionable. Because of his respectful silence, Jessamine had begun to suspect that Regalis understood what she was feeling better than she did herself. She'd hardly noticed the scenery or the passing traffic. When they'd arrived in countryside that she recognized as being very near Dagevli, Jess gave a jolt—she couldn't remember most of the journey. There was one moment she could recall clearly, where

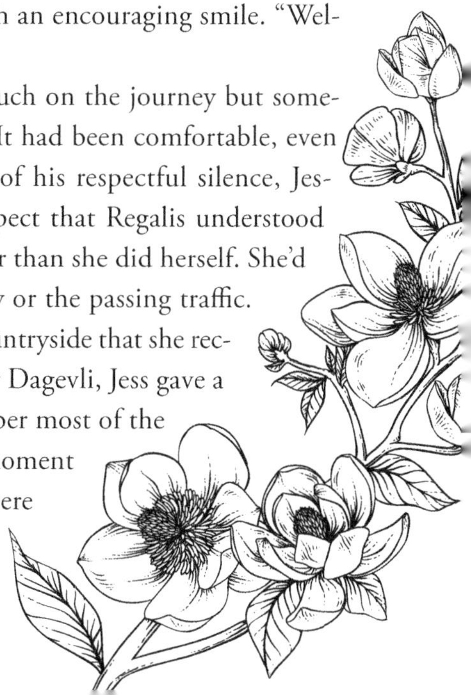

a rider went sprinting by them at top speed, one hand holding his hat to his head, the other urging his steed on. Clods of dirt flew up behind him as Regalis and Jessamine guided their horses out of his way. Otherwise, the entire journey home her mind had been a storm of questions, speculations, scenarios. What would Marion think of what Jess had done in Rahamlar? Or should Jess not tell her? At least not until after Marion had explained her own behaviors and secrets.

The self-righteousness of being the wronged party was still present as Jess bounced back and forth between speculating on the reasons her mother might never have told her about her twin, and how exactly she herself was going to explain that she'd invaded a foreign kingdom, poisoned a handful of unseelie guards, and rescued a lady. She and Laec had not just helped a woman in need, but someone important, someone that even King Agir and Queen Esha knew. Was Jess proud of herself? Was she ashamed? She examined her feelings the way a child examines an exotic insect or sparkly mineral, until she finally determined that she felt both… at the same time, which was overwhelming.

The breeze had a nip to it, lifting tendrils of her hair as she stood at the front gate. She felt Beazle shift against her scalp as he woke up.

We're home, Beaze, she thought.

The cottage looked smaller and the front garden—Greta's favorite place, Jess thought with a pang—had browned and decayed as summer's window came to a close. The garden beds behind the cottage that stretched almost all the way to the banks of the stream at the back of the property, would now be cleared and covered with mulch to rest for the winter.

An ache went through her as she took the paving stones to the front door, passing bare rosebushes, their thorns jutting every which way. Jess had always thought there was something a little humiliating about a rosebush with no foliage, all its charms stripped away, the fragrant petals gone and the bones and spikes exposed.

Jess paused at the door, hitching the bag Ilishec had loaned her higher on her shoulder, and pushed into the cottage. Would there be tension between her and Marion? Of course, but it couldn't be helped, and Jess was too eager for answers for it to matter.

"Mom?"

Hidden in her hair, Beazle gave a quiet chirp. Jessamine was too startled to focus on him. A woman who was not Marion was kneeling on the floor beside her mother's single cot. The woman gasped as she turned toward the door then struggled to her feet, bracing herself on the cot's wooden frame.

"Jessica? Good heavens, that was fast." The lady's voice cracked.

It took Jess a moment to recognize Hanna. Clair's mother's face was so ravaged by sorrow, pain and shock that it took Jessamine time to identify her neighbor. It took her several seconds longer to focus past Hanna… at the figure lying on the cot. Marion. Pale, eyes closed, utterly still.

"Hanna? What—"

"Oh, Jess." Hanna rushed to her, wrapping her arms around her and squeezing her tight against her bosom, one hand curled over Jess's skull, like she was still a little girl. "I didn't expect you to arrive so soon. You startled me, darling. Honey… I'm so sorry. It happened so fast—"

Jess stared at her mother's face over Hanna's arm, still confused. She pushed away, going to her knees by the bed. Marion's strong, calloused hands lay on her stomach, one crossed over the other. Jess was afraid to touch her mother, afraid of what she might feel. But she had to. She put the pads of her fingers on the back of her mother's hand, then, slowly, lay her whole hand over Marion's. Her mother was cool to the touch, cool and lifeless.

Hanna's warm hand touched her shoulder. "I found her on the floor last night. At first I was sure she'd fainted, maybe from too much wine. My own mam would faint from time to time, but"—Hanna took a shuddery inhale—"her face…"

Jess's gaze went to Marion's eyes, nose, mouth. Her mother appeared to be asleep, perfect in restful stillness.

"Her face… what?"

Hanna swallowed. "You can't see it now because she's… passed on, but the right half of her face wasn't working properly. So I knew it was more serious than fainting. She brushed me off, saying it would go away on its own. It took me an hour, but I convinced her to let me get Mr. Moody. I sent Tad, but before they returned Marion had a second spell. After that one she was just… gone. By the time Tad and Mr. Moody arrived, there was nothing he could do for her."

Gone. The word was a cold wind slicing through thin clothes. Gone. Gone, like Greta was gone.

I'll never see those eyes open again. She'll never look at me again, she'll never smile at me. She'll never know what I did… and I'll never know her secrets.

Jess's eyes felt dry. She rubbed them with her knuckles. Why wasn't she crying? She felt like she should be crying, but nothing was coming.

"…a stroke." Hanna was still explaining. "That's what Mr. Moody said it was. One stroke, then another. I'm sorry, love. I sent a messenger with a letter for you. You must have passed him on the road."

The sprinting horseman holding his hat down? He'd been carrying a message for her.

Beazle emerged from her hair and crawled down Jessamine's sleeve, slowly, creeping like someone inching down from a tower by a rope. He reached her elbow, pausing with his little snout in the air to sniff, full of caution. With a little hop, Beazle landed on Marion's stomach.

Hanna took in a quick breath, followed by a satisfied sigh. "Beazle! I haven't seen him in such a long time. There have been many days in the last sixteen years that I was sure I must have imagined him. Now here he is, the little darling."

"You didn't imagine him," Jess murmured.

Beazle sat very still on the rough fabric of Marion's dress. Then he turned big liquid eyes up at Jess, and something broke inside her. The truth was in his gaze. She hung her head, finally feeling a trickle of hot moisture gather behind her eyelids. Her mother really was dead.

"And the other one? The butterfly? It was Greta, yes?"

"Gone." Jess sounded so empty, like her voice was coming out through the hollow throat of a sculpture made of glass. "Greta was killed. Just last week."

"Oh, love."

Hanna knelt beside her on the floor, folding Jess's slender hand inside of her own. They were as rough and strong and calloused as Marion's hands, the hands of a mother. Jess pressed her shoulder against Hanna, feeling her solidity and warmth. They sat like that until the sound of subdued voices and a squeaky wagon wheel signaled the arrival of villagers.

"They're here to take her away," Hanna said. "Prepare her for burial."

Beazle flapped to Jess's shoulder but didn't crawl inside her hair. It was pointless to hide now. The one who wanted so badly to keep him a secret would never protest about him again.

Clair and Tad came into the cottage with two men. Her old friend's face was full of empathy and sorrow. Silently, Jess let herself be folded into Clair's arms, then Tad's. If they stared at Beazle, Jess hardly noticed, she was just thankful they didn't make her talk.

They watched as Marion's body was wrapped and carried to the two-wheeled cart sitting in the street, hitched to a dappled gray horse.

Regalis stood at the fence, watching, pale and quiet. When Jess emerged from the cottage with Hanna's arm wrapped around her shoulders, she felt the weight of the

Fahyli's gaze. Distantly, Ferrugin—Regalis's hawk familiar—screamed, a mournful and lonely sound.

Jess couldn't tear her eyes from her mother's wrapped body.

How could you leave me like this? I'm too young… far too young to lose you.

The world was a different place now.

With another squeak from the wagon wheel, Marion's body was solemnly escorted toward the village center. Watching the wagon grow smaller and smaller, Jessamine felt the last of her childhood fall away, like the two halves of a walnut shell.

The next couple of days were a blur of visits from villagers. Jessamine received many lingering and loving hugs from people she had known all her life. None of them had ever guessed at her true nature, at least not out loud. Since it was now widely known that she was Calyx, a few boasted that they'd always had suspicions, only to be laughed at.

She could feel their eyes on her, at times staring with admiration, while other looks were less friendly. Perhaps they didn't appreciate being fooled all this time. Beazle never hid, and Jess never once thought about covering her ears. Curious children hovered around her, wanting to talk to her, to ask her about her life in the shining city. But she had nothing to give them, nothing to give anyone. She'd barely stopped looking around for Greta, and now—without any warning—she had sunk to new depths of grief.

Could life really be this way? Someone you loved

was there one moment, and the next they were gone? It seemed too cruel to be real, too much for a heart to bear. How did people survive this kind of pain?

She got an answer as the days went by, anticlimactic though it seemed. She continued to wake in the morning, continued to eat to fill her stomach, even if she didn't enjoy the food, she continued to feel the sun on her face. Speckles of autumn rain fell on her hair as she stood with Hanna, Clair and Tad as the villagers lowered Marion's body into the earth. Kind words were spoken, mournful songs were sung, and sweet prayers were offered. Then everyone dispersed and it was all over.

For a long time, Jess stood alone in the graveyard. She felt tears on her face but was hardly aware of weeping. When she sat on her haunches, Beazle dropped into her lap and curled up there, perhaps sensing that Jess had no intention of leaving Marion's resting place any time soon. She put a hand around him and he snuggled against her palm; his tiny pink tongue darted out, licking her thumb.

Time passed. The light dimmed. More speckles of rain fell, like the tears of birds and faeries. The crunch of a dry leaf under a foot brought her back to herself. She turned to see Hanna and Clair. Clair was holding a coat by the shoulders, ready to put it on Jess.

Hanna touched Jessamine's back. "Come darling. You can't stay out here all night."

"I could," Jess replied. She really didn't mind the cold or the damp.

Hanna's look was freighted with something. Expectation? Concern?

"There's something important you need to see."

With tingly legs and a numb mind, Jess got to her feet and joined her neighbors for the walk through town. Clair put the coat over Jess's shoulders and Jess realized only then just how cold she'd really been. Clair stayed by Jess's side as they ate a meal of sourdough bread with butter, and a rich beef stew with homemade noodles. Warmth and Finn's laughter reminded Jess of the life still going on around her, life she felt so distanced from. Jess was grateful for his chatter. When the meal was over she tried to help with clearing the table, but Hanna took her by the hand and led her to a room at the back of the cottage. A bedroom, cozy with a fireplace and a large bed heaped with handmade quilts, pillows, and a knitted throw. A window overlooked the garden, which looked a lot like the Fontana's yard, filled with garden beds on the same sloped land leading down to the stream.

Hanna pulled a small trunk out from under the bed, opened it and withdrew a brown paper wrapping. She lay the package on the quilt and unfolded it with reverence. Inside were a dozen baby bonnets. Some were knit, others made of stiff and durable fabric, some had a little brim to keep the sun off a baby's face. Some were simple, others had frills and faded ribbons. Hanna picked up a small green cap made of brushed cotton.

"Half of these are yours, and half belonged to your brother."

Jess sucked in a breath. Marion was gone, but of course Hanna knew something. She'd been there when Jess and her twin had been born. When Hanna handed her the green baby's cap, she brought it to her nose. It smelled of must and old lavender.

Rubbing the soft fabric with her fingertips, she pictured it hugging the tiny crown of an infant. "Why do you have these?"

Hanna sat on the bed and patted the quilt. Jess sat beside her, stroking her palm over the bonnet.

Hanna picked up another, this one woven with fine yarn dyed the color of a dove's wing. "Your mother didn't want you to find them by accident. Not before she'd had a chance to tell you about him."

Jess felt something inside the cap and turned up the soft brim. A handmade name tag, with letters lovingly stitched in curlicues. Jess held her breath as the name imprinted itself on her heart. She'd had a brother, a brother named…

"Julian Fontana." Saying his name out loud for the first time in her life, she loved the sound of it.

Hanna sighed. "Yes. Jessica and Julian. You were the sweetest wee things, such good babies."

"What happened to him?"

"I don't know."

Jess's heart fell.

But Hanna added, "Not after he was taken away, anyhow."

Jess blinked. "Taken? He didn't die?"

Hanna shook her head. She lay down the gray bonnet and picked up another, this one knit from white yarn with a yellow zig-zag pattern encircling the crown. "These were to hide your ears until your hair was long enough to cover them. Marion hoped it would be enough to protect you."

Protect them?

Hanna turned toward her, her gaze soft but serious. "I can't tell you very much, honey. Marion made me take an oath of secrecy and the only reason I complied is because she also promised she would tell you everything when she was ready. I was sure she would have done years ago. I always believed it was wrong of her to keep it from you, but Marion… well, no one can judge another's suffering or force them to atone. But now that she's gone… I want you to know everything that I know. Especially since there is a good chance that Julian is still alive and he's the only family you have. I can't tell you much, but I can tell you a little."

Jess listened—afraid to move, almost afraid to breathe—as Hanna told her about events she'd been present for but was too young to remember. Hanna told her how excited she'd been when she saw the bat and the butterfly, how hopeful for the twins' future she'd been, and Marion's confusing and worrying response; how she seemed ready to kill the familiars. She explained Marion had had extreme paranoia that someone would discover she'd given birth to half-fae twins.

"I always thought she was being a little ridiculous about it, although I'd never say that to her. It was clear she was frightened of something, terrified even, but she never explained what she was so scared of. It wasn't until *that night* that I finally understood that the danger wasn't all in Marion's mind."

That night. The words made the hair on the back of Jessamine's neck prickle.

Hanna and Tad had awoken to horrible sounds coming from next door. Marion's twins were only ten months old. A baby wailed. There was yelling, followed by a bloodcurdling scream. Hanna hardly recognized her neighbor's voice.

Tad and Hanna had scrambled from their bed. Hanna went to comfort Clair, crying from her cradle, while Tad grabbed an axe from the pegs inside their front door—dashing from their cottage in his bare feet. Hanna looked out the open door to see two horses with hooded riders galloping toward the center of town. When Hanna arrived at Marion's cottage, she found her neighbor on her knees and weeping, with Tad crouched over her. Chairs had been overturned and there were fragments of broken plates and cups scattered across the floor. Bedding had been stripped and thrown on the floor, the narrow single mattress overturned. The ladder leading up to the loft sat askew, one rung broken. Hanna had expected to find things missing, but nothing of value had been taken.

Except Julian.

At first Hanna thought that both the twins had been taken, but a soft baby sound led Tad to the dresser behind the ladder. He opened the bottom drawer and Greta fluttered out. The glasswing had zigged wildly around the cottage then out the open door, disappearing into the night.

Jessica was inside the drawer with Beazle sitting curled up on her chest. Her big eyes looked out at them without understanding. She began to fuss only after the chaos was over. Weeping, Marion put the baby to her breast.

"Beazle must have kept you quiet," explained Hanna, stroking the bonnet as it lay over her thigh. "That clever little bat of yours must have known that if you had made any sound at all, you'd have been discovered and taken. Just like Julian."

"Taken by who?"

Hanna gave a long weary exhale. "I cannot tell you how many times I begged Marion to tell me who took Julian and why. She wouldn't. Only once, when she'd drunk too much, did she give me any hint at all. She said simply that he—she said he, not they, so I knew it was one person in particular who was responsible—was someone from her past, and that if she ever told me the truth I would hate her, that everyone would hate her. Even that she'd be run out of town."

It was not just difficult for Jess, but impossible, to imagine the responsible disciplinarian having done anything anyone would reproach her for, let alone revile her or banish her for. "She really said that? That you would hate her?"

"She really did. I believe it's safe to assume that its the same reason that she never told you either. She put it off and put it off because she couldn't tell you who took Julian without including whatever it was in her past that she is… was… so ashamed of."

Jessamine fingered the delicate fabric of Julian's baby hat, running her thumb over the nametag. "But Greta came back."

"Yes, the next day she returned and wouldn't leave your side. I guess she had tried to find Julian but couldn't. Wherever he'd been taken, she couldn't follow. I suppose no butterfly, even a familiar, can keep up to a galloping horse, even in daylight."

Jess brushed moisture from her eyes. "In the wild, butterflies only live for a month or two. If Julian died she should have died too, but she didn't. I always thought it was our bond that kept her alive, but maybe I was wrong." The gentle, motherly face she'd come to love as much as she'd loved Marion's blurred as Jess's vision swam with tears. "Is it really possible that Julian is alive? That he's been alive all this time?"

Hanna pulled Jess into a hug and kissed her head. "I'm so sorry, dear. It's a tragedy to lose your mother so young, and even more so before she had a chance to explain her past to you."

Jess sniffed, taking strength from Hanna's kindness. "There has to be a way to find him. There will be clues. I'll find them. I'll find… him." Julian was the only family Jess had now, aside from Beazle. He was her blood, her twin, and she needed to know what had happened to him, and what it was that Marion was so afraid to tell her. "Isn't there anything else you can tell me? Anything you remember from when my mom first arrived in Dagevli? Did she never talk about her parents or family, or where she came from?"

Hanna put the bonnet back on the pile. "Believe me, Jess, we tried. Tad and I tried so hard over the years to get Marion to open up. She wouldn't, and when she got fed up and angry with us and told us to leave it alone, we had to respect that. The only thing I can tell you is that Tad has always had an ear for accents. When Marion arrived she sounded like any other Dagevlian, except for when she drank too much."

Jess knew this. Marion's accent did change a little when she was drinking, but Jess had never read anything into it more than a drunken affectations.

"Tad thinks that she sounded like the peasants from Nasyk, but Jess, honey, he's no investigator. He's just a guy with a good ear, and it's just a guess."

"Nasyk." Jess felt something open up in her chest, a tiny flower of conviction that—if she allowed—would blossom into full-grown hope. "Where is that?"

"East of Solana, on the edge of a big forest."

"Have you ever been there?"

"No, but Tad has."

As though he'd overheard, Tad appeared in the doorway wiping a wet dish with a towel.

Jess felt swallowed up by the compassion in his dark eyes. "You thought my mom was from Nasyk?"

But Tad only shrugged. "My guess is that she was raised there. The way that people talk is pretty fixed by the time they are ten. I think she spent her formative years there, but that's as much as I would guess at."

"How do you know what a Nasyk accent sounds like?"

Tad smiled, his eyes crinkling the same way Clair's did. "I traveled quite a bit before Hanna and I settled down. I was a musician for a little while."

Jess hadn't known that about Clair's father. It struck

her just how much more of life these adults had lived than she had, so much that Tad had had a whole different occupation before he'd married Hanna, had a family and become a farmer.

"Nasyk is a village much like Dagevli, but every region has its dialects and local sayings. Your mom sometimes used phrases when she was drinking that I never heard used anywhere else except there. Phrases like 'let us away,' which no one in Dagevli uses. She also used to say she was 'seeing snakes' when she was tipsy. I only ever heard that phrase from a Nasykian, which is famous for being snake-infested in places, by the way."

Jess chewed her lip. It wasn't much to go on. It was highly unlikely her grandparents were still alive, otherwise surely Marion would have kept in touch with them—family had meant a lot to Marion. But there might be someone in Nasyk who remembered Marion as a young person. Someone who could give Jessamine another clue.

Chapter Two

Laec

THE CROFTER AND three human soldiers followed Laec to the old well. Jess had shown Ian its location the previous day before leaving for Dagevli, and the crofter had recruited Laec to lead them down into it.

As Laec threw his leg over the edge of the well, he commented that it was Jessamine who had had the courage to climb into it first. The crofter expressed the first real emotion Laec had seen on his face that day… the cock of an eyebrow. It was hard to read the man's face; he never smiled, his heavy eyelids and the pouches under his eyes made him look disinterested in life, even bored, which Laec suspected was far from the truth. There was a toughness in the set of Ian's mouth, not a cruelty exactly, but a rigidity and stoutness that made one feel that the crofter shouldn't be crossed. Given that his familiar was a bear, that was probably true. Laec hadn't seen the bear since the map room, and supposed there was no point bringing a bear to a well. However, Erasmus was a handy scout, while Sy's familiar—a racoon named Mae—had an excellent nose and sharp ears. A raccoon's sight was their least keen sense, but underground that wouldn't be a problem. Sy had the look of people from Tryske: lean and graceful, with golden skin, dark hooded eyes and glossy black hair.

Aside from the soldiers, a young man with the most beautiful hummingbird familiar had joined them just as they were leaving the palace yards. Laec hadn't even noticed them until he had looked back over his shoulder to answer a question while they were crossing the field enroute to the well. The bird sat on the young man's shoulder, head twitching, wings snapping and ruffling as the wind brushed against her. She had black feathers with a teal throat and bright purple crests on her wings and forehead, and was so small she could drown in a teacup.

"Who's the guy at the back?" Laec had asked Kite as she highstepped through the long grasses.

Erasmus screamed as distant thunder rolled over them from the mountains. The air had turned cool and the wind gusted, tugging Laec's hair out from under his collar. A smattering of rain began to fall. He dug in his pocket for his Solana military-issue woolen cap, pulling it down over his ears, then tugged up the collar of his dark-green jacket, also part of a Solana soldier's autumn uniform.

Kite glanced back, her head turning quickly, like she herself was part bird. "That's Lucas, he also goes by Digit."

"He's got a hummingbird."

"That's Ania."

Hummingbirds were pollinators, so that made Digit flora fae. "So, they're Calyx?"

"No."

Laec waited for more but that was all the information she gave, and as usual, her expression said she wasn't inclined to share more. Laec shrugged and put his head down.

"What is winter like in Solana?" Laec asked.

Kite glanced at the sky. "Short, rainy. It's not that cold but some days it feels cold because the air is humid. We sometimes get a little snow, not every year, but if we do it doesn't stay long. Melts within a few hours most times. What's winter like in Stavarjak?"

Laec wished he'd been issued a pair of gloves. He jammed his hands in his pockets. Kite was right about the humidity making it feel colder. "Winter? In Stavarjak? The Spring court?"

Kite dimpled. "Right. I forgot. No winter."

"No, there is. It's just really mild. We still have cycles, they're just not very noticeable. It's still green and warm, and there's always something blooming."

"Do you miss it?"

The answer that came into Laec's mind abruptly surprised him. He didn't miss it. He missed Fyfa and a few other friends, but she'd recently been reunited with Byrne after a long separation and they had re-fallen in love. Thinking about Fyfa and Byrne made him think about Çifta. Laec's heart gave a little lurch. He would never regret saving her, but he was afraid of where it might lead. She'd been tended by palace healers, given a beautiful room and all the clothing, shoes and supplies she needed—while Laec had basically been put under house arrest and fallen into an untrusted position. He was still annoyed at Çifta for not telling him when they'd first met that she had been betrothed. He'd allowed himself to relax around her and enjoy her company for a couple of days. He'd allowed himself to care, just like he had with Georjie. The sooner Çifta went back to Boskaya, back to her life, back to her father to be married off to whoever he found worthy, the better off Laec would be.

The crofter, soldiers and Fahyli followed Laec into the well without complaint. There had been some grunts of annoyance as the brambles snagged at their clothes, but they all passed through the liquid barrier without fear or hesitation. When their boots touched down, the soldiers produced etherlamps, throwing long coins of amber light across the rubble. Mae scampered ahead, snuffling under rocks and in corners. She soon disappeared into the gloom, followed by Sy, who stayed close to the wall on the left. Erasmus whooshed off down the tunnel while Kite strode along the wall to the right.

The soldiers, the crofter, and Digit spread themselves across the tunnel, inspecting the state of the passage. Laec trailed at the back. He'd done his part, and he'd already been down this road. He was tempted to head back to the palace but he knew the crofter wouldn't allow it. The group walked on in silence for a while, until Erasmus materialized, kicking up dust with his wings. He landed on Kite's shoulder.

"Rahamlar soldiers," she murmured. Their own soldiers brought their hands to the hilts of their swords, almost as one, but relaxed when Kite added: "Four and a half miles ahead." She paused and Laec realized with a start that she and Erasmus were communicating silently.

"Sorry. Just four," she amended.

"What are they doing?" The crofter's profile was dusted with etherlight as he turned toward Kite.

"Same as us. Walking. Exploring."

The crofter grunted and the party carried on. When the sound of boots on the dirt echoed down the cavern, Ian looked back at Laec, a silent command in his face.

Laec understood. He was to keep back, keep to the shadows. As one of the "offending party" who had sneaked into Rahamlar and taken the prince's betrothed, the crofter didn't want Laec to be too visible, in case one of the Rahamlar party could identify him. Laec thought this highly unlikely. It had been dark, he had been hooded, and only seen either fleeing on horseback at breakneck speed, or by combatants in the frantic and tension-loaded moments of sword-fights beneath the boughs of leafy trees on a cloudy night. Still, it was better to be careful.

"Who goes there?" The voice had the Rahamlarin slight nasal twang.

"Lord Peneçek," called Sy. His voice sliced confidently through the air, like a razor-sharp blade through paper. "Who comes?"

"Captain Yorin," came the reply. "May it go easy for you."

How polite. This was a Solanan response that villagers

and city-dwellers exchanged in markets and other public places. Sy glanced back at the crofter, whose nod was barely perceptible, before calling back, "And you."

Minutes later the crofter held up his hand to indicate a stop and they waited as the Rahamlarin party stepped into the light thrown by the etherlamps. Laec stayed behind Lucas's narrow form, visible enough to be counted but only as a silhouette wearing the same livery as the others.

"Captain Yorin," said the crofter in a flat but not hostile tone.

"Crofter." Yorin stopped several feet back and his soldiers halted just behind him. They were big unseelie guards, nothing like the older sentries Laec had seen throughout the interior of Rahamlar. These were bulky and broad, extra wide at the shoulder—ears sharp enough to scream their unseelie nature if their taloned fingers hadn't done it first.

"You're in Solana territory," Ian said, resting the palm of his hand on the pommel of his sword in a relaxed way. "It's difficult to tell down here, I'll grant you."

"That it is." Yorin's gaze flicked around the group, weighing, calculating. "We wouldn't be in your territory if some of yours hadn't come into ours first."

"Is that so?"

"It's so." The captain paused. "You wouldn't be down here if you didn't already know that, Ian."

Kite slowly moved into a crouch. Erasmus walked across her back from one shoulder to another, his sharp beak opening and closing. One of the unseelie soldiers had his gaze glued to the bird, his arm crossed over his chest, hand gripping the handle of a short sword. There was a chittering sound and Mae emerged from the shadows where the floor met the wall. Her appearance drew a hiss from one of the unseelie. With a look, Sy brought Mae to his ankle where she curled up into a fat little ball of fur, sniffing at the air.

"Lady Çifta presented herself to King Agir and Queen Esha two nights ago." The crofter moved his weight from one hip to the other, his big shoulders shifting beneath his tunic.

Captain Yorin's lip curled, just a little. "Prince Faraçek would like his bride back. If she is returned within the day, he may be willing to go easy on those who perpetrated such offense."

"Those who perpetrated—" Ian sounded surprised and confused. "And who might that be, pray tell?"

"The ones what took her," Yorin snapped, starting to lose a grip on etiquette. "The same ones responsible for taking the lives of my guards. I have three dead and two missing."

Ian spread one hand wide, an apologetic gesture. "The Lady Çifta arrived alone. If she had help, she admitted no such thing to us."

Laec was surprised at how easily the lie slipped from the crofter's mouth, how believable Ian's tone. His respect for the man inched upward. Good liars had to be taken note of.

Yorin's brows came down over his eyes. "She had help. There were two of them, and one was a woman. We have evidence that suggests she was one of your flower fae."

Ian scoffed. "You obviously don't know anything about the nature of our Calyx if you think one of them would have the courage—or skills, for that matter—to take Lady Çifta out from under Prince Faraçek's nose. Out from under your accomplished guardsmen, no less. Really, Captain?"

Captain Yorin looked uncomfortable, but lifted his chin. "Nevertheless, Rahamlar demands justice. Lady Çifta must be returned and the criminals punished. You wouldn't stand for such an insult, and neither shall we."

Laec's heart started to race, but Ian was admirably calm. "As for the matter of Lady Çifta, I believe her father has already been notified that she is taking shelter in Solana. King Osvitan can take the matter up with Kazery Unya. What becomes of the betrothal is none of our affair, so you can expect that Solana will not interfere on that front."

Captain Yorin looked satisfied with this, but a dark look came over his face as Ian continued.

"But we also have laws that protect fugitives and victims of unlawful incarceration, so neither will we return her to Rahamlar against her will. If she wishes to go, we will provide an escort. If she wishes to stay, she will have our protection until we hear further from her father. As for the perpetrators, we are not aware of any. As I said, Lady Çifta arrived alone. However, for the sake of being thorough, we shall do our own investigations and will keep you informed should we uncover any who may have helped her flee. I must comment though, if the lady had not been mistreated, she would not have been so eager to leave. Perhaps there is something to be learned about the welcoming of a future princess into your kingdom?"

The captain did not rise to Ian's stinging rebuke, would not be distracted from the topic he cared most about. "With all due respect, Crofter, the prince will not accept such watery terms, or your ignorant criticisms. We suspect a member of your Calyx. Possibly two members, although we believe the second was male, and it is not certain he was fae. If I am right, then by law you must hand them over."

"You risk great insult here, Captain Yorin," said Ian tightly.

The captain lifted his chin and raised a placating hand. "I do not accuse King Agir of anything. Given all I know at this moment, I'm inclined to believe the villains acted of their own accord. I saw how you reacted when the prince… during the performance. You showed a level of cool-headedness when others would have allowed emotion to prevail and lead to disaster. So neither do I suspect you of anything."

Laec wondered if Captain Yorin really believed these words or if he was just using flattery to get what he wanted.

Ian shifted his hands behind his back. "I see. And how do you propose to uncover these potentially fictional miscreants identities?"

The captain took a thoughtful pause. "I have an idea, but I would prefer to present it to King Agir himself."

The cave fell silent for several long moments. Laec hardly dared to breath. What did the captain have up his sleeve?

The crofter gave a nod. "Very well. Be at the Gate of Stars the day after tomorrow, at dawn. I'll escort you to His Majesty's presence myself."

Captain Yorin looked satisfied. "I'll be there." He swept an arm around, indicating the passageway engulfing them. "And this?"

"The law applies beneath ground as well as above it," said the crofter. "We have borders which must be respected. Keep to your side and we shall do the same—unless or until some other arrangement changes it. Does that suit you?"

"Certainly. Until the Gate of Stars, then."

Captain Yorin gave a subtle signal that Laec was too far back to see, but the unseelie soldiers retreated. The gloom soon swallowed them. The captain spun on his heel and followed his men, leaving the Fahyli and Solana soldiers to retreat in the other direction.

Chapter Three

Çifta

Dear Gemma,

In the several days that have passed since I arrived, I have decided that Solana Palace must be hiding some horrifically dark secrets—adulterous trysts, sinister political intrigues, gossips with vile intentions, murderers masquerading as charming nobles. What kingdom in Ivryndi doesn't have murderers?

I came to this suspicion after witnessing a superior member of the palace staff get to his knees to help a kitchen wench clean up a pile of broken crockery and leftover oatmeal that she had accidentally dropped.

It wasn't this kind and humble gesture alone that has pushed me from simply admiring outsider, to bemused guest, to full blown skeptic. It has been three and a half days of witnessing the flawless outplaying of harmonious palace life everywhere I look. Can this place possibly be real? At first, I just marveled at how polite the courtiers were among themselves, how sweetly the Calyx treat every visitor no matter where they're from or their station in life. But soon I couldn't fail to notice that it isn't merely the upper classes and celebrity citizenry (after all, they are expected to behave in a genteel manner anyway) who seem to value decorum the way people in Boskaya treasure gold.

Servants are kind to stable hands, launderers laugh in the yard with the herbalists, chemists chat with the arborists in an easy and sociable manner, soldiers are polite to the boys who shine their boots with shoe-black and oil their leathers with green-tinted salves.

Yesterday, I returned from an early morning stroll and entered the main courtyard in time to witness two blacksmiths rush out of the forge. Their objective? To help a scrawny young farrier-in-training get a spooked stallion under control. Without being asked, gardeners bring the last of the late harvest blossoms to cleaning staff whom they know like them, just so they have something pretty and fragrant in their own rooms to enjoy after a long day's work.

As if this all weren't enough, I have been given a beautiful suite of rooms in the East Keep and enough clothing, shoes and accessories to be mistaken for a member of the royal family. I have been better treated here as a refugee than I ever was as a princess-to-be in...

Çifta paused and sat back in her chair, touching the end of her quill to the tip of her nose. It would be better if she kept her accusations out of the letter, in case someone other than Gemma read it. She reached for the blotter and soaked up the still wet ink of the last line. Over the smudge, she wrote anew:

I have been welcomed to sit alongside the most distinguished guests in the banquet hall, and no one has pried into my personal affairs, although there is a warm level of interest in my person and my presence. I tell you, Gemma. These Solanans cannot be trusted.

Çifta chewed her lip and looked away from the page, wishing that a certain red-headed fae male from Stavarjak had shown a warmer level of interest in her person and her presence. She couldn't complain to Gemma that Laec had not sought her out—other than to perfunctorily ensure that she was not injured from their escape, that she had everything she needed—including parchment, ink and a quill, with which to write to her father post-haste—and that her suite was warm and comfortable—a suite that was an apartment consisting of four rooms all decorated with varying botanical themes, and were luxurious to the point of absurd.

Gemma would cheekily tell her to have a dalliance if it was what she wanted, it was Gemma after all. But her sister would also reply that Çifta had no right to expect anything from Laec, especially not after she'd let him think she was available, and Gemma would be right.

The irony was that now that she had damaged Laec's trust in her, she was very close to becoming available—she hoped—again. She wouldn't make matters worse by telling Laec any of this. She had to finalize things with Kazery first. What might Laec have to offer that would satisfy Kazery's appetite for wealth and influence? Çifta didn't know. She had doubts about the big-eyed, wild-haired Stavarjakian with the too-long eye-teeth. It was stupid of her to think of it, really. Childish. It was only a girlish crush for a handsome and unavailable male. Too bad the message wasn't getting through to her heart. A day did not pass since she'd been rescued, where Laec had not come into her thoughts. And nights? Çifta blushed to think of the manner in which he'd come into her dreams as well.

Laec's expectation had been clear: Çifta would write

to her father, and he would send an escort for her in a matter of days. Already, she'd lingered at Solana for too long. Already, she'd been on the receiving end of a calculated look from Laec in passing, a look that she read as *still here?*

She was supposed to return to her home city and her former life so her father could begin the hunt for an appropriate husband once more. When she thought of it, dread piled up in her heart like rocks. She wasn't ready to think about another match, not after what had transpired in Rahamlar.

Truthfully, she didn't even want to go home.

Her father had a lot of business at this time of year. He traveled up and down the rutted, windy coastal roads in a carriage—at breakneck speed—forging new relationships, renegotiating contracts, networking with suppliers, and seducing new partners. In other words, re-establishing Unya Shipping & Trading as the foremost merchant on the continent. He was in Boskaya now, but Çifta knew the foyer of the Unya manor would be stacked with boxes, full of paperwork, samples and supplies, waiting to be loaded on carriages. By the time Çifta arrived home, it would be empty except for Cook. The idea depressed her. Why go home to such loneliness when Solana was so welcoming and diverting?

While she wasn't brave enough to directly suggest that she be put in charge of arranging her own advantageous marriage, she planned to recommend that—after he invoked the clause allowing him to dissolve her betrothal—he visit her in Solana himself. It was only a slight detour on his way to Cardagenya, and she felt certain that if he saw this kingdom for himself, and saw her in it, that he would feel better about giving her the long leash she so craved.

She hadn't quite figured out how to say it, which was why she was practicing—procrastinating—by writing to her sister instead.

She instinctively knew that sending her father a direct and truthful report of what Prince Faraçek had put her through was a terrible idea for many reasons. Firstly, there was no genteel way to describe it. No linguistic acrobatics could gloss over the horror, abuse and insult she'd been subjected to. Secondly, she abhorred the idea of putting it down in writing, not only was it very unladylike, it could fall into the wrong hands. This had happened many times before to the Unya family, usually thanks to untrustworthy servants. Thirdly, she quailed at the thought of her father's face when he learned of it. The idea that she had been mistreated in the slightest way would shame Kazery deeply, as it shamed her, albeit for different reasons. Kazery was proud of his ability to sniff out opportunities, both in business and family matters. His poor judgment in choosing Prince Faraçek would be on display for all of Boskaya to gossip about. Çifta was beloved by many, and could already hear the town prattle: he saw a prince and nothing else mattered, not even the safety of his own youngest daughter, what a fool. Not only that, her suffering would infuriate him, and a furious Kazery Unya was a force no one could control.

By the time she finished her tongue-in-cheek letter

to Gemma, Çifta felt ready to tackle the daunting task of writing to her father. She could delay it no longer.

King Agir had sent a formal letter to Kazery already, informing the richest merchant of Ivryndi of his daughter's whereabouts, confirming her safety and the open arms with which Solana welcomed her. Çifta greatly appreciated this kindness; it had given her a little room to breathe. But now she'd waited a little too long to write her own. A day was understandable, given her bruises and exhaustion. Two days was concerning but forgivable, given the ordeal she'd weathered. Three days was bordering on rude or alarming depending on the perspective her father chose to take.

Four days was unforgivable. She had to get this letter written and into the hands of the postal service before noon, before her father sent an assassin to dispatch whoever had murdered his daughter.

Setting a fresh piece of parchment in front of her, she dipped her quill, took a deep breath, and had the letter finished within five minutes.

Dear father,

As King Agir has informed you, I am currently in Solana, alive and well. The events that led to this development must be discussed in person. As you must have already concluded, the betrothal needs to be dissolved. Prince Faraçek and I were not a good match. I am confident that King Osvitan will accept this without alarm or injury. On the contrary, he will be expecting it.

I know you will soon depart for your annual journey. Why not stop by Solana on your way to Cardagenya?

Your loving daughter,

Çifta Unya

Çifta signed it with a flourish and sat back to read it.

It was terribly formal, not her usual tone at all. But it was not prudent to embellish, too much information could easily be misinterpreted, and she needed more time to ruminate over what she'd say when the time came.

Before she reconsidered, she folded up the letter, sealed it with gold wax using her personal seal. It was in the postal services hands by half eleven, after which Çifta joined a small group of Calyx and courtiers for lunch.

CHAPTER FOUR

JESSAMINE

DREAD WEIGHED ON Jessamine's heart like a wet woolen blanket as she and Regalis stepped through the side gate and into the courtyard. What waited for her? She felt like she was treading water in a deep, cold lake, unsure of how long she could stay afloat before help arrived, and just as uncertain about whether help would arrive at all.

She had stayed in Dagevli for five days. The villagers had closed in around her, taking care of her, supporting her, but everywhere she looked Jess was reminded of her mother. Everywhere she looked she saw pity in people's eyes. Even her pony, Apple—whom Hanna and Tad had taken into their care—looked at Jess with a sorrowful sympathy that kept her grief fresh. She slept, but restlessly and with unpleasant dreams about Marion's coffin. She ate, but food tasted like dust. She read, but her mind wandered.

Finally, she could not take Dagevli any longer. She sorted through her mother's things, cleaned the cottage and locked it. If she was going to be dismissed from the Calyx she might need her childhood home, although she couldn't imagine living in it without her mother. Hanna and Clair had been reluctant to let her leave. They tried to convince her that she wasn't ready to go back, but Jessamine knew she couldn't stay. It was too painful. She needed to be busy, otherwise she felt trapped in her pain, like she had a wound that would not heal as long as she kept looking at it. She needed to look away, focus elsewhere.

On the journey to Solana City, lulled by the sound of their horses' hooves clopping along the road, Jessamine ruminated on the future. She had no idea what to expect when she met with the king and queen—some kind of punishment no doubt. Ilishec was disappointed in her, that was certain. King Agir was unhappy with her too, but at the end of the meeting with her, Laec and Çifta—after the king had been told the whole story—she thought his frustration had softened. Also, the king knew that Jess had lost Greta in Rahamlar, and now he would learn that she'd also lost her mother. The only good thing to come out of losing them might be a little leniency.

Stable hands took away the horses, leaving Jess and Regalis standing in the courtyard with their bags. Regalis turned to Jessamine. "Come on. I'll walk you to your room."

"Thank you," Jess mumbled, stretching her back before shouldering her bag.

They headed for the entrance to the East Keep. Regalis had been a silent oak for Jess during her stay in Dagevli, never far from her side. He stayed in Marion's cottage while Jessamine slept at Hanna and Tad's house, sharing a bed with Clair.

Regalis was a fae of few words, but the compassion in his eyes and the actions he took said more than enough. When Jess told him he should go back to the city, he'd refused, claiming that his orders were to escort her and keep her safe, however long it took. He'd helped Hanna organize Marion's funeral, he'd even cooked for them one day—a vegetarian dish from his home village of Kitrell made of rice and lentils with a spicy tomato sauce. He'd talked when she needed to be distracted, although she couldn't remember anything he'd told her except that his mountain town was so far north that it was close to the border of Silverfall. He was quiet when she needed silence, somehow always sensing her rightly. Jess thought his hawk would get restless, but Ferrugin was hardly around. When Jess asked about her, Regalis said she was out exploring, and that she loved spending time away from Solana City.

Jess looked up, realizing they were in front of her suite.

Regalis gave her a look of dark intensity. "It gets easier, you know."

"What does?"

"Grief. I'm sorry to say that it never fully goes away. But it does get easier to bear."

She hugged her bag to the front of her chest and swallowed. "Thanks for being my escort, Regalis. You were… so kind to me. I'm grateful. I'll see you around."

"Anytime." He squeezed her shoulder and walked away.

Jess watched him go down the hall and turn the far corner. Then she pushed into her room and looked around, feeling dazed. It felt like a year since she'd been here, not less than a week. Beazle squirmed out of her hair and flapped into the rafters with a squeak. Jessamine tossed her bag on her bed and went into her bathing room to clean up. She was combing out wet hair and wearing sleeping clothes before she realized that it was too early to go to bed. She should at least go and tell Ilishec that she was home. Home. She quietly acknowledged that this place, and not Dagevli, was more her home now than her cottage.

A knock on her door made her put down her comb, but before she could open the door, Rose opened it a crack and poked her nose in, peeking around. Her gorgeous eyes widened. "You're back!" She came striding over to hug Jess when she noticed Jess's clothing. "Going to bed?"

"Not yet. I just had a bath."

"Ah." Rose nodded, but she had yet to smile. Rose was the smiliest Calyx aside from Snap.

"What's wrong?" Jess perched on her bed and pulled her feet up under her, continuing to disentangle her long hair with her fingers.

"There's trouble, Jess." Rose sat beside her, pulling up her own feet. "Ilishec told me… about… what you did."

Jess gasped. Shock went through her like electricity. "No one is supposed to know."

"None of the other Calyx do… except for Aster, of course. I had to tell her because she kept pestering me. She knew something was up. Sorry."

"But why did Ilishec tell?"

Rose looked as puzzled as Jess felt. "I'm not exactly sure. Maybe he just knew you'd need a friend. Someone who knows everything and can support you. Anyway, I'm glad he did." She pulled Jess into her side, giving her a fierce half-hug. "I'm so proud of you, Jess. What you did was incredibly stupid, but incredibly brave. I wish I had that kind of courage."

"Thanks," she whispered. Moisture gathered in her eyes. To hear Rose say she was proud of her made a lump form in Jessamine's throat.

"He says you're supposed to meet with King Agir?"

Jess nodded and rubbed her eyes, tired at the thought of it.

"Don't think about it yet, Jess. You need to keep yourself together and focused on tomorrow."

She blinked at her friend, looking through blurry eyes. "What's tomorrow?"

Rose took her hand. "Captain Yorin arrives. He's made an agreement with the king. He has one hour to inspect the Calyx. He's looking for whoever kidnapped Lady Çifta."

Jess struggled to breathe, hardly believing what she was hearing. She wanted to ask why King Agir would allow such a thing, here, right in the heart of the kingdom.

Rose saw the terror in Jess's face. "We can't hide you because the captain knows there are fifty of us and we all have to be present at once. The inspection will take place in the Breynia Ballroom. If he finds the culprits, he is allowed to take them back to Rahamlar for punishment. If he doesn't find them, he's sworn never to bring it up again. Well, Prince Faraçek has sworn, I guess. The captain is just a representative. Obviously, I wasn't there when they made the deal, but Ilishec told me that Captain Yorin made the accusation to Queen Esha and King Agir's faces that the culprits were from the Scented Court. When asked why he suspected us, he produced a sleeve with sweat on it that smelled strongly like plant oils. Also, we were just there—I guess he figures that someone from the group that performed in Rahamlar saw Çifta, thought she looked miserable, and made the decision to break her free. Even so, he wants to see everyone, just in case."

Jess was at a loss for words. Was this the punishment for her wrongdoing? King Agir and Queen Esha would leave it up to Yorin, *if* he could catch her. A tightness Jess had never felt before crept across her chest, making her heart throb painfully with anxiety.

Rose squeezed her hand. "Don't worry Jess, Ilishec has a plan. You're not going anywhere if he has anything to do with it. I'm really sorry to spring this on you the minute you return. How was it by the way? I've been dying to hear what your mom had to say about your twin."

Jess looked into her friend's big beautiful blue gaze. "My mom… she had a stroke. Two strokes."

"Jessamine!" Rose gasped. "Why did you come back so soon? Is she okay?"

"She died. She was gone before I even got home. Our neighbor sent a letter when the first stroke happened, we passed the postal service on our way to Dagevli. If I'd left sooner, I might have arrived in time to see her."

"Oh, Jess." Rose's voice was thick, her eyes shining.

Jess didn't know people could feel this much sorrow, this much emptiness. She missed her mother with a desperation she never thought possible. Marion was all she'd known of family, love and safety. Jess had been in such a hurry to grow up, in such a hurry for adventure that when the opportunity came, she'd pounced on it like a cat on a cricket. If she'd known Marion only had months to live she never would have left home. Why hadn't she begged Ilishec to let her go back to Dagevli the moment she learned she had a twin? Why had she gotten involved in Lady Çifta's affairs?

Jess's face crumpled. "If I hadn't gone to Rahamlar—"

Rose shook her head, her eyes soft with compassion. "Don't do that, Jess. Don't torment yourself over might-have-beens, what you could or should have done differently. That doesn't lead anywhere good. It's not your fault." Rose hugged Jess a third time in as many minutes. "Oh Jess, I'm so sorry. You poor thing!"

Rose's incredible scent enveloped Jess as she laid her head on her friend's shoulder. Her mind whirled, her stomach felt like it had shrunk to the size of an olive pit. Hanging over everything was the kind of bitter sadness Jessamine had never known existed.

"I should have stayed longer in Dagevli," Jess murmured. "I just couldn't. There are too many memories…"

Rose held Jess in her arms, her cheek resting on Jess's damp hair. "As far as the inspection goes, it wouldn't have made any difference. The moment the crofter got the letter from Regalis letting him know you were on your way, he had to tell the king. Captain Yorin insisted all Calyx be present, so it's not like you could dodge it."

Jess straightened, brushing her hands across her wet cheeks. "What am I going to do?"

Rose's perfect brow wrinkled. "We have a plan to throw him off course. I'll explain tomorrow. Why don't you put on some clothes and come have dinner with me and Aster? She's missed you as much as I have. The only reason she isn't here right now is because she has a mountain of nomenclature homework to get through. You need to be with friends right now, people who love you."

Jess thought about the pity in the villagers' eyes that she'd so needed to get away from. She didn't want to have to face the same thing here, not yet. She stood and crossed to her as-yet-unpacked bag, rifling inside and pulling out a tunic and leggings. She shucked her night clothes and dressed. "I don't want to talk about my mother."

"You don't have to. I promise." Rose went to Jess's closet and pulled out a pair of shoes and a vest.

Jess swallowed the lump in her throat. "Everyone will feel sorry for me. I can't bear that."

"You'll have to tell them eventually," Rose said softly. She drew Jess's hair back and tied it in a low knot at the nape of her neck, out of the way.

Jessamine pulled on her shoes and wormed into her vest. "I will. I promise. Just… not tonight."

Rose nodded. "If that's what you want."

"That's what I want."

Jessamine sat in a chair positioned in front of one of the tall windows—in what she had learned the Calyx referred to as "the tailors' den"—where the morning light fell over her face. All around her Calyx sat at vanity tables, doing their own makeup or letting another do it for them, as Rose was doing for Jess. Makeup was not commonly used by the Calyx since the flora magic gave them an otherworldly beauty that didn't need to be accentuated—except for Jess, who looked no different than when she'd arrived. Aster had comforted her by saying that flora fae changed at their own pace and there was nothing to be worried about. When Jess complained that Peony had changed so much that she looked like she'd been in the Calyx for years, Aster had murmured, "But she's a prodigy."

Jess couldn't tell if the comment had been sarcastic or not.

The tailors' den didn't have the air of buzz and excitement that it usually had before performances. The Calyx had been told that they were going to be inspected, but not by who, nor why. They'd been instructed to remain quiet and calm—just to stand in place for the duration.

The articles that Olinya and her team had unearthed for the Calyx to wear transcended any outfit Jessamine had worn or seen before. These were outfits of stunning design and proportion. Costumes. Already a few of the Calyx had finished their hair and makeup and were being dressed on the second level in front of the mirrors. Diaphanous gowns with crystals sewn into the fabric, structured suits with wide sweeping features at the shoulders to accentuate masculinity. Headdresses for some, tiaras for others, incredibly high hairstyles that required pounds of pins and a fixative to stay in place.

Some of the Calyx exchanged confused looks about how they were being prepared. Jess could see the questions in their eyes. Why so elaborate? Why the makeup? For an inspection? It didn't make a lot of sense. Olinya, with her usual smile and good cheer, speculated that it might be a kind of inventory taking. Such a thing had happened once or twice before. But when it came Jess's turn to be dressed, she suspected that Olinya knew more than she was letting on. Her kind dark gaze had concern that wasn't usually there. She tutted and murmured as Jess was enfolded and swallowed by her costume, then put final touches on Jess's headpiece. When Olinya moved out of the way so Jess could see her reflection, she stared at herself with a species of horrified amazement.

She looked… well, like someone else. Which was entirely the point.

She'd been wrong; these weren't costumes, they were distractions, disguises. They'd be presented to Captain Yorin looking completely different from how they normally looked, and worlds apart from how they had appeared when they'd performed at Rahamlar in veils and long-sleeved, high-necked gowns. Jess began to feel a little better as she turned this way and that, inspecting her disguise. Rose had applied cosmetics with a heavy hand, and cleverly: Jess appeared to have much juicier lips than she actually possessed, her cheek bones appeared wider and higher, her eyes looked properly huge, and the eyelashes that Rose had glued to her lids were pale green to match her gown and draw attention away from the fear in her gaze. Layer upon layer of pale-green gauze cascaded over her hips and thighs, all the way to the floor. Strapped to Jess's feet were a pair of platform shoes, invisible beneath the gown. They made Jess's legs appear longer and brought her to a height similar to the most mature Calyx. Beazle couldn't burrow his way into Jess's hair, with its tight updo and coatings of glue, so Olinya installed a many-petaled rose blossom which he could hide beneath or inside.

Ilishec slipped between the mirrors to inspect Jess with thoughtful satisfaction. "Wonderful job, Olinya. She looks like an entirely different creature. Turn for me Jess. How are the shoes? Giving you any trouble?"

"No. They're fine." Jess stepped off the platform and walked around, her spine erect, one hand on her hip, showing Ilishec how poised and confident she could look.

"Good." Ilishec took her hands and looked into her eyes, his expression sober. "Remember: honeysuckle, *cleome*, and *ergeron*. Think about no other botanicals but them. For today, they're all you can conjure. The others do not exist."

"I understand." Ilishec and Rose had explained earlier that these were her most benign and pleasantly scented plants.

"Do as I say, and they won't identify you. I have every confidence." He released her hands and stepped back.

Jess glanced in the mirror. Seeing herself this way made her feel less exposed—she barely recognized her own face. "Won't the captain be upset that we are so heavily altered?"

The gardener pressed his lips into a line. "That's his problem. When he made this agreement with King Agir, he didn't stipulate what the Calyx were to wear. It's too late for him to take issue with how you are presented. If he implies that we are hiding someone, we will ridicule him. He knows nothing of the Calyx, our routines, our practices. As far as he knows, you are dressed this way because we have a private performance this afternoon." He let out a long-suffering sigh. "I don't even care if he doesn't believe me. When he can't nail down a perpetrator, that will be the end of it."

Jess nodded, eager to get on with it. She wanted to get it over with *now*. Her scalp was starting to itch and blinking felt weird.

At precisely ten-forty-five, the Calyx made their way to a little used ballroom. Staff stepped to the sides of the halls to let the Calyx pass, watching the fae with expressions of awe. Jessamine wondered what they'd been told, if anything. Fifty flora fae decked out in Olinya's most extravagant costumes and wearing enough makeup for a circus must be a bit of a shock to the palace servers accustomed to seeing them bare-faced and wearing tunics and sandals.

Without any of the usual music or ceremony, the Calyx stepped into the large, windowless ballroom. It smelled musty, and the wooden floorboards creaked and groaned as they lined up in rows of ten.

Jess's heart leapt when she saw that Captain Yorin was

already there, flanked by two human soldiers; two more unseelie soldiers were seated in a shadowy corner. With narrowed eyes, the captain watched the Calyx arrange themselves into neat lines. The chandeliers and sconces were lit with etherlight, but they gave off an unflattering blue glow, different from the orange lighting they'd been under in Rahamlar. Jess suspected this was another way Ilishec expressed his annoyance with Captain Yorin. Rahamlar was allowed to do an inspection, but the gardener didn't have to like it or make it easy.

When Yorin uncrossed his arms, she began to sweat. He held the torn sleeve from her tunic, the one she'd worn *that* night. When the captain held the sleeve down for a dog to sniff—a dog that had been sitting so still and quiet that Jess didn't see it until it moved—Jess's heart began to run hurdles.

She closed her eyes, swallowing down the lump in her throat, mind racing. Sifting mentally through her magic the way a chef picks through crates for the right produce, Jess banished all the toxic botanicals and focused on just one that Ilishec had suggested. Honeysuckle: mountains and mountains of sweet, fragrant, benign honeysuckle…

Yorin didn't speak, didn't address the Calyx, didn't ask questions or complain about their ridiculous costumes and makeup. He didn't need to, not with a hunting dog at his side. Jess opened her eyes just as Yorin unsnapped the hound's leash. With an upward glance and a couple of tail-wags, the dog sniffed the sleeve one last time then trotted across the floor to the nearest Calyx: Proteas. Quickly moving on, the hound sniffed its way through the fae, pausing here and there. The speed with which it moved through the company was a little disconcerting.

Jess could feel the fabric at her armpits growing damp. Beazle moved beneath his rose, feeling her discontent. Jessamine closed her eyes and tried to think of something that made her feel safe. She summoned images of Marion: rolling dough at the workbench, whitewashing the front of the cottage, weeding the squash patch, chatting with villagers as she sold berry bread wrapped in waxed cloth printed with paisley. A flush of warm nostalgia filled Jess's heart. Marion had loved her deeply and had always protected her, which Jess now understood had been an outcome of what had happened to Julian.

Jess had brought the baby bonnets back with her to Solana, tucked carefully in a side pocket of her bag. When she'd unpacked, she'd put them in one of the jewelry drawers inside her wardrobe, moving everything else out so that they could lie flat and unwrinkled. They were proof. A tether to the only family she had left, unless her father was still alive. He'd always been a blank spot too.

Jess heard the dog's nails click on the floor beside her. She held thoughts of Marion and Julian against her heart, emitting honeysuckle perfume, as the dog sniffed at her hem. It nosed her dress up, cold nose touching Jess's ankle. Just as quickly though, the dog moved on to Aster, then to Rose. Jess's Calyx friends emanated a confidence and a calm strength that seemed to seep into Jess's very bones and fill her with a rare serenity.

Yorin began to pace unhappily. When the dog ran back to him and sat looking up at him as if to say, *What's next?* Yorin held the sleeve to the dog's nose, shaking it impatiently. The dog wagged its tail, sniffed the sleeve, and promptly sat again. Jess bit her cheeks against a smile as she imagined the dog's thoughts; *Yeah, I got it the first time. There's nothing like that here.* Captain Yorin looked at his fellow soldiers with annoyance and disbelief.

Ilishec approached him and the two exchanged words that Jess couldn't hear. They talked for several long moments, with the captain gesturing at the group of Calyx standing like elaborate stone pillars. Ilishec looked like he was trying to hide amusement, which annoyed the captain even more. Finally the gardener just shrugged and nodded his head. Jess caught the final words, "—nearly out of time, I suggest you not waste it."

The captain barked at his soldiers and they spread out, strolling among the Calyx with vigilant eyes. One of the unseelie strode to Jess's row. He could be the soldier she and Laec had nearly run down in the road, he was the right height and shape, but Jess couldn't be sure. She kept her gaze straight ahead until he appeared in the line of her vision, then she watched him with a bored expression. He looked her up and down, circled her, studied her, even sniffed her. Jess resisted the urge to lean away from him in distaste.

"Are you the fae what lost her moth?" he asked in a gruff tone.

Before Jess could answer, Ilishec was there. "Hers is a bat familiar."

The soldier's feral gaze went from Jess to Ilishec. "Where is the one who lost the moth, then?"

"Gone." Ilishec didn't even blink as the lie came. "She

left. I don't expect a brute like you to understand what the grief of losing a familiar does to a flora fae's magic, but… well, she's gone. Ruined."

The soldier grunted and moved away, dispassionate.

The Calyx were inspected repeatedly until the full hour was up, much to the captain's clear irritation.

"You are dismissed," called Ilishec to the Calyx, then added, for the captain's benefit: "Thank you for your patience and please accept our apologies for the humiliation you were subjected to today."

The Calyx turned and filed from the room, heads held high. Only when they were down the hall and nearly back to the tailors' den did they clump together in little groups, talking in scandalized whispers to one another.

Snap came up on Jessamine's right. "What was that about?"

"Why are you whispering?" Rose replied at full volume. "The captain obviously mistook some fugitive for a Calyx. Clearly, he was wrong." She began to pull the pins from her hair, loosening the structure of her enormous queenly updo. "This tiara is killing me."

Snap looked puzzled. "Then why did the gardener lie about—"

Rose hissed and Snap didn't finish.

The Calyx returned to the tailors' den to change and wash up. Conversation lingered on the inspection but soon turned to what lay ahead for the day. When Aster was finished cleaning her own face, she helped Jess with her false eyelashes, gently detaching them and setting them in a protective case.

"When do you see the king?"

"I'm not sure. He said that I wouldn't have to wait long." Jess surprised herself by how calm she sounded. Or maybe it wasn't calm, it was denial. Was she really in this situation? Orphaned and about to be dismissed?

Cleared of all makeup, and with her hair loose and her tunic donned, Jessamine looked at her reflection. She'd been told all her life that she was a pretty girl, sometimes followed by the assumption—by the more outspoken individuals—that she must have taken after her father. It might be true. Jessamine had never seen much of Marion in her face. Jess had a narrower bone structure, and pale gray eyes where Marion's were dark brown. But now, looking at the sad girl in the mirror, Jessamine saw more of her mother than she'd ever seen before. Maybe it hadn't just been Marion's heavy eyelids that had given her a look of deep longing, of melancholy. Maybe it was loss.

"You okay?" Aster leaned against the vanity, looking at Jess with concern.

The majority of Calyx had left the tailors' den. She, Rose and Aster were the stragglers.

She looked up at Aster. "How would I go about trying to find a missing person?"

Jess's question brought Rose scampering over from her own mirror, her expression electrified. "Who's missing?"

"My brother."

Aster and Rose exchanged a look of shock. Both dragged chairs over from the nearest vanity tables.

Aster spun her chair and threw a leg over the seat

in an uncharacteristic tomboyish move. "What did your mom tell you?"

Rose gave Jess a sympathetic look. Jess swallowed down the lump in her throat. Aster and Rose had become good friends to her, it wasn't fair that Rose knew but Aster didn't. Aster listened quietly, her eyes shining with empathy, as Jessamine told her everything. When she was done, Aster enfolded Jess in a fragrant hug.

"With my mom gone… I'm alone in the world. But there's a chance my brother is alive. I need to find him. I don't care how long it takes or how far I have to go."

"You're not alone," Aster said. "You have us."

"Yeah, we're your family now, Jess," Rose added.

"I know, and thanks, but—"

Aster sat. "I understand. I'd want to find him too. We'll help."

Rose nodded with enthusiasm. "The first thing to do is visit the Registry. We're lucky because the records office for all of Solana is right here in the capital, not far from the Perfume Shop. What's his name?"

"Julian Fontana."

"Did he have a middle name?"

Jess shook her head. "I don't think so. I don't, so probably not."

"Okay, so that's where we'll start. I'll make an appointment." Rose scratched at her scalp, pulling out a few missed pins, which she tossed into a tray on Jessamine's vanity. "The records office is a bit of a labyrinth. They keep everything there, not just birth records. We have to send a letter of inquiry and then give them time to do a search. If there has ever been a Julian Fontana registered in Solana, they'll have a record of him."

Hope rose in Jess's heart like a dove winging toward the sun. She looked from one beautiful fae face to the other. "Thank you. Both of you."

Aster dimpled. "What's family for?"

Chapter Five

Jessamine

Standing outside the double doors with the sculpted lion pride above it, Jessamine's heart thumped slow and hard within her ribcage. When she was summoned by a page, she suppressed the urge to pepper him with questions about what she was about to face. He wouldn't know anything anyway.

In anticipation of her meeting with the monarchs, Jess had put on a long simple dress, set her hair up and adorned it with primrose blossoms. She hoped that seeing her looking unassuming and feminine might erase the memory of the last time they'd seen her: filthy, exhausted, and blood-encrusted, with feet too swollen to fit inside her boots.

With the unnecessary statement that the king and queen would see her shortly, the pageboy left her standing by herself in the quiet hall. She backed up until she felt the paneling then leaned against it, her knees trembling. When the door opened, she straightened fast, like a soldier at attention.

Ilishec poked his head out. Behind him, Jess heard murmurs of a group discussion. She could see the crofter, Panther, and two others. King Agir's voice drifted from the room.

Ilishec closed the door behind him. He put his hands on her arms. "Are you okay?"

Jess lied in the form of a nod. "What's going to happen?"

"I can't tell you, Jessamine. They've heard my point of view, as well as the crofter's and Captain Bradburn's. They've even consulted lawyers, but they haven't voiced any personal opinions. Whatever they have to say, I'm going to hear it just before you do. Did you eat something? I asked Mrs. Tierney to make you an elixir to help with nerves."

"I got it, thanks." Jess hadn't been able to finish the bright green cocktail, but she appreciated the thought.

"I'd better go back in. It won't be much longer."

Ilishec opened the door and the murmur of voices swept into the hall again. For a brief moment, Jess locked eyes with a young man standing beside Panther. Just before the door closed Panther followed the young man's gaze and met Jess's eyes—he might have given a slight nod, but she could easily have imagined it.

Five minutes later a group filed out, among them was Panther with Tulliana at his side. Another Fahyli followed with a racoon perched on his shoulder, then a barrel-bellied man with grizzled hair and many scars. He had to be Captain Bradburn. Two human soldiers followed and the door swung shut. Jess was unsure if she should knock or wait further. There was still someone left inside—the young man she'd seen standing beside Panther.

Minutes passed. Jess expected to see him come out, but instead, Ilishec opened the door and beckoned her inside. Jess entered, trying to hide that her hands were shaking.

King Agir and Queen Esha sat on marble stools set on the low dais. Esha's gown, a buttery yellow velvet with dark-green trim, flowed over the back of her seat and pooled on the floor. The crofter stood to the right of the king. Ilishec took his place to the left of the queen. A small spry fae man, with glasses perched on the end of his nose, sat at a small desk in the corner. He watched the proceedings with professional interest, holding a quill poised over a stack of parchment. Jess looked around for the young man she'd spotted but there was no one else in the room. There was also nowhere for him to hide. Jess hid her puzzlement behind a flat expression.

"Come." King Agir beckoned her to stand on the carpet in front of the group.

She walked forward, noticing a pot of soil sitting on the floor to the side of the dais. She curtsied as gracefully as she could manage with her quaking knees, then stood and put her hands behind her back. She lifted her chin, pretending she was ready for whatever came.

"State your name and position, please," said Queen Esha kindly. "For the record."

Jess cleared her throat. "Jessamine Fontana, member of the Calyx and citizen of Solana."

The scratching of the quill filled the silence. When it stopped, the queen said, "State your parents' names and your place of birth as well, please."

Jess blinked, caught off guard. This was for the record, she had to be truthful, otherwise it might come back to haunt her later. "Uh… I never knew my father, but my mother is… was… Marion Fontana. I was born in the village of Dagevli."

Ilishec blurted, "Oh, Jess!"

Queen Esha brought a hand to her mouth to cover a gasp.

"Your mother is deceased?" King Agir's brows hiked nearly to his hairline. He shot a dismayed look at the crofter. Jess suspected that the crofter already knew because he didn't react.

"A little over a week ago, Sire."

"We're very sorry for your loss, Jessamine." Queen Esha put a hand on her husband's forearm and the delicate fingers squeezed some silent communication.

The king's gaze softened. "How unfortunate. Was she ill?"

"The healer in Dagevli says it was a stroke. Two strokes, one after the other." Jess's throat closed up. She was afraid that if she continued to talk she would burst into tears, the last thing she wanted to do in their presence. She closed her mouth, breathing deeply through her nose and swallowing repeatedly, struggling to keep her emotions under control. The scratching of the quill came again, reminding her that all this was being recorded for posterity. She'd rather be whipped for her crimes than have it forever in the record that she'd turned into a blubbering mess while facing her sentence.

Queen Esha's next question took Jess off guard again: "Where is Beazle?"

She gestured to her hair. "He's here."

"He'll be asleep, darling," murmured the king. "He hunts at night and sleeps all day, remember?"

"That is normally the case, yes. But actually, he is awake right now, Sire." Jess was tense, so Beazle was also tense.

Esha looked pleased. "May we see him? This concerns him as well."

Jess lifted a hand to the warm lump at the back of her neck. Beazle crawled into her palm and hugged her thumb. He looked out at the people across from them, yawned and shook his tiny head like a dog, as if trying to clear his ears.

"Thank you. He really is just as tiny as I remember," the queen said with a smile.

That smile dissolved some of the tension in Jess's shoulders.

"Before we begin, we have a request," said the king. "You have the ability to find lost objects with your flora magic. Will this magic also work to find a person?"

Jess didn't know what she had expected, but she had not expected any of what had happened so far. They were being so kind, and now a request? She wanted to make the king happy, but she also had to be truthful. "I don't know, Sire. I've never tried."

"Would you be willing to?"

Now the pot of soil made sense. "Of course. Who?"

"Two people, actually. Most likely they are together. Princess Serya and Princess Isabey of Rahamlar. King Osvitan has asked for our help in locating his daughters and we've agreed to do what we can. Bradburn has men searching the kingdom, but if the princesses do not want to be found, then it may be very difficult. We're hoping your magic will do the trick."

The queen produced a piece of parchment and held it out to Jessamine. "Here is a recent drawing that King Osvitan sent us, in case you need a visual."

Jess took it and looked at the simple line drawings of two young women, one clearly fae and the other clearly human, both with dark hair and a similar nose, mouth and chin. She studied the images and then knelt on the carpet by the pot of soil. Beazle flapped down and landed on the rim. Jessamine chewed her lip as she thought about the older princess, the queen-in-waiting. She put a hand over the soil, conjuring *solidago*. The tendrils curled delicately as they emerged from the dirt, unfurling, expanding, reaching upward. Shoots grew from stems and tiny yellow buds formed. The little flowers opened and pollen puffed into the air, but Jess received no information, nothing rose in her mind, her consciousness didn't travel anywhere, and Beazle remained on the edge of the pot, watching the *solidago* grow with no more interest than a bystander.

He jumped onto the back of Jess's hand before crawling up her arm.

Jess looked up at the expectant royals and shook her head. "I'm sorry, Sire, Ma'am."

The king looked disappointed but not surprised.

Ilishec spoke apologetically. "The folklore does specify that it is over objects that the magic works, not living entities."

King Agir waved a hand. "Thank you for trying. Let's move on."

Given Çifta's experience of Faraçek, Jess thought there was also a good chance that the princesses might no longer be alive, but she kept the thought to herself. She got to her feet and moved back in front of the dais.

"Returning to why we are here," began the king, templing his fingers. "Jessamine Fontana, do you see that what you did could be construed as treason?"

Jess's pulse sped up. "I didn't mean it that way, Sire. I only wanted to help someone who was in trouble—and maybe in some small way take vengeance for what had happened to Greta. I am sorry for the problems it might have caused between Solana and Rahamlar. Truly, I am. If I could go back in time knowing what I know now…"

…that my mother had only days to live…

"…I wouldn't have made the same decision. I have regrets." Not about rescuing Çifta of course, but certainly about not getting to see her mother one more time before losing her. Not something Jess would ever voice aloud in this company.

The king's expression closed against her flimsy

response. "Be that as it may, there must be consequences for civilians who take matters into their own hands. Solana is a civil society founded on laws and principles. We cannot have our citizens sneaking into neighboring territory and getting involved in foreign affairs, especially not members of our own household, and we do consider the Calyx to be part of our household."

"I understand," Jess whispered.

The king continued as if she had not spoken. "The gardener is clear with every member of the Calyx when they contract with us, acts of treason will get you dismissed. In some cases, most cases in fact, treason is cause for execution."

Jess looked at the floor, feeling as though a huge hammer made of stone was lifting—slowly—over her head, and that it could be released at any moment. With Marion gone, ousted from the Calyx, what would she do? She couldn't bear the thought of returning to Dagevli.

"But there is another side to the matter, and another opportunity," the king was saying.

Jess found the courage to lift her gaze.

"What you did—and do not mistake me, I am not endorsing it—was remarkable. With only one other person, you infiltrated a fortress, are responsible for the deaths of several unseelie guards, and your familiar saved you and Laec from certain death with duplication."

Jess opened her mouth to protest—had she really killed those guards? And the king had used the word "duplication" before in reference to the myriad of bats who had rescued them in the underground passage.

King Agir put up a hand. "I know, I know. You claim they were not duplicates because they were large, some of them massive, and your little fellow there is tiny. But there is much you do not know. Duplication is a Fahyli trait. The smaller the familiar, the more duplicates they are able to produce. The more duplicates they are able to produce, the larger those duplicates become. We've never seen a mammalian familiar as tiny as Beazle before. Which makes what he is able to do… well, possibly some kind of record."

Jess felt her jaw sag with disbelief. She glanced down at Beazle. He cocked his head as if to say, *took you long enough*.

She looked up, mystified. "What are you saying? That Beazle… can split himself into a thousand bats?"

King Agir looked at the crofter.

Ian answered in his deep, detached voice. "It's part of the Fahyli magic, Jessamine. Fahyli familiars are able to reproduce themselves in times of need. Some are able to do it at will, others can only do it in times of stress or extreme emergency. To date, the smallest familiars we have worked with are birds. Large birds are able to produce in multiples of tens, the smaller birds in the hundreds. The largest familiar we have is mine, a bear. She can duplicate herself only once—because the larger the familiar, the more magic duplication requires. It can leave both the animal and the fae exhausted. You were very tired after your underground excursion, not only because you had a tense and adrenaline-fueled night—including a fight for your life—and you walked all the way there and back again, but also because you and Beazle produced all those bats, perhaps numbering in the thousands. We don't know. But what we do know for a fact is that the other bats were not summoned *by* him, they were duplicates *of* him."

Jess stared at the crofter, hardly able to absorb what he was saying.

"Jessamine, you are fauna fae," Ian said, not unkindly.

"*And* flora fae," Ilishec was quick to add. "You're both."

The quill scratched and scratched, then stopped. Waiting for her reply.

Jess wished she had a chair to sit in, she felt shocked enough to topple over. "I'm… both?"

The crofter nodded. "Beazle is a mammal and a pollinator. It's rare but it can and does happen. We have another like you among the Fahyli already."

"Do you remember the less desirable compounds we profiled in your sweat?" Ilishec asked.

"Of course." How could she forget?

"You're adept at producing toxins, which is how you were able to fatally poison those guards."

She already understood that—poison, yes, it was the "fatally" part she was having trouble with—but she was still trying to wrap her mind around what the crofter had said.

The king interjected. "Given what we've learned about your nature and abilities, it appears that you are well equipped to serve the kingdom in other ways beyond that of a Calyx. So, Queen Esha and I would like to present you with a choice: either accept dismissal from the Calyx and the kingdom of Solana for treason, never to return, or remain in the Calyx under the condition that—for a period of five years—you will also serve as Fahyli when required."

Jess's mind raced. Aster had told her and Snap at the inaugural ball that the duties of Fahyli included translation, scouting, escorting, guarding, things of that nature. That didn't sound so bad. It even sounded interesting.

"What would my role be as a Fahyli?"

"If we can cultivate your natural talents, given what we've already pointed out about Beazle—his exceptionally small size—you may be well suited to gathering intelligence," said the crofter, adding with no small amount of irony in his tone, "If you've the temperament for it, which I daresay has already been proven by your extra-curricular escapade to Rahamlar."

"Intelligence…" Jess was finding it hard to breath. "You want me to *spy*?"

The king tilted his chin down. "Naturally, you would have to keep the specifics of your new position to yourself, and you would be required to juggle Calyx duties alongside your new role."

Jess shot a glance at Ilishec—it looked like thunderclouds were gathering behind his eyes. The crofter, on the other hand, seemed energized and engaged in this discussion. It struck her like a bolt of electricity: he wanted her. He thought she had value. The realization made her feel a bit dizzy. She could join the Fahyli… but secretly.

"Would the other Fahyli know that we are one of them?"

"Of course." The crofter looked surprised that she

would ask. "Some among them will have to train you. Panther and Tulliana can coach you on telepathy, Regalis can teach you to handle the weapons suitable for women of your stature. Sy can coach you on accents and Kite can help refine your remote vision. There are others who can help."

Small weapons? Telepathy? Jess's hearing fuzzed in and out. "I… don't know what to say."

"You have three days to make a decision." King Agir spoke calmly, plainly, matter-of-factly, like he gave ultimatums of this magnitude all the time. Maybe he did. It was another thought that struck Jessamine with all the speed and velocity of a cobra. *Of course* there were spies working for Solana, every kingdom must have them. It just had never occurred to her before. Her life at the palace had been all about making beauty, she'd been sheltered from any business that did not concern the flora fae.

"Three days," she croaked.

"If you have questions Jess, seek me out," said the crofter. "I'm at your service."

"Me as well," added the gardener quickly.

"Thanks… thank you. Am I… is that all?"

The king gave another of his royal waves. "You are dismissed."

Queen Esha nodded. "You'll be summoned in three days. We will expect your answer."

Numbly, Jess backed away after an awkward curtsy. Beazle licked the pad of her thumb as if trying to tell her everything was okay. She hauled the heavy door open and backed out of the room, dazzled by what fortune had doled upon her.

Chapter Six

Çifta

For as long as she could remember, drawing had helped Çifta process her thoughts. The sound of a pencil stroking a page as it left its marks, separating substance from negative space, interpreting even mundane elements in life in a wholly unique way. The feeling of charcoal, chalk, or wood gripped gently between the fingertips. The pleasure of controlling the shade, depth of color and shadow on a subject. She had started with animals, flowers, trees, and other beautiful things from the outdoors. But faces had soon displaced nature's creations to become Çifta's favorite. There was so much to see in a face, so much of a life lived came out in the eyes, in the tension of a person's lips, in the way they held their head, their jaw. Faces expressed a vast inner world and history, and spoke volumes in a way no landscape or still-life could. Thoughts and feelings could be hidden as one went about their day, but it was exceptionally difficult to hide oneself from the probing eye of a skilled artist. Talent was how it started, skill came after years of sharpening the connection between the eye and the hand—the way a smith hones the edge of a knife. Çifta knew she had ability, but it was more than just a gift, it was a meditation, a form of expression that had become a comfort to her.

So when the day dawned bright with not so much as a wisp in the sky, Çifta looked out over the city of spires, terra cotta roofs and softly turning weathervanes, and had an overwhelming urge to explore, find something new to draw. She dressed in a rush, packed her sketchbook and a selection of pencils, grabbed some fruit from the breakfast room, and made her way out of the palace into the streets of the city. The palace grounds were beautiful, but Çifta craved the kind of drawing opportunities that only life in the streets could provide. She hoped to capture something unique to Solanan citizens, and in the process, maybe she'd come up with how she might explain her predicament to her father when he arrived.

The streets were flooded with sunlight. It was not cold, but neither was it warm, and the air held the scent of fall: mulch and dead leaves and rich soil. She shook her head against the memory of Faraçek's strange breath, forcing thoughts of the prince out of her mind. None of that. Not today. Today she was a free woman, free to walk, free to draw, free to capture something beautiful. She wandered the wide white stone streets, then the narrower offshoots, quaint passages that smelled of baking, stew and hops. These side streets were elegantly serpentine and lined with painted wooden doors of private homes, each a bright singular color not used by any of the others, as effective as an address. Some stood open while parents chatted as their children sprinted up short stairways only to turn and leap off. Çifta had to flatten herself against the walls more than once, lest she be bowled over by a dirty-faced youth.

When she came to an open yard with old, twisted olive trees and garden plots, she took a seat on a bench to give it a proper assessment. Women in long skirts and colorful headwraps, knotted at the neck, worked in the plots pulling up plants, spreading wood chips, wrapping shrubs in burlap, and stacking the last of the autumn vegetables in wheelbarrows and carts. On a blanket on the grass sat a baby girl in a yellow bonnet, no older than a year. In her chubby fist was a soft handmade rattle which she shook as she babbled nonsensically with her sweet baby voice.

It was a nice scene and would make a good warm up sketch.

Çifta opened her sketchbook and selected a pencil. Laying down broad strokes first, she captured the scene as a whole. The stone walls of the open square, the gnarled olive trees and tilled earth, a wheelbarrow, women's skirts and smiles, the baby. Too soon, the baby was bundled up and the women wheeled their goods out of the courtyard.

Çifta turned to a fresh page and closed her eyes. In the bloom of red sunlight through her eyelids she imagined the halls of Rahamlar's fortress. She saw the courtyard churning with unseelie soldiers, horses, and nobles, hunting dogs wagging their tails. She could almost feel the damp, smell the cold mineral scent of the rivers, the green fragrance of the algae creeping up the stone walls. She heard Faraçek's voice again as she was partway up the steps of the aviary.

She shoved thoughts of the prince away, again, but the faces of Serya and Isabey took his place: one so very human, the other unseelie but tender with kindness and the naivete of youth. Another face came to her, that of the young man who had knocked on her door late at night and shown her Serya's seal.

Çifta opened her eyes and drew his face from memory, intending to sketch now, then render it in color on a canvas later, when she had access to paint. She'd seen him in torchlight but that had only made the bones of his face more prominent and highlighted the coppery blond of his hair. He'd had a kind face. Though she couldn't recall the color of his eyes, she clearly remembered the concern in them. A man whose boyhood years were not long behind him. She sketched him as she remembered him, swathed in the amber glow of fire and half hidden in gloom. His face came to life on the page, his youth and earnestness bursting from his gaze.

"I say, that's very good."

Çifta looked behind her. A young fae male with messy blond hair and a studious expression hovered at her shoulder. He was narrow shouldered with long limbs and long hands. His nose was pinched and pointed, but his fae eyes were set above wide cheekbones, and they stared at her sketch, big and interested.

"Thank you." She shifted over on the seat, happy to make acquaintance with someone who appreciated art.

He slid onto the bench beside her, his attention fully on her drawing. "Is it true to life?"

Çifta tried to look at it objectively, holding the drawing away from herself. "True to my memory anyway."

"May I?" The young man gestured at the sketchbook.

Çifta let him have it and he held it out and up so their shadows wouldn't fall over the page, gazing at her handiwork with open admiration. "Very good. Bravo. While I cannot say if it is a good likeness, I can see your mastery at work here. Simply splendid."

Çifta had been complimented on her work all her life. She said thank you without embarrassment or false modesty. "I've been drawing for a long time."

He gently turned the page back, making sure not to touch the drawing. Only artists treated drawings with such reverence.

"You must be an artist," she observed.

"I am, yes. Though I can stand to admit that I still have much to learn. Look at the way you've captured the light, and with only gray scale. Remarkable. Truly." He flipped past the women working and the baby, coming to sketches she'd made of Laec. "Oh, I know him! Of him, I should say. We've never met, but I have seen him around the palace. I never forget a face. You couldn't have captured him any better." He lifted powder-blue eyes to hers. "What is your name?"

She held out a hand. "Çifta Unya. Pleased to meet you. And you are?"

He lay the sketchbook in his lap and took her hand, shaking it gently. "Auvo Feteky, an artist for the Scented Court. Are you a guest or a citizen?"

She gave him a regretful smile. "Guest, unfortunately. I'm from Boskaya."

He looked disappointed and made no effort to hide it. "I supposed as much from your accent, although we do have many foreigners who come to visit but never leave. How long do you plan to stay?"

Just when she'd put her troubles out of her mind. "I… I'm not sure."

He handed her sketchbook back with reluctance, then ran a hand through his floppy hair. "If you were looking for an occupation, I would make you an offer on the spot."

Çifta blinked, wondering if she'd heard him correctly. "An offer?"

"To work in the portrait tower. I have someone retiring after the Midwinter Festival, and haven't found a replacement yet. It is very difficult to find artists of your caliber. We hire only the best. We document the Calyx as they come into the retinue, and frequently—sometimes as often as once a month, depending on how quickly they change—until they leave. It's a wonderful career for an artist who enjoys portraiture and has an eye for detail, so I don't often have openings. I will need to place an advertisement soon, I suppose." He gave a melodramatic but heartfelt sigh, even as he shot her a sly sideways glance.

Çifta's heart surged with desire and excitement. *Work as an artist?* She didn't need money, but the idea of an occupation that involved the use of her skill left her body covered by goosebumps. "That sounds as though it was made for me. I cannot tell you how much I would love it! I could be here for months, please let me help while I am here. Won't you?"

Auvo's fine pale brows lifted. "Months you say?"

"Well, I..." She wasn't about to drag this young fae male into the complicated workings of her situation. It would be prudent to temper her excitement and his hope. She had no idea what the outcome of her conversation with Kazery might be. She could be sent back to Boskaya at once.

"I have often wished to join a society of artists, but I've never"—she was about to say "been allowed" since Kazery, while he was very proud of her talent, did not see the point in encouraging her to develop relationships with a group of poor artistic souls when she was destined for much greater—"found any," she said diplomatically.

Auvo beamed. "There are many artists in Solana. It would be an honor to introduce you. Do you know where the portrait tower is?"

Çifta shook her head.

He lifted a hand and twisted his torso, about to gesture back at the palace. "Let me give you directions—"

She put a hand on his forearm. "Are you going there now?"

He cocked a brow. "I am."

"Why don't you show me yourself?"

A smile split his face in half and he nodded. As they stood, he held his elbow out to her.

Çifta put her things in her bag and took her new acquaintance by the arm. They climbed their way back to the palace, chatting like old friends.

Chapter Seven

Laec

With Erasmus trailing behind him, landing on beams and furniture and whatever else suited his fancy, Laec went to the dining hall in the West Keep and took breakfast without sitting down. Feeling the weight of the limbo he was in, he itched to do something active, to exercise his muscles and his mind. He needed a distraction from his arrest. The view from the window of the dining hall, on the second floor of the keep, reminded him that there was plenty of activity happening in the yards to the west of the palace.

He downed breakfast as he watched soldiers training in one yard, and Fahyli training in the one beside it. Dumping his plate, he grabbed a large apple from a fruit bowl and headed for the door. Erasmus squawked and flew after him, his ever-present shadow.

Laec entered the gate to find some Fahyli in conversation

while they lolled in the grass, others sparring with wooden sticks or swords, and still others shooting at an archery station. Familiars busied themselves in their own ways.

Erasmus winged over to Kite, sitting in the grass. When her familiar landed on her shoulder, she lowered her head for a moment as if listening, then lifted her gaze to watch Laec approach. She nodded to him in greeting.

Above the yard, the glittering palace with its many terraces, windows and spires, blocked out most of the sky. Courtiers could be seen on the second floor terrace—a level which connected the East Keep to the West via a busy hallway—chatting and drinking, playing games, or watching the activity in the yards. Often they came to observe the Fahyli as they trained. Laec recognized a few Calyx among the courtiers from their height alone.

"Oi."

Laec just had time to react as Panther tossed him a wooden staff.

"Let's spar, Stavarjak. These Fahyli are letting me down."

Laec and Panther moved to an even patch of flat, worn earth. Tully lay in the grass with her head up, her lime-green gaze tracking them as they warmed up. She got distracted when a grasshopper bounced in front of her. She flopped a paw on top of it and sniffed at the quarry she'd pinned against the earth. When she moved her paw, the grasshopper bounced again, this time off Tully's forehead. She gave a half-hearted swipe and it hopped away. With a frighteningly large yawn, she flopped over onto her side, tail twitching.

Laec hefted the staff, feeling its weight. He stretched his neck, tilting his head side to side and hearing it crackle. "I haven't fought with wood since I was a wee faeling. Please tell me you upgrade to steel from time to time?"

Panther flashed his teeth in a cocky grin. "Show me you're worthy to taste my steel, then we'll talk."

Laec laughed as Panther advanced, blocking a quick flurry of blows. Panther danced back, giving him a calculating look that said, *okay maybe you are a worthy opponent.* They shuffled back and forth, parrying, deflecting, attacking. The sound of wood striking wood filled the air with loud cracks and the Fahyli shifted in the grass so they could watch.

Kite shouted instructions. "You must be quicker, Laec. What are you, an old man? Steady your stance, Pan. Jump!"

The sparring pair were soon barraged by so many commands and criticisms that it was impossible to tell who the advice was meant to help.

"Thrust! Spin away!"

"Get low. Augh! So sloppy."

"Raise your left arm. Your hands are too close together. Ooooh! That was a sharp one."

"Attack, attack, attack! Cut low! What a mess."

"Take off the blindfold, Geez! Who trained you?"

Laec's blood was up, competition glimmered in Panther's eyes. The two were well matched though they had different techniques. At one point Laec thought he heard Tully give her distinctive bark but he was too focused to look over.

"Protect your head. Dodge, then parry!"

"Steady! Pivot, watch that ankle, Pan!"

Sweat trickled down Laec's back as he deflected a furious attack, then delivered a blow to Panther's midsection with the butt end of his staff. The Fahyli went sprawling backward. Laec was sure he was going to fall, and he did—but Panther turned the momentum into a reverse somersault and was on his feet in a flash, coiled to spring, chest heaving. The Fahyli grinned, perspiration dripping down the sides of his face and into the dark shadow on his jaw.

"Not bad, for a Northman."

Laec wiped a forearm across his brow. Movement from the terrace lifted his gaze; blue-black hair glimmered in the sunlight as Çifta shook her head at someone in the crowd of courtiers watching the sparring. Even from here, Laec felt caught by the brightness of her eyes.

"Oof!"

Laec staggered back as Panther caught him in the stomach with the end of his staff. All the wind left his lungs as he landed hard on his back, trying but failing to reinflate his lungs. For a moment he was back on the road in Syrgana Forest—horses milling around him, neighing with fright as they were ambushed. Panther loomed over him, poised to deliver another blow, but pulled back when he saw that Laec couldn't breathe. He extended a hand and helped Laec to his feet. With a hand against his chest, he finally managed to inhale.

Panther looked up at the balcony then back at Laec, pointedly. "Who distracted you?"

Laec coughed, thumping his chest with a fist. "No one. I let my guard down."

"Sure." Panther smirked. "Need a minute?"

Laec lifted his staff into position.

Panther grinned. Laec had never seen the Fahyli smile so much before. They launched into a fresh round, and were once again barraged by useless advice by their Fahyli audience. They fought until their muscles shook and their throats burned, took a break to drink water, then went for round three.

"Where are you from?" Laec called between parries and thrusts. His strength was being tapped now, but every blow Panther delivered seemed as strong as the first.

"South."

Laec ducked beneath a thrust, panting. "How specific."

Punctuating his efforts with grunts, Panther added, "A jungle place you've never heard of. Very far south. Worlds away, and not just on the map."

Laec spun, parried, thrust, leapt over a swipe intended to trip him. "How did you come to be here then?"

Panther's dark eyes flashed. "I was bought." He bent away from a thrust, flexible as a sapling. "I mean, we. We were bought."

Laec danced in close and delivered a combination from his youth that he thought he'd long forgotten. He marveled that the body had a memory of its own. Sometimes it just needed to be reminded. He was also astounded by Panther's admission. Buying and selling fae was an old world activity that Laec thought no longer happened. "Who bought you?"

Panther deflected, took a blow to the shoulder, then spun away from Laec's advance. "The crofter."

As he turned, Panther's gaze lifted to the balcony. Laec saw his chance and went for it, jabbing Panther in the ribcage twice before the Fahyli could rally his defense.

Panther gusted air and doubled over, groaning and laughing at his own folly.

Laec stepped back and looked up. Some Calyx had joined Çifta watching the fun happening in the yard.

He turned back to Panther, teasing. "Which one is responsible for your demise, Pan? The blond? The redhead?"

Panther groaned as he straightened, one hand on his ribs. "They shouldn't be allowed up there." His cheeks were flushed. Laec couldn't tell if it was from exertion or embarrassment—perhaps a little of both.

Laec chuckled. "I'd make fun of you if I hadn't just been a victim myself."

Panther cocked an eyebrow. "You have your eye on a Calyx?"

Çifta was not Calyx, yet to Laec, she exuded just as much exotic beauty and allure. She shouldered as much responsibility as the flora fae for her powers to distract in the middle of a sparring match. "No. You?"

"Good. Because that would be unwise, my friend." Panther held out his hand for Laec's staff. "Shall we let the others have a go? Sy and Regalis are chomping at the bit to show us up."

Laec was happy to hand over his staff. His muscles burned and his heart was slamming around inside his torso, but some of the anxiety he'd built up over the last few days had fizzled away.

His gaze returned briefly to the balcony. His heart fell a little when he saw that Çifta was no longer there, for which he immediately rebuked himself. Panther had said it would be unwise to fall for a flora fae, but it was even less wise to fall for the daughter of the wealthiest merchant in Ivryndi. Yet, how could Laec stop his feelings from blossoming where they wished? His heart was an untamed stallion, not a draft horse bound to the yoke of reason and logic—however unfortunate that might be for him.

Laec settled in the grass as Sy and Regalis began to circle each other. As the first sharp cracks of wood on wood, Laec realized that Panther had done what Laec himself was famous for in Elphame's court: dodged a direct question.

Chapter Eight

Jessamine

As promised, three days after the ultimatum, Jess was summoned to the room she was beginning to think of as the Lion's Den. The door was open. King Agir and the crofter stood by the window, conversing quietly, but Queen Esha was not present. The crofter's knuckles bumped softly against the table, emphasizing whatever he was saying. The king listened, head partially bowed as he stroked his beard. When Jess entered they both looked up. She curtsied as Beazle dropped out of her hair and crawled to her collarbone, where he sat in the hollow.

"Good afternoon, Miss Fontana." The king moved to the stool on the dais. The crofter watched her with hooded eyes.

"Good afternoon, Sire. We've come to accept your offer." Jess didn't see the point in wasting time. "It was kind of you to give me three days to decide, but it wasn't a difficult decision. We belong here, whatever role we play. So we accept."

The king and crofter exchanged a pleased look.

King Agir said, "You have no questions? No reservations or doubts?"

Jess couldn't prevent a dry smile. "I have doubts that I have the nature of a spy, but since we cannot stay in Solana otherwise, I haven't any choice."

King Agir returned her smile. "No, I suppose you don't. But I would argue that you've already proven that you have the nature of a spy. You are young. When we are young we have yet to learn what we are capable of. You may find yourself better suited to it than you think."

Jess shifted her hands to behind her back, hoping she appeared relaxed when she felt anything but. "So what's next, Sire?"

"Take a knee, Miss Fontana." The king came to stand in front of her.

Jess went to one knee.

"Hold your left hand out, palm up."

She did so.

"Little one?" The king tapped her palm.

Beazle hopped into her hand and looked up.

"A very smart creature you have there," murmured Agir. He put his left hand on the top of Jessamine's head. Warmth flowered through her crown as the king gently touched the top of Beazle's head with the pads of his fingers.

"Lift your eyes to mine."

She did so.

King Agir's strong voice flowed around her. "By the blood flowing through your veins and hearts, do you swear allegiance in good faith never to cause me or my kingdom harm?"

Jess's gaze was locked on the king's. "I swear it, Sire."

Beazle squeaked. Jess thought the king looked like he was trying not to smile.

"Do you promise yourself to me against all other persons and without deceit until your term here is finished?"

"I swear it, Sire."

Beazle squeaked. This time, Jess thought she heard the crofter stifle a snort of laughter.

"Do you promise to uphold your duties to the best of your ability and to keep all secret things of the crown concealed, upon pain of death?"

Jess gulped. "I swear it, Sire."

Beazle squeaked.

"And so I swear my protection to you, and will defend you as my own. Rise, Jessamine Fontana and Beazle Fontana of Solana's Fahyli." The king withdrew his hand and stepped back. "My part here is finished. My liegeman Ian Peneçek, your crofter, is your master. Follow him in all things, just as you would follow me."

"Yes, Sire."

Jess looked at the crofter, whose heavy eyes hid all thought and emotion. She wondered what manner of master he was and suppressed a shiver. Ilishec didn't seem to like Ian, which made her not want to trust him. She'd sworn to obey and serve King Agir, and by extension the crofter, but that didn't mean she had to like him. Could she separate her feelings from her service?

The king surprised Jessamine by excusing himself, leaving Jess and Ian alone. They didn't have long to stare at one another before Jess sensed someone else was present. She turned.

The same young man she had caught a glimpse of while waiting to hear her "punishment" was standing just behind her. She had not seen him leave that first time, just like she hadn't seen him enter today—and the king had closed the door as he left. This young man had not been in this room a second ago. She would swear to it.

A soft hum passed Jess's ear as a small colorful bird zipped by and landed on the top of the young man's head.

"Where did you come from?" Jess asked, unsure if it was the man or the hummingbird she was addressing.

He smiled and held out a ring. "This is for you. You don't need to wear it, in fact its best if you don't, unless you need to invoke the protection of the king."

She took the small gold ring. It had the tiny wreathed lion's head of Solana wrought in gold. Two phrases were etched around the inside of the band. "Solana, *cor meum*," she read aloud. "*Pulchritudo nostra fortitudo*."

"Solana, my heart and—"

"Beauty is our strength," Jess guessed.

He dipped his chin. "I'm Digit. This is Ania. We're going to show you around."

Jess glanced at the crofter, who gave her a cool smile that she couldn't read. "Enjoy."

"Show me around?" Then it occurred to her. "Oh, do you mean the West Keep?"

Digit shook his head. "I'm going to show you Solana Palace as very few get to see it." He moved to the wall. With a featherlight touch of the stones, a section of the wall slid back into itself and then to the side. The entrance was jagged with bricks and mortar, leaving a toothy hole. A narrow passageway was revealed, but when it was closed, one would have to look very close to see that it was even there.

Jess's eyes widened. "That explains how you come and go without using the door."

Digit tilted his head. "Now you can, too."

Jess's pulse jumped with excitement and curiosity. Digit slipped into the passage and disappeared from view. With a final look at the crofter, she followed him.

Squeezing into the passage way, she saw that it went both left and right and that small stones planted in the mortar gave off a red glow to light her path. Excited, Beazle flapped off into the gloom. Jess couldn't tell which way Digit had gone, but Beazle knew. As she moved away from the trick door, the grinding of stone on stone signaled that it had closed behind her, leaving her in the narrow dusty gap between two walls.

Cursing under her breath as a spiderweb tickled her forehead, Jess crept along the passageway and followed it to the left, where—thankfully—it widened. The light improved due to a cluster of vertical slashes in the stone, through which fresh air drifted. Digit waited for her in a small alcove, his hair moving in the slight breeze. Ania hovered in the air beside him. Beazle crawled up the wall toward one of the vents to sniff at the air coming in.

Digit turned his back to the vents and pointed to a large, whole stone in the wall. A complex collection of lines and angles drawn on the surface drew Jess in for a better look. It took her a moment to figure out what she was looking at.

"It's a map?" She cocked her head at it, trying to discern what was wrong with it. "But it's incomplete."

"They all look like that. But after a while you won't need them anyway."

"Them?" Jess looked at Digit as Ania landed on top of his head. Beazle landed beside her in Digit's hair, where he sniffed at Ania. She was tiny herself and yet still three times his size.

"Beaze! I'm sorry, he doesn't usually sit on other people."

"That's alright." Digit dimpled. "Everyone likes Ania."

"She is lovely. So, what do you mean "them." I won't need them any more."

"The maps. These are all over the palace, and even in some places in the city. There is a way to go through the palace from one side to the other without ever being seen." Digit brushed dirt off the front of his tunic, a simple black long-sleeved shirt belted at the waist. "It's a little dusty, but you'll find you get used to it. You have to remember to clean yourself off before going back out in public, or you'll get questions."

Jess ran a finger over the map, feeling the recessed

lines of the etching, which had been filled with some kind of pigment.

"I get that a spy has to be stealthy, but what are you usually up to when you use these passages?"

"It could be delivering a private message or a secret item. It could be to hide. But more often than not it is to listen to conversations or to search the rooms of guests that are under suspicion."

"Oh." These were behaviors her mother had raised her not to do. Granted, she had eavesdropped on her mother several times, she'd also looked through her mother's things when Marion wasn't around. Marion had known she would, or she wouldn't have hidden Julian's bonnets. Jess wasn't sure if she felt comforted or ashamed. "Who else knows about these passages?"

"Only those who need to know."

That made Jess's stomach tighten. She needed to know because she'd be asked to do something that needed to be done in secret. The idea made her feel a little too warm. "You seem awfully young to be doing work like this."

Digit continued down the passage, keeping his voice low. "Young people make better spies. We have faster reflexes, sharper senses. We're not as good with weapons as those who have had years of training, so we're better utilized in this way rather than combat. You'll still have to learn how to defend yourself—all the Fahyli have to know how to fight."

Jess had to touch the grimy walls on either side to keep from stumbling. "F-fight?"

"Relax. You'll learn." Digit's voice drifted back to her,

confident as a promise, bouncing off the walls, which now felt like they were closing in. Around a corner, they arrived at a narrow set of uneven steps that disappeared into blackness.

"Watch yourself here. Use Beazle's eyes if you can."

"We can't do that on command." Jess kept her hands on the walls as she toed her way down.

"You'll learn that too."

"Can you do it? With Ania?"

"No." Digit was almost entirely invisible ahead of her.

Jess almost missed a step. "Wait, you have a hummingbird familiar. Ania is a pollinator. But… I'd have seen you before if you were Calyx."

"I'm flora fae, but I'm not Calyx. I wanted to be once but…"

The sound of their shoes scraping over dusty stone steps echoed off the walls. Jess wrinkled her nose as the urge to sneeze tickled her sinuses.

"But what?"

"But my father wouldn't hear of it, so I'm Fahyli instead," he whispered. "Quiet now."

Jess held her breath as muffled voices came from the other side of the wall—a couple of men and at least one woman were talking. There was laughter and the sound of chips or games pieces being tossed on a table or a wooden board. She and Digit moved silently by the party, coming to the bottom of the steps. The voices faded as they continued on.

Digit led Jess through the warren of secret passageways and showed her where they were on the partial maps in little alcoves. They were able to look down into ballrooms and council rooms, galleries, certain alcoves near the libraries, the queen's parlor, the kitchens and many of the guest suites. Jess was introduced to a layer of secrecy that she had never suspected was part of Solana.

"Is there anywhere we can't spy on?"

"A few of the royal chambers have rooms that are completely private, but if the king wants someone to think they're having a private audience, yet he wants us to overhear what is going on, he'll host a conversation where it can be heard."

"So… he wants to be eavesdropped on?" Jess traced her fingers along the wall as they descended to a lower level, then quickly snatched them back. The walls felt damp, and very dirty.

"Sometimes."

"But why?"

Digit sighed. "We don't always know. Just because we're spies doesn't mean we're told everything that's going on. More often, it's best that we don't know, and by best, I mean it's safer. We have to compartmentalize tasks, keep them separate from everything else. Pay attention to where we are, Jess. Do you recognize it?"

Jess pulled up. "We've been here before?"

He sighed again and looked back. In the gloom his face looked like a half-moon on a cloudy night. "You have to memorize these passages, Jessamine. One day you might be required to cross the palace very quickly. You can't be stumbling up and down stairs, getting lost or coming out at the wrong place."

"Sorry, I'm… this is all new to me."

Digit faced front. "That's obvious. Pay attention to the features around you, and keep up. Let's do another circuit. I only have you for another forty-five minutes, so we'll have to hurry. Ilishec is expecting you after this, right?"

"Yes." Jess felt nervous about her meeting with the gardener.

Digit seemed to sense her concern. "It'll be fine, Jess. Put it out of your mind so you don't get lost."

She nodded, and off they went again.

"Come in, Jess." The gardener sat at his worktable with folders and scrolls spread haphazardly about him. He looked unhappy as he turned to her, but his expression shuttered. "How are you?"

Jessamine sat beside Ilishec. "I'm…" *Sad. Empty. Lost. A little scared.* "Fine."

Beazle climbed up the fabric of her shirt and came to a stop on her shoulder. He could sense the current of anxiety that hummed through Jess's body. She felt like someone had hooked her up to the ether to keep her heart beating. She hadn't slept well since returning to the palace and wondered if she would ever sleep through the night again, or wake without moisture on her cheeks. She swallowed down the lump in her throat.

"We haven't had much time to talk. Are you angry with me?"

Ilishec folded his fingers on the tabletop and looked

down at his hands. "Angry? No. I'm disappointed that you would risk your life and your position by doing something so foolish."

Jess nodded as a cold fist wrapped around her heart.

He looked at her with soft eyes. "But I also remember being young, impulsive, and making stupid choices. More importantly, I remember learning from them. We adults can impart advice and share our life experiences with young people, but no matter how much we wish otherwise, we can't make you understand risk the way that decades of living can. So here we are. I am thankful that you suffered nothing more serious than a few cuts and bruises, and I'm deeply sorry about your mother. We're never really ready to lose a parent, but at your age it is exceptionally difficult."

"Thanks." Her voice was a husk.

"Are you sure you want to do it, Jess? Work with the crofter? Join the Fahyli? Be a spy?"

"What choice do I have? I don't want to go back to Dagevli and live in my mother's cottage. Dagevli is…" *A river of sad memories I would drown in.* "…not my home any longer. As much as I love my neighbors, I'm not one of them. I belong here, with the other flora and fauna fae."

Ilishec cleared his throat and spoke slowly, as if picking and choosing his words delicately. "I understand. I would never speak against King Agir's decrees, but…"

"You don't like it," Jess supplied. "I can tell."

He let out a long exhale through his nose. "Working with the crofter will turn you into something else—someone else—and frankly, I don't like sharing. To me, you were Calyx first and that is your true calling. But since it's not my decision, I must do my part." He reached across the table and drew a brown folder toward himself with one hand, while hooking a finger of the other hand on the edge of a paper box, which he tilted so that Jess could see the contents. Inside were tissue wrapped packages. "These are the clothes you were wearing when you returned from Rahamlar. I had them analyzed."

"So that's where they'd gone. I thought someone had thrown them out."

"The reason I told you to focus on honeysuckle, *cleome* and *erigeron* for Captain Yorin's inspection is because the chemical blend that saturated your clothing came from other botanicals. I knew that as long as your body wasn't oozing the same fragrance as your tunic from that night, even a dog wouldn't be able to identify you as you." He paused, as if unsure how to continue. "Your mix of plants and flowers is very interesting, Jess. Some of what you produce is fragrant and beneficial, while others are…"

"Deadly? I didn't realize until the king's ultimatum that I had killed those guards."

He nodded as he flipped open the folder. "Yes. We found carboxyparquin, atropine, scopolamine, and a lot more."

Jess shook her head. "I figured out that I was making poison when the first guard passed out after sharing a waterskin with me, but I wasn't doing it on purpose. I promise. I can hardly believe that such a small dose could… kill."

"And therein lies the problem. Jess, you must—and

I mean *must*—learn to control what your magic is doing, otherwise you're a threat to everyone around you. The only ones immune to your poison are you and Beazle." Ilishec shot her a sideways look. "Tell me, what were you feeling that night?"

Jess let her mind journey back to the events in Rahamlar. A distinct memory of—initially—enjoying herself: she'd been adrenalized, excited, she'd felt strong, maybe even invincible. That's not what Ilishec was asking her about, though. "All kinds of things, but after I got caught I was mostly frightened." She thought about the way she'd been kicked, beaten, ridiculed. "Frightened and angry."

A series of conflicting emotions ran across Ilishec's features, landing on solemnity. He held up a finger. "Listen to me, Jessamine. Learning to control one's emotions is important for anyone in service to the Scented Court, but for you, it is absolutely critical. I'm talking about a level of control that will never be required from the rest of the Calyx. You need to be able to take a slap across the face—metaphorically speaking—and still produce fragrant honeysuckle. You need to be able to produce *erigeron* in life threatening situations. You need to be able to control the production of *datura* and *atropa belladonna,* even *ipomoea* and certain varieties of *solidago*. I'm not going to mince words here, Jess. You're extremely dangerous."

Extremely dangerous. Jess felt wonder and a touch of disquiet. Of course, she now knew this, but to hear someone in authority say it out loud and so plainly gave her shivers. It was like the deed to a property being stamped, only this stamp went on her forehead.

Before her label could really sink in, Ilishec returned to the folder. "I had Hazel cross-check your profiles with a dictionary of active phytochemical agents to help us categorize your abilities. Their effects include—and this is not a complete list—headaches, vomiting, severely dry mouth, slurred speech, disruption of cognitive capacity such as learning and memories, miscarriages, paralysis, confusion, heart problems, digestive problems…"

Jess half wondered—in spite of the gardener's earlier assertion—if she might be capable of poisoning herself because her mouth was dry and her hearing was fuzzing in and out.

"…liver damage, depression, irritability and weakness, loss of appetite, coma-inducement, convulsions, blindness, dilated pupils, violent beha—"

"Stop! Stop!" Jess grabbed the gardener's forearm. "Please stop."

Ilishec looked at her, compassion softening his brown eyes. "And of course, instant death."

Jess covered her eyes with her hands. "I'm a killer."

"You're not a killer, Jess. At least no more than anyone else. Many Calyx can produce poisonous compounds, we just don't cultivate those abilities because we're focused on fragrance. Part of your penalty is to face this side of yourself, to understand it and control it. But my dear, you would need to do this anyway, even if you had never interfered with Lady Çifta. I am sorry that you're in this situation. I wish I could change it, but wishing is worthless. You have a duty, and so do I. The crofter will train you for your Fahyli role, but this is mine. Mine and Peony's."

Jess took her hands away from her eyes to stare at the gardener with dismay. "Peony?"

He nodded. "No one is better at isolating and compartmentalizing flora magic. Already she has surpassed Rose with her natural talent, which is really saying something."

"But…" Jess sputtered. "Peony hates me, and I'm not particularly fond of her either."

"I'm sure she doesn't *hate* you," Ilishec murmured.

Outrage lashed at Jessamine's heart. Peony?! It was adding insult to injury. She pulled a face. "Peonies aren't even toxic."

"Not particularly no, but that's beside the point. The principles are the same whether you are producing perfume or poison. You don't have to be friends, but you must pay attention to what she teaches you. Part of growing up is learning how to cooperate with people in a civilized manner in order to meet a mutual objective—keeping your personal feelings out of it." He added with an ironic twist of his mouth. "Believe me, this is a challenge that occurs at all ages."

Jess's tummy felt like a snarled coil of wire. "Does Peony know she has to tutor me?"

Ilishec gave Jess a grim smile. "Not yet, she's extremely busy and I haven't had time to talk with her, but she will. This is what you agreed to, Jess. I suggest you make the best of it. I'm going to have to make the best of it, as will Peony. I daresay she will help you greatly in both directions. Even if your… darker side… had been left in the dark, I might have asked her to tutor you at some point. You were struggling with—"

"I remember," snapped Jess, then immediately murmured, "Sorry."

"That's alright. I'm sure you're feeling a little overwhelmed." Ilishec went to the sink and filled a glass with water for Jess. "Shall we start with *belladonna*? It has some truly spectacular ill effects. But then again so does *datura*. Do you have a preference on where we focus first?"

Jess took a sip of water as Ilishec pulled another folder toward them and flipped it open. Jess could read a poem that someone with pretty handwriting, probably Hazel, had scrawled in the corner. It was entitled "Traditional Mnemonic" which was followed by:

Blind as a bat
Mad as a hatter,
Red as a beet,
Hot as a hare,
Dry as a bone,
The bowel and bladder lose their tone,
And the heart runs alone.

Jess's own heart felt like it was running alone. Glumly, she shook her head. "I don't care where we start."

Ilishec put a pair of glasses on. "Good. Then let's begin."

Jessamine's lessons with Regalis were a shock to her system. She'd been under the impression—based on her time with him in Dagevli—that the tall, lanky Fahyli was a soft-hearted fae who preferred to keep to himself, read books, cook stews, and sleep in long grass beneath trees. While all of that was true, she now learned that it was also true that he loved weaponry and had a savage streak a mile wide.

He exposed her to at least twenty different kinds of weapons, watching as she handled them—poorly—with a measured look in his eyes that reminded her a lot of his hawk. He wasn't pleased with the thickness of her wrists (too delicate) or the length of her fingers (too long) or the way she moved her limbs (too ladylike). When she became irritated with him (I'm Calyx, I'm trained to dance) he wouldn't tolerate her cheek. She would simply have to overcome the habits she learned from her dance masters and she was, he affirmed, more than capable of learning both.

Regalis was annoyed that she'd have to settle for a short, light dagger, but Jess was delighted when he handed her the knife that would become hers—should she ever have a mission that needed a blade—the lighter and smaller her weapon, the better. She figured she wasn't a soldier meant for battle so self-defensive techniques should be sufficient; and further, she had poison. Regalis had disagreed, but after talking to the crofter he drilled her in self-defense maneuvers until her body was bruised and sore. He taught her a few attack combinations, usually with one eye on the keep, and Jess suspected he didn't have permission to do it, but he loved fighting strategies so much that he couldn't deny himself the pleasure of sharing his knowledge.

Four days a week in the early mornings she was put through a rigorous session in the fields of the West Keep. She'd return to her room before breakfast, sweaty and stinking of overripe *cleome*—the raw material she channeled during her sessions, just to keep things safe. While she bathed, she readied her mind for dances, court etiquette, and fragrances.

From Sy she learned to identify accents from all over Ivryndi, and ways of extracting information without exposing one's true purpose or even letting the one being interrogated realize that they'd given up something of value. From Kite she learned to open herself further to Beazle's sight, but given that bats don't have great eyesight, and Jessamine was not equipped to receive sonar from him, they achieved only modest success. Certainly they could never expect to achieve the kind of telepathic vision that Fahyli with birds of prey had. Still, Jess was delighted with their progress. At least now she could signal Beazle for help rather than rely on him to decide when to send her images, which could be disorienting.

Two days a week she roamed the secret passageways with Digit until she was able to get around without aid. Beazle helped her in the beginning, but his memory was so much better than hers that he got bored and returned to his usual naps. When she was able to take a book from Digit on one side of the palace and deliver it into his hand on the opposite side, without ever being seen, and under a pre-set length of time, Digit proclaimed her a master of the palace.

Three times a week, and always at night with Beazle flying above her to make sure they were alone, Jessamine did the sweat sessions that resulted in her most toxic substances. She never touched the equipment, she only did explosive sprints up the steepest incline the garden had to offer, to produce sweat as quickly as possible. She thought she'd have to repel the wee harvesters but they never came anywhere near her while she was slick with poison. They knew what was deadly and what was not. She did her best to get as much of the raw materials into the special bottles the gardener had assigned her, without any help. She then corked, labeled and delivered them to a lockbox in Ilishec's workshop. She kept meaning to ask him what he did with them, but she was so busy with her schedule that they hardly entered her mind. After every session, she put her sweaty clothing into a special bag for cleaning, then showered and scrubbed until her skin was red and glowing before slipping into bed, exhausted and satisfied with the fruits of another productive day.

CHAPTER NINE

LAEC

LAEC FROWNED AT Erasmus as the raptor fluttered to the top of the stone wall surrounding the courtyard and gave his classic, piercing cry.

"I know, I know. I'm not going anywhere. You won't let me," Laec muttered under his breath, even as he reached into the pouch he'd begun to carry around and retrieved a piece of meat. Erasmus cocked his head and gave a chirp that slid up at the end, like a question. Laec held out the raw flesh and Erasmus swooped over, snatching it from Laec's fingers and swallowing it in one smooth motion. The kite returned to his post, watching Laec with one beady eye.

"You could at least make it last. Honestly, where's the joy in swallowing everything in one gulp?" He frowned. "Are we ever going to be friends? Or are you just going to stalk me?"

It had been weeks since the king had commanded Laec

not leave the palace until further notice, and since then, Laec had been followed by animals wherever he went. Most often it was Erasmus, but sometimes it was Ferrugin, occasionally Mae or one of the dogs. Laec had taken to carrying food with him in the hopes that he could befriend the familiars. They always took the food, but they never got friendly. He was beginning to think the manipulator was the one being manipulated.

For a short time, there was no animal in sight and Laec thought it might be safe to celebrate an improvement in his status. But then he went by the library and saw Tully, Pan's black panther, emerge from beneath a table. She slunk along after him, keeping to corners and shadowy places, silent as a ghost. His illusion of increasing freedom went up in smoke. How ironic that the largest, most intimidating animal was also the least visible. But most often it was Erasmus, which meant it was Kite who'd been assigned to watch Laec. He wondered how she felt about that.

Laec glanced longingly through the open gates of the courtyard at the city beyond. Solana was a city of diversions and wonders, of gossip and trade, of quaint shops and bustling fragrant markets. Palace life was luxurious—even for someone who was not allowed to leave, and under constant supervision—but it wasn't real life. Putting his back to the gate, Laec trudged up the steps. A clattering of horses on the courtyard stones made him turn.

A group of human soldiers came into the yard, trailing a man in a wide black hat with a huge plumed feather. A flurry of stable hands and groomsmen swept into the yard, taking bridles and holding horses while men dismounted.

The leader, in a red coat with brass buttons running down the front and knee-high black boots, got off his mount and stretched. Laec cocked an eyebrow. The man was enormous. His uniform would have been impressive enough, but in addition to his clothing and the long, curved sword at his hip, he had a thick black beard, impeccably groomed. He even had a wax-tipped mustache with a fullness Laec doubted he could achieve even with magical enhancement. Laec absently rubbed the stubble at his jaw.

The man's soldiers mingled with Solana's servants as they led the horses away, chatting and laughing. Some of the soldiers gawked up at the palace spires, the gaping rose window illuminated with its soft light, the flowering vines trailing along the walls and winding up the columns along the steps.

When a stable hand passed close to Laec's elbow, he stopped the boy. "Who is that?"

"A merchant from Kirkik, sir," the boy retorted before scampering away.

Laec's curiosity lit like dry kindling. This huge bearded man had to be Çifta's father. Çifta shared no likeness to him except for shiny blue-black hair. Laec kept back and waited a few moments before following Kazery inside the palace. Çifta's father didn't glance his way as he chatted with a servant in Solana livery. The palace entrance was a large space with many tall columns. One wide staircase ascended a level before splitting off into two, each leading to different wings of the palace. The servant led Kazery up toward the East Keep.

Keeping his distance and thankful for the near constant busyness of the palace hallways, Laec followed unnoticed. They made their way toward one of the small libraries but didn't enter. The servant peered into a few of the alcoves, drawing each curtain back with an apology ready for the inhabitant. His heart thudding, Laec pretended to be looking out a window as he heard Çifta's delighted voice and Kazery's booming laugh. He glanced over his shoulder to see Çifta swept up in her father's arms and spun in a circle. Servants and guests narrowly avoided Çifta's flying feet. The man who had led Kazery strode away, an amused smile on his face.

Laec faced the window again just as Erasmus flapped down the hall and landed on the back of a gilded bench. He blinked at Laec as if to ask, *what are you up to?*

Kazery and Çifta disappeared inside the alcove. Laec stuck his tongue out at the bird. Hiding behind a servant carrying a tall stack of linens, Laec passed Çifta's alcove and slipped into the neighboring one—sitting against the wall nearest her, straining his ears. He heard Çifta and Kazery talking, voices too muffled to understand. Three small stained-glass windows lined this alcove. Laec propped one open and sat resting his elbows on the sill, as if innocently enjoying the brisk late-autumn air. Kazery's voice, which was as powerful as his presence and carried like it was amplified, came clearly to Laec's ears.

"…sorry I cannot stay," he was saying. "My business in Cardagenya is somewhat urgent. I left my carriages with Hashe and came on horseback to save time."

Çifta didn't sound surprised. "Surely, you'll return for

the Midwinter Festival though? This year is the Decennial and many important people are coming."

"These are not my people, little minnow. What happened to your cheek?"

Laec's gut tightened like the string on a lady's purse, but Kazery sounded more curious than alarmed. Çifta's bruises had almost fully healed, but there was still a faint patch of blue on the curve of her right cheek.

Çifta gave a fake laugh. "It's nothing. I got up to relieve myself in the middle of the night and accidentally walked into the door. I'm not used to my surroundings yet."

Laec made a face. Why was she lying?

"I thought you'd grown out of your clumsiness, my girl. Apparently not." There was a crinkle of paper. "But I didn't come all this way to admonish your lack of nimbleness."

"My letter." Çifta sounded reticent now, even apprehensive.

"Of course your letter. I received two letters within a few weeks of one another, one reported that you'd arrived safely in Rahamlar, had met your betrothed and all was well. I was elated to read your permission to arrange the shipment of the bride price. I made all the necessary preparations and you cannot imagine all the coordination that was required, separating the valuables and packaging them individually for some level of insurance, and so on. But just before I was to send the first instalment, I received *another* letter." Kazery's tone was growing in incredulity. "This one reported that you were no longer even *in* Rahamlar, but Solana. You're fine, but you wish to annul the betrothal. Imagine my shock. You wrote nothing of the circumstances which led to this. There was no explanation, only a request to come and see you, but no wish to come home? Forgive me, darling. I don't think I have ever been more perplexed in my life, and as my secretaries will tell you, that is really saying something."

Laec shared the man's confusion. She hadn't explained anything at all to her father?

Çifta was apologetic but firm. "We weren't right for one another, father. Can you trust that I would not ask for an annulment unless it was absolutely necessary?"

Kazery let out a frustrated breath. "You're not giving me anything to work with Çifta. Do you not understand that I agreed to your betrothal with goodwill and honor? We made a promise to one another, King Osvitan and me, a commitment. He is not some lesser noble, he is a king. You have embarrassed me, daughter, and you seem unable or unwilling to help me to understand why. It cannot be borne."

Laec's esteem for Kazery emerged like a tender sprout. The man was huge and intimidating, but he spoke to his daughter in the gentlest tone. His irritation came through, but Laec thought the man was making great efforts to keep it veiled, at least until he understood more—an admirable quality.

There was a squawk from Erasmus as the kite landed on the floor and bounced toward Laec. Laec put his finger to his lips. Erasmus croaked again.

There was a moment of silence from the adjacent alcove before Kazery commented. "There are a lot of animals here."

There was a smile in Çifta's voice. "They're part of Solana's charm."

"If you say so. Come, let's not get distracted. Were you mistreated? What crime was committed that could not be worked out with talk and reason?"

Laec bit his lip. There it was. He'd laid it out exactly. Like a tongue going to a tender molar, Kazery had found the sore spot. Would Çifta lie to his face directly? She had no reason to protect Faraçek. He couldn't hurt her anymore. She was safe now, she owed her father the truth… Didn't she?

Çifta didn't respond audibly, but when Kazery added, "No? Then what? My dear, I am at my wits end."

Laec's eyes drifted shut with disappointment. She must have shaken her head no. He flexed his fingers and balled them into fists.

"I'm sorry then," Kazery replied simply. "You leave me no choice. Your sisters have done their duty, Çifta. Unless you can produce a better reason to annul the betrothal, you simply must return to Rahamlar. You must do it soon, and with sincere regrets on your lips. As far as I can tell, the prince still desires to marry you, in spite of your bizarre behavior, bless him. You will return, you will apologize, and you will wed."

"But—" Çifta sounded distraught now. "You built a clause into the contract!"

Kazery grumbled. "I told Gemma not to tell you."

"Why ever not?"

"Because that clause was inserted for dire circumstances only. I expected you to put your heart into making this alliance work, as all of your sisters have done with theirs. You can be flighty and emotional, little minnow. If you found that it was not a smooth start with the prince, this can only be expected. Love can take time, but it will come. You'll see."

"I don't think it will." Çifta's voice was small.

Kazery's voice finally rose a little. "And is this your reason for shaming me and the Unya name? This is your reason for destroying my access to the twin rivers, something I have coveted since I began my enterprise? Because you don't *think* you'll fall in love with him?"

Çifta's voice now had tears in it. "If the twin rivers are so important to you, surely we can find another way to secure them. Why must it involve my future? My life?"

A quiet astonishment seemed to leech from the alcove.

"What is the motto I raised you under, Çifta? Have you so quickly forgotten it?"

"Duty above all," Çifta replied meekly. "But father, I am dutiful. I have always been dutiful, I love you more than my own life."

"It doesn't look that way, Minnow."

"Let me try to secure the rivers for you without having to bind myself to… him. He is so…"

Laec leaned toward the window, holding his breath in anticipation of Çifta's chosen adjective.

Kazery was also apparently anticipating the conclusion. When she failed to finish her sentence he finally prompted: "So what?"

"Unseelie," Çifta cried. "I do not trust him, father. I cannot."

"But why?" Kazery now sounded on the edge of tearing out his own beard.

"Please. Let me find another way. Give me a chance. Could we not pay them for access, like everyone else does? Money can buy anything."

Kazery let out a weary sigh. "Our alliance was meant to ensure permanent access without the expensive tolls. A uniting of our families, my wealth with their power would give us something we cannot buy. You are meant to become a princess. Do you not understand what that means? You want to throw away a royal title and all that comes with it, like so much garbage? This is madness."

Çifta was on the edge of begging. "Please, let me try, father. If I fail…"

A long, freighted space of quiet passed, during which Laec had to make real effort to keep from yanking out his eyebrows.

"…then I'll do as you wish."

Kazery grumbled something inaudible. "I will return from Cardagenya when my business concludes. I am not certain how long it will take, but I have much to do so it will probably be after the Festival has finished. Am I to understand you wish to stay here, in Solana?"

Çifta sounded relieved. "Yes. It suits me and I am welcome here."

"I am not saying I agree, I am saying that I will send a letter to Osvitan asking for a little time. We will resume this conversation when I return. If by then you have somehow miraculously come to your senses, or found another way to make a meaningful alliance with Rahamlar without sewing your hand into it, then I'll listen to what you have to say."

"I'm grateful, father. I cannot tell you how grateful."

Kazery mumbled again, something about how having a favorite daughter would be his downfall.

Çifta sounded like a different woman now. "Are you sure you will not stay tonight? Solana is very beautiful, and has much to offer its guests."

He grunted. "No. I have hours of daylight left and time is not to be wasted."

Their voices moved away from the window.

Laec sat in the alcove while Erasmus watched him—neck feathers ruffled and head low, like the bird was either bored or tired—trying to work out why Çifta would conceal her abuse. Eventually Laec left the alcove and, keeping to the upper level, returned to a terrace overlooking the courtyard. He peered over the railing in time to see Kazery and his soldiers canter away. The man was true to his beliefs and wasted no time. Çifta stood on the steps of the palace, watching them go. She hugged herself, wrapping her hands around her elbows, looking small and cold. She stood there for a long time and Laec watched her, unmoving, and wondering what she was thinking.

Erasmus made a throaty noise, then yawned and stretched his wings.

"Would it make things easier for you to sit on my shoulder or on top of my head?" Laec asked the bird with fake courtesy.

Erasmus squawked, bounced once on the railing, then landed on Laec's shoulder.

"I was being sarcastic." But Laec let the bird stay. He waited at the top of the steps for Çifta to come back inside. When she entered the foyer, he waved to get her attention.

Even from a distance, Çifta's smile filled Laec's heart with warmth. It was a feeling that Laec rebelled against but was powerless to prevent. This was not what he had left Stavarjak for, and he really *should* be keeping his distance. Elphame would not be impressed. Then again, Elphame didn't need to know. That was the beauty of providing reports written from his perspective only, he could slant things any way he liked, and leave out what he deemed irrelevant.

Laec returned Çifta's smile as he went to meet her.

She pulled her shawl around her shoulders and held it at her bosom, her long tapered fingers curled around the fabric. "You've been avoiding me."

"Can you blame me?"

Erasmus's head swiveled back and forth from Çifta to Laec, like an old ladies' maid hungry for court gossip. Laec wondered for the hundredth time just how much the bird understood.

Çifta sighed. "I should have told you right away that I was betrothed to Prince Faraçek."

"Yes, you should have." Laec looked down at her, keeping accusation out of his tone as much as he could. "Why didn't you?"

They strolled together toward the gardens.

Çifta's lips compressed. She looked down at her hands. "I didn't want to… break the spell. We were having such a nice time. I was afraid of how quickly it would come to an end. I was afraid you'd distance yourself from me."

He would have, and he did. After she'd told him on the road—and before they parted ways—a wall went up between them. But the wall had gaping holes, because her admission, late though it was, only made Laec like her more. She could have let him find out some other way, but she'd not taken the coward's way out, and he admired that.

She looked over. "I'm sorry. Truly I am. I won't conceal anything from you again. Friends?"

Laec grunted. What Çifta could have taken as a sound of half-hearted agreement was actually guilt. Now he was concealing something from her.

They stepped out into the autumn sunshine, entering a garden crisscrossed with walkways lined with fragrant flowerbeds and shrubs. Couples and small groups of beautifully dressed courtiers strolled throughout, in conversation or just admiring the space. A group of musicians played a sweet symphony beneath a pretty pergola swallowed by *bougainvillea*.

"Where did you—" Çifta began.

At the same time Laec said, "I have to apologize—"

They laughed nervously.

Çifta said, "You first."

He cleared his throat. "I was just going to say that I have to apologize as well. I'm hoping after I tell you what I've done, you'll consider us even."

"Oh?"

"You and your father"—Laec took a breath—"I was sitting in the next alcove."

Her forehead creased and she squinted as they stepped out of the shade of a fat oak. Laec couldn't tell if she was upset or if it was the sun. Çifta stopped walking and put a hand in the crook of his elbow to stop him, the other she lifted to block the sun. "You were eavesdropping?"

Laec forced himself to look her in the eyes. "Yes."

Erasmus squawked as if to say, *I was there, I saw him.*

Çifta considered this, her gaze probing. She seemed to be torn between giving him hell and forgiving him. Finally, she let out a sigh and looked away. "I suppose that does make us even." Çifta's gaze shifted to the bird. "Friend of yours? I feel like I've seen him before."

Laec scoffed, annoyed. "Hardly. I can't get rid of him. He's reporting my every action to Kite as part of my punishment for rescuing you."

"I'm so sorry, Laec." Çifta paused and cocked her head. "Who is Kite?"

"One of the Fahyli, the fae you see around here in Solana livery, often accompanied by an animal. Erasmus visited you in your bedroom back in Rahamlar, that's why you feel like you know him, you have met before."

Çifta's glacial eyes widened. "Of course! It was so dark then. He looked so different. Thank you, Erasmus, for your part in helping me to get out of there." Çifta reached slowly toward the kite. Erasmus ruffled his feathers and shook himself proudly, letting her stroke his breast. "He's so beautiful."

"Beautiful and irritating." Laec watched Çifta while she stroked Erasmus, trying to read her expression. "I don't normally eavesdrop on people. Actually that is a lie. I eavesdrop a lot, but I don't normally eavesdrop on friends. This is… what shall I call it… an extenuating circumstance?"

Çifta began to walk again.

Laec fell in step with her. "Why didn't you tell your father the truth about Faraçek?"

"You don't know Kazery Unya." Çifta kicked a pebble off the path. "If he knew, he'd do something terrible."

"More terrible than forcing you to marry someone despicable?"

Çifta looked down, her expression doubtful. "He won't force me. You'll see."

Laec shook his head. It hadn't sounded like that to him. "He said he wouldn't let you break the betrothal."

Çifta exhaled, letting her cheeks balloon, which made her look heartbreakingly young. "I have a little time. I just have to find a reason for my father to break the agreement while not putting anyone in danger."

They walked a winding path bordered with a rainbow of fragrant flowers. Bees and butterflies droned this way and that, fluttering from blossom to blossom. The air smelled of mulch though, and the blossoms looked wilted and faded. Winter was on its way.

"Doesn't Kazery deserve to know the truth?"

Çifta held her hand out as a butterfly flew close. It landed briefly on one of her knuckles before taking off again. "It's not about what he deserves, Laec. I thought long and hard about what to tell him. Believe me. My father is… vengeful. He's not afraid of anyone, even when he should be."

Laec looked down at her in surprise. "He should be afraid of Faraçek?"

"Maybe. Faraçek has powers I don't understand, but even without that, he's a prince. He commands ranks of unseelie guards. You saw them. If Kazery knew what had happened to me while I was in Osvitan's care, he'd… he'd get violent. He might even start some kind of war. I won't, I can't be responsible for that."

Laec chewed his lip, supposing she must be exaggerating. Çifta's gaze flicked to his face and away again, perhaps registering his doubt.

"When I was little, my eldest sister Fetre told me stories about how our father became a merchant. He started as a pirate, the most fearsome pirate the Valdivian Sea has ever known. His career was short—only four years—but it was savage; by the end he had enough wealth to start his business and earn his fortune by more honest and less risky means. He had a different name then, one she wouldn't tell me. She only knew of his past because some old woman at a market pulled her aside and whispered in her ear, but Alana—my sisters' mother—pulled her away before the woman could tell her very much."

"Is it true?"

Çifta lifted a shoulder. "I think so, because shortly after that my father sent his men to all of the libraries and records offices in every town and city in Boskaya. I suspect he sent them beyond our borders too. Through blackmail, bribes or force, he had all records of his previous life destroyed. Now, only old sailors, doddery captains, and other pirates who tell exaggerated tales to pass the time remember him. Soon, no one will remember who he used to be."

Laec thought of the long row of captains and privateers standing outside the Unya Shipping & Trading office in Cardagenya. "But they are happy to do business with him?"

"Well first of all they don't have a choice, and second, they respect and fear him. The world of sailing merchants is different. Reputation is everything. And fear is a currency."

Laec understood that. Queen Elphame held that same currency. Although she wasn't as volatile as Çifta made Kazery sound, the infamous Stavarjak queen wielded powerful and ancient magic, one that both her citizens and those beyond Stavarjak's borders feared.

"Okay, so your father has a violent history and you're worried that if you tell him Faraçek beat you and imprisoned you, that Kazery will do something rash."

Çifta sniffed. "It's not just a worry. I know he will. I know my father."

"So what are you going to do? How are you going to get out of it?"

Çifta hooked her hand into the crook of Laec's elbow. "There's always a way."

Chapter Ten

Jessamine

The streets of Solana City bustled with life. Jess's first experience of the City had been from atop Ilishec's horse, and every time since then she'd been on her way somewhere, which meant passing too quickly through the high street to enjoy the shops and outdoor markets. She hadn't even seen the Perfume Shop yet, the flagship for all Solana's perfume stores in Ivryndi. It was two blocks closer to the palace than the Registry, so Jess would see it on the way.

Jess and Rose walked arm in arm along the white marble walkway that snaked its way through the busiest part of the city, Aster and Snap ahead of them, smiling and nodding politely to citizens who took notice of them, which was pretty much everyone.

The Calyx were on their own time today, but even so they had to follow certain rules when out in public because people would recognize them.

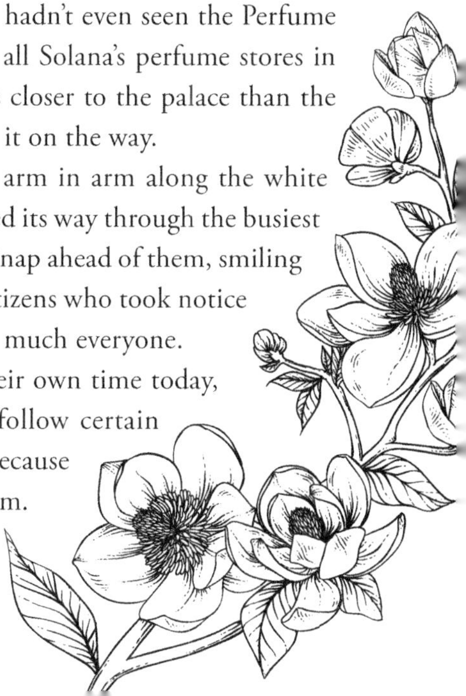

They were to expect to be stared at, even approached. They were to look and behave exactly like what they were: Calyx on their day off, which meant casual but fetching clothing, and hair done nicely. Jess wore a long-sleeved, body-hugging dress and slouchy calf-high boots. Her hair was pinned into a low side-bun—loose enough for Beazle to crawl in and out as he wished—decorated with *cleome* blossoms. The day was cool, so she also wore a fuzzy shawl.

As they made their way toward the Registry, Jess was—for once—grateful that her appearance hadn't changed. People noticed Rose and Aster, but barely wasted a glance at Jessamine and Snap. The streets grew busier and busier as they descended the gentle slope. Jess had never seen so many beautiful shops or elegant stalls in one place—the market in Dagevli was a sparse and shabby affair in comparison. Brightly colored façades announced shoes and clothing for sale, kitchen wares, furniture, art shops, book shops, coppersmiths, chandlers and milliners, bakeries and restaurants. The smells in the air varied from spicy and mouthwatering cooked foods, to the peculiar, pungent scent of ink and glue as they passed a bookbinding shop. Elaborate finishing around windows and balconies layered the city with charm and warmth.

A two-story building with a white façade and marble steps gleamed in the sun, standing out like a diamond among pearls. The blade sign hanging over the door pronounced in a hand-painted script that this was the home of Solana Perfumes & Fine Fragrance. An entrance and an exit, each consisting of a set of double doors, allowed people to go in one side of the building and out the other. Inside, the air was cool and fresh, moving softly from some ventilation system, yet the place still smelled mildly of sweet herbs and flowers. Customers milled about in front of a long counter where pretty frosted glass vials cradled the pure botanical essences that the Calyx worked so hard to produce. Along another wall was a collection of colored glass ampulla containing precious transparent perfume blends and creamy, opaque emulsions mixed artfully by Solana's chemists.

Peony occupied one corner of the shop, talking to a group of customers. She lifted one hand gracefully in front of a young girl's face and a chromatype of a peony spun into life. The girl gasped with delight and watched the mystic bloom drift on the air. Peony said something to her and the girl shyly touched the little chromatype with the skin of her wrist. It popped, and Peony showed her how to rub her wrists together and touch them to the sides of her neck to spread the perfume on her pulse points. When the girl lifted her wrist to her nose and inhaled, her eyes widened with amazement. Peony touched the girl's cheek and turned to another customer to produce a different kind of chromatype, this one with many petals and darker pink in color.

"Would it kill her to be that nice to us?" Rose murmured.

"She's a businesswoman," replied Aster under her breath, a smile plastered on her face. "I've never met a more calculated fae. She'll leave here with an absolute fortune."

"I didn't know we were allowed to come here and talk to customers." Jessamine was a little dazed at Peony's excessive charm. She could be so sweet when she wished to be.

Aster lifted an arm and sent a spray of tiny mystic aster blooms spinning into the air to float over the customers heads. "Of course we can. This is our business. Peony is making fans and growing her brand. You can too."

Sounds of pleasure filled the shop as the customers noticed that Peony wasn't the only Calyx present. Once the crowd closed around them, Rose used both hands to conjure a spectacular mystic bloom: a red rosebud the size of a horse's head. A woman reached out to touch the rose, but Rose held up a finger to wait. The woman paused. Rose took in a deep breath and blew on the chromatype. As her breath pushed the mystic bloom, it blossomed wide open and then broke into a hundred small rosebuds. The crowd laughed and touched the chromatypes, inhaling their scent.

Jess exchanged a frown with Snap. Jess wasn't able to chromatype, at least not yet, and Snap was more adept at producing green paint than mystic blooms. Trying to impress customers while Peony, Rose and Aster were here would be fruitless. Jess didn't mind that. Aster and Rose were very talented, but in Jess's opinion, Peony didn't deserve such status.

While Aster and Rose made fans, Jess and Snap wandered along the counter, sniffing samples and admiring the pretty decor. The register at the far end was never quiet for long, as a clerk continuously returned to tally customer's purchases and take payment. As they passed Peony on the way out the door, she gave a nod of acknowledgment to Rose and Aster, but nailed Jess with a sharp, knowing look.

"See you soon, Jess," Peony said before turning her back and ignoring Snap completely.

Rose cocked a questioning eyebrow at Jess as they went out the door.

"She's going to tutor me," Jess muttered with a glower. "Please don't ask how I feel about it."

"I don't need to," Rose murmured before taking Jess's arm and giving her a comforting squeeze.

The market grew crowded as they continued down the street toward the Registry. Word spread that there were Calyx in the market and vendors offered them food, clothing and other wares. A short woman in a bright red knitted hat held out a pair of fingerless gloves for Jessamine.

"Touch them, Miss. You'll not feel anything softer."

Jess felt the fuzzy knit material. The wrist warmers were a pale blue interwoven with green bands around the knuckles. "They are very soft."

The lady's eyes nearly disappeared in nets of wrinkles as she smiled. "They are cashmere from the wool of the mountain goats of Kitrell. I would be honored if you would take them and wear them as my gift. Please, Miss. Your hands are bare."

Jess looked at Rose in surprise, wondering if she'd misunderstood.

"If you want them, take them. That's very kind." Rose

smiled at the woman, then explained: "It helps the vendors' businesses for their product to be worn by Calyx."

Jess tried to get the woman to take something for them but she refused. Finally, she put them on and thanked the vendor, who looked fit to burst in pride.

"I'm Paisley, Miss. My name is inside the wrist so you won't forget me."

Jess flipped up a cuff to see delicate stitching inside that said Made by Paisley.

They moved on, having already lost Aster and Snap in the crowd.

By the time they found them in front of the Registry Office, Jess had been offered a handmade ceramic mug, a pair of slippers, feather clips for her hair, and a bun stuffed with spiced meat. Rose had been offered a pretty black mare, which she turned down with profuse thanks. Snap's cheeks were pink from the cool autumn air and his eyes sparkled with excitement.

"Look!" He held up a ceramic mug, the same kind Jess had turned down. "It was free!"

Jess held up her hands, showing off her new wrist warmers. "So were these. Rose was offered a horse."

Snap's eyes almost fell out of his head. "Did you take it?"

Rose laughed. "I already have a mare and she's pregnant. What do I want with another?"

"You could sell her, or breed her. I could look after her for you."

Rose's cheeks colored. "I don't want to take expensive

things from them. The small things, yes, because it helps them. But a horse is so expensive and I've no need."

"But—"

"Rose is wealthy already, Snap," Aster reminded him. "In a few years, you will be too."

Snap's laugh had an edge. "From green paint? I doubt that. The next time someone offers you a horse, please take it. For me."

Aster pushed open the door of the Registry and they passed into what looked a lot like the small postal office in Dagevli. A clerk came through a narrow archway behind a big solid desk. He was wafer thin and had sharp fae ears and an even sharper nose. "Welcome to the Registry Office. Do you have an appoint—oh! Calyx. How delightful. Hello." His professional expression melted into a smile. "Follow me please."

They followed the clerk through the archway and straight into what seemed like a never-ending closet full of drawers. They were led single file past the drawers and into an open seating area. Clerks worked at desks, some seated across from a civilian, some working on their own.

The clerk whispered, "Which one of you is Aster?"

"I am. I made the appointment." Aster put up a hand. "But we are here for her." She pulled Jess close to her side.

The clerk seemed to have difficulty pulling his gaze from Aster. When he looked at Jess, some of his enthusiasm faded. "Are you Calyx too?"

Jess nodded.

"Right. Well, have a seat if you like. Harper will be right with you." He pointed at a set of wooden chairs across from a desk piled high with papers and books, then he left the way they'd come.

A few minutes later, an elderly man shorter than Snap came bustling down the hall carrying a stack of small wooden boxes. Setting the boxes down on top of the already jumbled desk, he combed their faces, adjusting his glasses. "Aster?"

"That's me. But the inquiry was for Jessamine," Aster repeated.

"That's fine. I'm Harper, I did find what you were looking for. One moment. It's here somewhere." He began to dig through the papers on his desk, several sheets seesawed to the floor. "I just had it this morning… ah, yes. Here we are." He produced a single sheet of yellowed parchment and handed it to Aster.

Aster held it while Jess, Rose and Snap leaned close together to read it.

In a beautiful hand-written calligraphy, two names were written side by side: Jessica Fontana and Julian Fontana. Born the seventh day of Trexi to Marion Fontana of Dagevli village, Kingdom of Solana. There was a set of tiny baby's footprints beneath each name. Jess ran a finger lightly over Julian's footprints, which made him more real to her than anything else had. And there was her mother's signature, a jagged scrawl she'd recognize anywhere.

"Our birth certificate," Jess breathed.

"May she keep this?" Rose asked, and Jess could have kissed her because she didn't trust her own voice.

The clerk frowned. "No, I'm sorry. This is an original. Strictly speaking, no one should even touch it except a clerk, but for Calyx we've been known to bend the rules a little." He held out his hand for the certificate. Jess reluctantly returned it to him. "For a small fee, a signature, and proof of identity of course, I can make a copy of it for someone with the last name of Fontana, or someone with proof of relation to a Fontana through marriage or adoption."

Jess dug in the pocket of her dress. When she'd joined the Calyx she'd been given a silver pin with her birth name and her court name engraved against the shape of one of her blooms. She handed it to the clerk.

He peered at it through his glasses. "That will do. Just one copy?"

"Yes, please."

He returned her pin, turned to leave, but paused as he remembered another matter. "There was something else. Your request was documents registered for Fontanas, and two documents were found, but I've only showed you the one. I almost forgot." He rifled through the parchments on his desk again. "I know it looks like we're not very organized here but we do have a system… ah, here we are." He pulled out another page, this one as yellowed as the first but rather than parchment, it was a thinner, smoother paper.

He handed it to Jessamine. "It's a certificate of death for Julian Fontana."

Jess froze as she grasped the certificate. "Wh-what?"

The clerk was perfunctory, like he hadn't actually registered that she was Julian's twin. "Yes. It seems the boy didn't live very long. Would you like a copy of that one too?"

Jess stared at the clerk, hardly seeing him. Dead? Jess put a hand over her heart. He hadn't lived very long… but to her, he'd only just been born. She felt like someone had socked her straight in the stomach.

Aster took the certificate, sliding it gently from between Jess's numb fingers. She and Rose and Snap looked at it.

"Less than a year old," Rose murmured, putting an arm around Jess. "Poor lad."

Jess finally shifted her gaze to the document, struggling to read it, struggling to calculate. An "X" sat at the bottom where a signature should have been.

Aster had seen it too and looked up at the clerk. "Why is it signed with an X?"

Harper scratched at his chin. "That could be one of two circumstances: either the signee was illiterate, or they were signing on behalf of someone who was unable to sign at the time the registration was made, but was meant to come in later and finish the process… and then never did."

Rose's gaze sharpened and she squeezed Jess harder, as though concerned she might need help standing. "Since it was never signed properly, can we assume the person who made the registration was not Marion Fontana, and illiterate?"

Jess couldn't look away from the name of Julian Fontana, written beside the word "deceased."

"It could be assumed…" Harper replied, sounding a little doubtful. "It's difficult to say what occurred here. Who isn't literate in Solana? Everyone is educated, everyone learns their letters, and have done for many centuries."

Jess found her voice as confusion overtook her grief. "But aren't you supposed to have record of who made this registration? It wasn't my mother. She would have signed her name, like she did on our birth certificate."

Harper adjusted his glasses and scratched his nose. "Well, we know which clerk took the registration from the number, but not which citizen came in to notify us. To be honest, most of the documents with an X for a signature are extremely old. This document is only 15 years old. It is unusual."

"Can we talk to the clerk who took the registration, then?" Jess asked.

"Jess," said Aster, nudging her arm.

Harper gave her a sorry look. "I'm afraid she passed away at least three years ago."

"Jessamine," said Aster, more urgently this time.

"What?"

"Look." She pointed to the bottom of the page where a small line of text had been written—off-hand and possibly even unofficially, since it was floating there in the corner of the page. Spidery handwriting proclaimed: *Cause of death: accidental poisoning.*

The clerk continued talking but Jess wasn't listening anymore. She snatched the death certificate, ignoring Harper's tsk of disapproval. She held it close to her face. Accidental poisoning? Her throat constricted, she struggled to breathe. Her heart pounded, her body heated up. She felt like she was suffocating.

"Jess?" Rose put a hand under her elbow.

Harper interrupted himself mid-speech to peer at her with concern. "Are you alright?"

The room tilted as Jess clutched the certificate. It crinkled between her fingers. Her legs felt wobbly. The edges of her vision went fuzzy as she gulped, trying to fill her lungs. "I can't… breathe. Can I—?"

She went to her knees with Snap's help, then lay down on the cool wooden floor.

Harper gasped, clearly dismayed. "Miss, you can't… oh dear. Do I need to call a doctor?"

"…just need… minute," Jess wheezed as she lay on her back. Tears trickled from the corners of her eyes and into her hairline. Beazle stirred at the back of her neck and crawled out of her hair, squeaking into her ear.

"I'm okay, Beaze," she whispered, closing her eyes. "I just need a minute."

She felt someone take her hand but kept her eyes closed.

Rose's voice was soft. "Just breathe, Jess. It's a panic attack. It'll pass. Breathe, honey."

She focused on pulling air in and pushing it out. Already her heart had slowed and embarrassment was beginning to settle in. Was she really lying on the floor of the Registry Office? Ilishec would be ashamed.

The words danced behind her closed eyelids: accidental poisoning.

Oh Julian. What happened to you?

Memories circled like hungry wolves: hands tied behind her back, her body shoved forward, crushed against the horse as the guard sagged on top of her.

Accidental poisoning.

The guard who'd grabbed her off the back of the horse as she'd tried to get away, his hands on the slick and sweaty skin of her bare arm.

Accidental poisoning.

The last guard. She hadn't known that she was deadly. She'd only thought to give herself a chance to escape. Intentional poisoning, but accidental murder.

How could these words be on her twin brother's death certificate? Was it possible that she had had something to do with it, even as a helpless baby?

When control returned, she sat up, feeling anxiety migrate from her body into her mind.

"Let's get her up, please," Harper said, relieved. "I can't have Calyx fainting in my office. What will people think?"

"I'm so sorry. Please excuse me. I feel better now," Jess said.

Snap and Rose helped Jessamine to a seat. Beazle clung to her neckline until she was upright, then crawled to her collarbone where she could feel his tiny warm body against her skin. He vibrated like a leaf in the wind—as disturbed as she was—then went still.

She found a smile for her friends as they waited for the clerk to make copies of both documents, which took half an hour. While they waited they were given tea and biscuits. She thanked Harper and paid at the big front desk. The copies were rolled into a tube and slid into Jess's shoulder sack. She was highly conscious of them, as if each word bore considerable weight.

They stepped out into the fresh air and sunshine and joined the flow of traffic going back up the high street toward the castle. Rose and Aster walked on either side of her, quiet and serious. Snap went to a tent where they were selling wine. He returned and handed them each a cup.

Jess took a sip of the spiced drink, feeling it nudge away the cold feeling she'd developed in her bones. Her friends weren't pushing her to talk, but she could feel their concern.

A set of draft horses with shining brown hides and long lustrous tails sent Snap into fits of pleasure. Jess, Rose and Aster stepped into the shelter of an awning as Snap launched a tirade of questions at the driver, who looked only too happy to have found someone who was as passionate about his huge animals as he was.

"Are you feeling better?" Aster gently cradled Jess's elbow.

Rose and Aster hadn't turned away from her in disgust or fear. She could tell them, because she had to tell someone or she'd burst.

Jess kept her voice low, her cup near her lips. "Death by accidental poisoning. That's how Julian died."

Rose and Aster exchanged a look Jess couldn't unpack.

Rose put a metaphorical finger on Jess's concern with pinpoint accuracy. "You don't think you had something to do with it, do you Jess? I mean, you were an infant."

Jess took another sip of wine before answering. "I'm not sure I believe in coincidences."

Aster shook her head. "No, Jess. It's impossible."

Rose added, "Hanna told you Julian had been kidnapped, taken from your home. He was alive when he was taken. Whoever registered his death was illiterate, so we know it wasn't Marion."

"What if I poisoned him before he was taken? What if the kidnapper took him and he died that same night, from me? I wouldn't have known what I was doing, but if I was frightened… like if I heard sounds of an argument and my body did what it did back in Rahamlar. Who knows what I might have been capable of as a baby."

"But Marion hid you in a drawer, you weren't with Julian, according to Hanna," Aster reminded Jess.

Jess rubbed at her temple where a dull throb had begun. "Hanna saw Tad open the drawer and find me inside. I had been quiet, so I wasn't upset, but still… Julian died close to the age I was when the kidnapping happened. It just seems too fortuitous, in a bad way."

"There are a lot of ways someone can get accidentally poisoned, Jess. Just because it said that on his death certificate and you are his twin and capable of making poison doesn't automatically mean you're guilty." Rose tossed her empty cup into a nearby bin, glancing at Snap stroking the muscular neck of one of the horses. He grinned, pointing at the beast. Rose waved and smiled.

Aster took her last sip and tossed her cup after Rose's. "You have to let it go, Jess. You can't torture yourself over this. There's nothing you can do about what happened. Its very tragic, and I am sorry you had to find out this way, but maybe now you can… put it behind you?"

Rose's voice grew passionate. "How can she though? Who took Julian in the first place, and why? Just because he's dead doesn't mean she can put it in the past. For Jess, it's fresh."

Jess shot Rose a grateful look. She made Jess feel understood. "I have to know what happened."

Aster's brows stitched together, her voice soft. "I want to know too, but I don't see how."

"Someone knows," Rose muttered. "Someone took him that night. Marion has a past. You told me once that your mother was forty-nine when she gave birth to you. She lived almost a whole lifetime before you came along. Someone has to know the truth."

"Really? Forty-nine?" Aster's eyes went big.

Jess nodded, chewing her lip. "It's true. She always said I was her miracle baby, she just never told me there were two of us."

Snap said goodbye to the driver and the horses and joined them. He'd been given an invitation to the driver's farm and was so excited that he couldn't stop talking about the breeds he'd get to see and the connections he would make for when he started his own barn. He didn't notice the mood.

Jess was thankful. She needed some time to retreat, time to think about what she should do. Beazle gave a little squeak. When she put her hand to him, he climbed beneath the cashmere of her new wrist warmer, curling up in the warm palm of her hand. He stayed there as the group walked back up to the palace but he didn't fall asleep, or even drowse. Jess wondered if Beazle was thinking about Julian. He'd been there that night, just as Greta had. She wondered, did familiars have better memories than the babies they bonded with?

Chapter Eleven

Jessamine

When the crofter had told Jess that Panther was to be one of her tutors; she got so excited that she would see Tully again that she barely listened to the subject matter. She was to meet Panther and Tulliana at the Thistle Yard in the West Keep during the block of time she normally had nomenclature scheduled. She donned the leggings, tunic and boots that she wore during her lessons with Regalis and Kite, and took great pains to braid her hair into a coil on the top of her head so it would be out of the way. Despite Beazle flapping along beside her, she had to ask for directions to find the Thistle Yard.

Pushing her way through a gate, she entered a small grass yard with what looked like a running track at the bottom of a gentle decline. Jess thought she must have arrived ahead of Panther because the yard appeared to be empty, but his

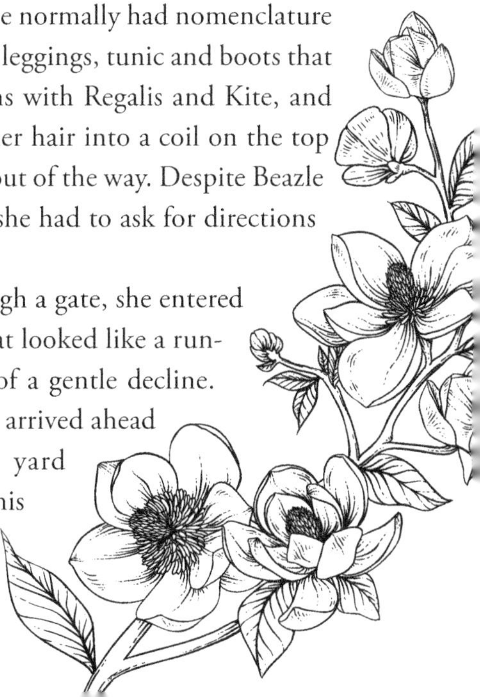

dark head lifted from the grass on the slope. Tully's head popped up a second later. Her glossy black face shone in the sun, her eyes half closed against the bright light. Panther looked over and lifted his hand in a lazy wave. Didn't look like they'd be doing anything too active.

Jess picked her way through the long tussocks, noticing a brown burlap sack sitting on the ground beside Panther's hip as she reached him. He patted the grass, inviting her to sit, as he came up to a cross-legged position. Tully flopped over on her side with a grunt. Picking up on the mood, Beazle plopped onto the top of her head.

Jess grinned at Panther's wind-tousled hair. "Am I going to learn the art of napping in broad daylight?"

"Not quite." He dimpled as his dark eyes flicked to where her bat perched in her braid, like a jewel set in a crown. "Beazle, was it?"

Beazle squeaked.

"How is his vocabulary?"

Jess cocked her head. "His… vocabulary? Hmm. Well he's smart, if that's what you're asking."

Panther put a hand on Tully's huge flank, pinching her fur between his fingers and tugging it upward in a repetitive caress. "I'm sure he is. That's not what I'm asking. I'm asking about his words. I have no doubt that he can understand most of what we say, but how much can you understand of what he says?"

Jess frowned. "Beazle can't talk."

Beazle squeaked again. Was there something a little indignant in that squeak?

Panther seemed to think so. "Yes, he can. At least, to

a degree. Every familiar is different, perhaps limited by species. We don't really know. But trust me, your communication is limited more by you than by him. That's what I'm going to teach you. How to communicate with him. Silently."

Jess gaped, doubt rising strong in her chest.

Panther withdrew his hand from his cat. "Let me show you. Sit still. Don't be afraid."

He looked at Tully. She didn't react at first, but several seconds later her long tail lifted out of the grass and curled into the air before falling back to the ground. Panther didn't take his eyes from her. Tully lifted her head and gave a short bark. It sounded like she was a little annoyed. With a second snarky chirrup, Tully got laboriously to her feet, rippling with muscle and bulk. Jess's heartrate doubled as the panther stretched her nose toward Jess's face. Her breath blew across Jess's jaw and cheek as the cat sniffed her. Tully swung her head and looked at Panther with a snort before sniffing at Jess some more. Satisfied, the cat flopped over, paws curling and uncurling.

"You had an egg popkin with bacon for breakfast, along with some…" Panther dimpled. "Rabbit food, for breakfast."

Jess laughed with surprise. "She's right. Although I would hardly call Mrs. Tierney's amazing elixirs rabbit food."

Panther grinned. "Tully doesn't have a better word for plants." He reached inside the burlap sack and pulled out three small copper cups and a white ball of yarn. "You're going to turn your back while Beazle watches me hide this ball of yarn under one of these three cups. We're not leaving this paddock until you can tell me which one Beazle has *told you* contains the yarn. Three times over, so we know it's not just a fluke."

Dismay pooled in Jess's belly like cold pondwater. "Beazle and I have been together all of our lives. If we were able to communicate silently, don't you think we would have done it by now?"

"Did you know it was possible before now?"

"No."

"That makes all the difference. Fauna magic can do all kinds of things. We are limited by our faith in ourselves, and our understanding of the magic linking us to our familiars. Magic doesn't have limitations, Jess. We only think it does—which makes *us* the limitation. Most fauna fae live their whole lives not realizing their potential, simply because they're not aware of it. They think that the bond they forge shortly after birth is the extent of it, but that bond is what you get without trying. It's not unlike talent and skill. Kite has a talent for archery because she is blessed with good hand-eye coordination, but her accuracy is thanks to the hard work she put into developing that skill. Our connection to our familiar is similar. The magic has given you a taste of what is there, but if you don't nurture it and practice wielding it, then it'll never improve. You are Fahyli. You are duty bound to put everything you have into developing your fauna magic. So is Beazle, but he knows it already."

Heartened, Jess turned herself around in the grass. "Okay. Let's give this a go."

She felt Beazle crawl to the back of her head where he could see what Panther was doing. She could hear the sound of the cups being set up in the grass.

"Ready."

She closed her eyes and listened, all of her awareness going to the warm little body on the top of her head.

"Which cup did he put the yarn under, Beaze?"

The wind ruffled the tops of the grass. Birds twittered, a raven called from somewhere far away, a lonely sound. Male voices from a nearby yard floated on the breeze. Tully gave a big sigh. Panther changed position, his weight crushing untouched grasses. A horse gave a high-pitched whinny from the faraway stables.

Beazle chirped twice, a touch frustrated.

"Can you hear him?" Panther asked.

Jess shook her head. "Nothing."

Beazle squeaked again, truly indignant this time. He tugged on a strand of hair, making her wince.

"I'm sorry Beaze. I can't hear anything aside from the noise around us."

Panther's voice was calm and unruffled, like he'd expected her to fail. "You're using your ears, Jess. Use your mind."

She blew a frustrated raspberry. "What does that even mean?"

"He's not communicating with his voice. Animals don't have the equipment needed to form words. Ignore what is coming into your ears. Push it into the background, and put Beazle in the foreground. He's got information to give to you."

Jess tried again, trying to ignore the sounds of the world around them. She thought only of the sweet, warm lump on the top of her head. Beazle climbed down her hair and dropped onto her shoulder, facing Panther. No information entered her mind. She wrestled with impatience, the desire to tell Panther that maybe it couldn't work when a familiar was as tiny as Beazle. Tully was an enormous animal, with a brain as large as theirs. What if Beazle didn't have the capacity?

Beazle scratched the side of her neck and bit her earlobe.

"Ow! Beaze!" Jess put her hand up and he climbed into it. Her ear stung. Beazle had teeth like needles. "That really hurt! What was that for?" She pinched her earlobe then looked at her fingers to see a little smear of blood.

Beazle wrinkled his nose and bared his little fangs, then let loose two sharp barks, a sound she'd never heard him make before. Simultaneously, a thought burst into her mind like an angry bull crashing through a locked gate.

...my brain!

Jess gasped, staring at her familiar. "Did you... was that you?"

Beazle hissed like an angry kitten. If he wasn't so cute, she might have recoiled. She bit her cheeks to stifle laughter, but she'd never seen him ticked off before and it would have been frightening had he been larger. As it was, he was simply adorable. Her enjoyment and surprise must have opened her to him further. More words slipped into her brain.

My mind isn't limited by my smallness. You're the slow one. Don't blame me.

"Alright, I'm sorry." Jess felt a little breathless with excitement. "I never thought there was anything wrong with your brain. I promise. You're just... so wee." She lifted Beazle to her cheek. "I'm sorry. Please forgive me. You're right. I'm the slow one. I've always been the slower one of the two of us. Be patient with me, okay?"

Beazle chirruped and licked her cheekbone. Jess felt tears line her lower lids, though she felt anything but sad. Love surged in her heart for her familiar. Love, and a new feeling: the excitement of new magical possibilities opening up to them. Conjuring botanicals and making the raw materials for perfume was exhilarating, but it all paled in comparison to being able to converse with Beazle. Beazle was her family. He remembered Greta, he remembered Marion. Maybe he even remembered Julian.

I do.

Jess sucked in a breath and fought back more tears as she held Beazle to her face. *Oh, Beaze. I'm so sorry I didn't know this was possible sooner. You're so right. I really am the slow one.* She sat still in the grass, holding him against her, savoring the feeling of his warmth and his soft fur against her face, tears trickling down her cheeks.

Panther coughed quietly behind her.

Jess wiped her face and turned back to him. Embarrassment heated her cheeks. "I'm sorry. We just... um. We need a minute."

"Success, I take it?" Panther cocked an eyebrow, studying her face.

Jess nodded, her chin wobbling.

His eyes softened. "It can be a little startling when

communication comes through clearly for the first time, but it's not supposed to make you cry."

Jess gave a laugh that was also half a sob. She looked down at Beazle. "You're the best, Beaze. You know that? And you're very handsome, too."

Beazle let his tongue roll out of his mouth, looking a little like a tiny smiling dog.

Tully, who had lifted her head to watch, got up and licked the side of Jess's face, her tongue hot and rough. Tully sniffed at Beazle then pulled back, panting a little as she stared into Jess's face.

"She wants to know if you're okay." Panther said.

Jess put her palm up to Tully. The cat licked her hand, a slow languid stroke filled with care. Jess lay her hand against Tully's cheek, feeling the dense pelt and the vibrant life beneath. She stroked the panther, still holding Beazle in her other hand.

"Thanks, Tully. You're so kind. Yes, I'm ok. I don't think learning how to do this is quite as emotional for others as it is for Beazle and me. You see, we had a twin. He's gone now, but Beazle remembers him. I never knew that until today."

Tully sat on her haunches then lay on her side with a grunt, her huge head in Jess's lap.

"You've done it now." Panther smiled.

Jess kept stroking Tully, enjoying the cat's beauty. When she stroked Tully's belly, the cat began to purr. Just like the domestic cats that populated Dagevli, this huge animal also loved attention and affection.

Jess laughed, glorying in the feeling of the cat's thick pelt. "I thought you were a soldier, Tully."

Panther leaned back on his elbows in the grass. "Who says that a soldier can't also be a sucker for cuddles?" He let Jess stroke Tully for a while, then asked Jess to try the cups again. This time it was straightforward.

"Let's hope duplication is this easy for you and Beazle," Panther said, looking impressed.

"Are you supposed to help me with that too?"

"Not me," Panther plucked a strand of grass and clamped it between his teeth. "Tully's too big. She can only produce three, four on a good day. It wouldn't make sense. You'll need to learn it from Kite, probably. Erasmus is the next smallest familiar, I think, after Beazle."

Jess canted her head. "Not Digit and Ania?"

He looked like the possibility had never crossed his mind before. "I was under the impression that she can't duplicate. Odd for a Fahyli, I know. Hmm. A question for the crofter, I guess. Come on." He nudged her hip with a toe. "One last time, just for good measure."

Chapter Twelve

Jessamine

Peony stood waiting for Jess at the door to the Perfumery, her arms crossed, a sour expression on her face. Her hair had been coiled into twists and pinned loosely on top of her head. Sphex, her villainous-looking digger wasp, clung to the side of her neck.

Peony's beauty took Jess's breath away, but Jess wouldn't give her the satisfaction of seeing the proof of how much her appearance had changed. Sometimes it made Solana's guests and nobles stop in their tracks. After only a few months—they whispered—and already as beautiful as Gardenia and Rose, as ethereal as Nypha and Lotus, and as exotic as Proteas. It made Jess feel inferior. She hoped Peony had reached her peak. How much beauty did one Calyx need?

A wave of Peony's natural scent drifted over Jess as she approached, attired in her skimpy white workout clothing, feet bare. A woman's scent: rich, floral and heady. No wonder it was in high demand.

Peony shifted her weight into a hip. "Well, well, well. Here she is. Jess of all smells, master of none."

Jess rolled her eyes. "I'm not here by choice, you know."

"I do know. Neither am I, and my time is much more precious than yours, so the sooner you master yourself, the sooner we can end this. I've looked over your botanicals and their profiles." Peony clicked her tongue in disapproval. "Not a lot to work with, in my humble—"

Jess snorted.

"—opinion." Peony acted as though she hadn't heard. "We can expedite your education by focusing solely on honeysuckle. The beauty of a fragrance is a matter of opinion, but I think *lonicera* has the most appeal to the general population. Do you agree?"

Jess hadn't expected to be asked her opinion. "Oh. Um. Yes. I guess I do."

Peony smirked. "Good. Then off you go. Make me some raw material. I'll meet you back here in twenty."

Beazle took off to find somewhere peaceful to nap as Jess ran to warm up. She made several laps around the Perfumery and hothouses, trying to focus on what she was doing. It was impossible not to be irked by Peony's superior attitude. Her mind wandered off task, trying to figure why Peony was so much further advanced. Her father was a perfumer, sure, but there had to be more to it than growing up in a household that was obsessed with the perfume business.

Jess made three circuits with the weights in the exercise course, not stopping until every muscle was burning and her skin was coated with sweat containing the fine oil of *lonicera*. Heart pounding, Jess stood for the faeries and pollinators to harvest her raw material.

Even with her eyes closed and the soothing music of the harvest filling the air, Jess's mind wandered like an untethered goat, nibbling at this and that. She felt impatient and annoyed. Why did Ilishec have to pair her up with the Calyx she liked the least? There were many other flora fae who were good at producing fragrance, Rose for one. Jess would have enjoyed being tutored so much more if it had been a friend giving her guidance.

When her skin was cleared of all moisture, she moved out into the yard, got a glass of water and watched other Calyx working out while she waited for Peony—who appeared with a small vial of clear liquid. Wordlessly, she handed the vial to Jess.

Jess lifted it to her nose and closed her eyes. Peony gave a world-weary sigh that made Jess pause. "What?"

"Never sniff straight from the bottle. Either wave the fragrance toward your nose with a hand, or put it on a piece of felt and wave that. You won't get an accurate reading on it if you snork it from the vial. Honestly."

Teeth grinding, Jess obediently wafted the scent of her raw material toward her nose and inhaled. "It smells like… honeysuckle." Sort of. It smelled like old honeysuckle, as it was decaying and falling off its stems.

Peony cocked an eyebrow. "No it doesn't. It smells like jealousy and disrespect."

Jess stared at Peony, shock etched into her features.

"Don't look so surprised. I'm tutoring you for a reason. Put your ego aside and think about why it smells like jealousy and disrespect." Peony took the vial from Jess and wafted the scent toward her nose. She made a moue of disgust. "Even a touch of scorn. How unfortunate. No wonder you're so far behind."

Jess was shaken. She had no response for these accusations except to admit Peony's dart of truth had gone straight to the bullseye. She was feeling jealous of Peony, that she could admit. But disrespect? Scorn? She had to dig deeper for those.

Peony waited for a response, those huge eyes combing Jess's face. "Well? Am I wrong?"

Jess briefly closed her eyes to draw on her small store of patience. She looked at Peony. "Not entirely. I may not like you, but I don't disrespect you. In fact, it's quite the opposite. I have enormous respect for your abilities."

Peony's eyes widened as if this was the last thing she'd ever expected Jess to say. Her features softened. She put a hand on Jess's arm and coaxed her toward a bench. "Sit down, Jess."

Jess sat, and Peony perched on the edge of the bench beside her with her knees tilted toward Jess. Disdain was gone from her face, which increased her already incredible beauty.

"I wasn't talking about your feelings for me. I was talking about the magic flowing through you and your relationship to it. Okay, maybe you might feel some amount of jealousy for me, which has tainted this batch, but what I'm trying to get at is that you don't have the respect for the magic and the process that you should have. Until you develop a healthy respect for your magic, you'll struggle to refine your raw material."

Jess was taken aback. "But… I respect the magic. I do."

Peony was almost kind with her response. "I'm sure you think you do, but something is getting in the way. You're too emotional."

"And you're not?"

"Not when it comes to perfume. I can admit that I'm not the easiest to get along with. My siblings teased that I should have been born with a connection to roses because I'm sharp and thorny. But when it comes to perfume-making, I have too much respect and love for nature to let my emotions defile the product that comes through me."

"So… how do you do that?"

"Self-sacrifice. Our thoughts control us if we let them, when it comes to this magic, we have to get out of the way and let the energy do what it does best: flow through us. You have to put your feelings to the side when you use flora fae magic, because the magic isn't actually yours. You're just the vessel through which it travels. You can be a crooked vessel, or you can be a straight one. You only become straight when you realize with humility that you're dealing with something that's much bigger than yourself, something that you must revere, treasure and respect enough to set yourself aside for it. Get it?"

Jess shook her head, like a dog clearing its ears. "Do you have any idea how weird it is for this advice to be coming from you? You're the most arrogant Calyx here, and you're lecturing me on self-sacrifice and reverence for the process? It borders on the ridiculous."

Peony, to her credit, did not look offended. "I don't claim to be great with other people, Jess. Getting others to like me isn't high on my list of priorities. I care about the magic, the art, and the end experience. You can think whatever you want about me, I couldn't care less. But no one can put themselves aside for the magic like I can, and I'll prove it to you." Peony got to her feet and gave Jess a meaningful look. "Watch. And be patient."

Peony kicked off her sandals and stood in the grass. She closed her eyes and tilted her head a little so sunlight fell across her face. She took a deep breath in and let it out very slowly, and as she did so her features relaxed. Long minutes passed. The wind lifted loose tendrils of Peony's hair and shifted the cobweb-light skirt of her dress. Just when Jess was about to tell Peony to stop wasting their time, the skin of Peony's arms glimmered in the sunlight. A dewy layer had formed along both shoulders and down to each wrist. The scent of tender white peonies in early spring drifted in the air, as soft as a blown kiss. In spite of herself, Jess inhaled deeply, amazed: quality raw material produced without physical exertion.

Droplets of oil beaded on Peony's skin then ran down her arms in little rivulets, tiny rivers of fragrance. Peony made cups with her palms. Jess watched with growing incredulity as fragrance pooled in Peony's hands—the moisture twined from her outer arm to her inner collecting so Peony would not lose a drop. Bees and butterflies and the tiny lights of fae began to buzz around Peony, wanting to harvest the oils.

Peony looked at Jess, her eyes softly illuminated with a pale light that dimmed as Jess looked at her.

"How did you do that?"

Peony smiled without ire. "I set an intention then got out of the way."

"But you did it without moving. That's… how is that possible?"

"Would you believe me if I told you that the physical exertion is an exercise more for the mind than the body? We think we need to build heat and sweat for the magic to flow, but its just not true."

"I wouldn't have believed you if I hadn't just seen it. Can I learn to do this?"

Peony poured the raw material that had pooled in her left hand into her right. "I can't teach you, unfortunately. But now that you know it's possible, you can figure it out for yourself."

Jess's heart fell. This seemed impossible. "Do you think any flora fae can do it?"

Peony thought about it. "I think… I think maybe some who suffer in life learn survival skills that others don't learn. Like how to find peace even in the center of conflict. I didn't have a great childhood. One of the ways I coped was to pretend I was someone else, somewhere else. I don't mean another fae, I mean another form: an earthworm, a bird, a mouse or a beetle. I always picked humble lifeforms because I find simple beauty in the way that they live. They were safe forms to be because they were beneath the notice of my tormentors, but they are also the closest to the earth and its gentle ways. When I'm Peony, I'm not the easiest to get along with. I know that. But when I'm *paeonia*, I am deeply connected to a magic and energy that is so much bigger than me. I love the process." She lifted her palmful of precious oils. "It allows me to stop being this." She put her other hand on her chest. "At least for a little while."

Jess wanted to ask Peony who her tormentors were, but Peony's expression had shifted. The pretty inner glow that had lit her eyes from within had gone and there was a hard edge to her again.

"You won't be able to do it overnight," Peony said. "If you're capable of doing it at all. You'll have to exercise to sweat because your mind is weak, and you're self-centered. Do another round and think about what I showed you. Try to get out of the way. Appreciate and respect the incredible power that nature has, and let it be what it is. There is no Jessamine Fontana. There is only the sweet innocence and beauty of *lonicera*. It has no ego, no preconceived notions of how life is supposed to be, no mental or social constructs. It fills the world with its special beauty without being aware of its gifts." Peony looked down at her palm, as though wishing she'd not said so much. "Now go, before I regret sharing all of this with you."

Jess shut her mouth, got up, and began to run.

For the next few weeks Jess's days were full, moving from Fahyli training to Calyx practice and back again. Toward the end of a group dancing lesson with two dozen other Calyx, Ilishec entered the ballroom to observe. He then snaked his way through the dancers to where Jess was dancing with Asclepias.

"Sorry to interrupt, but may I?" the gardener asked Asclepias.

"Of course."

Asclepias gracefully transferred Jess's hand to Ilishec's, then bowed and backed away. They resumed the steps, narrowly avoiding Gardenia and Proteas as they swung by.

"I wanted the chance to speak with you—"

She winced as Ilishec's hand touched a bruise on her lower back.

"Are you alright?"

"Yes, just a bruise. Go on, Gardener."

His expression darkened and he lowered his voice. "I knew he'd be hard on you. Calyx are not built for the rigors of combat or the intrigues of politics."

"I minded in the beginning, but now…" Jess shrugged. She wouldn't admit to Ilishec that she and Beazle were enjoying learning skills she would never have acquired if she hadn't joined the Fahyli. "What did you want to talk to me about?"

"While you were otherwise occupied, I addressed the Calyx about the upcoming Midwinter Festival. I wanted to make sure you are aware of what's ahead."

Jess had heard murmurs about the Festival in the halls. "When is it?"

"In five weeks, guests from all over Ivryndi will begin to descend upon our city. They'll continue to arrive until the Festival is almost over—it gets very busy. Before then, you'll know all the foreign and domestic dances, maybe you'll even have a perfume for sale. It's a great opportunity for Calyx to add to their coffers. But the Midwinter will be extra busy for you, given your… new duties, as you'll be required to maintain peak performance in both capacities for all twenty-one days of the Festival—"

"Twenty-one days?" Jess barked, then cringed and apologized when the dance instructor shot her a glare. She lowered her voice. "Three whole weeks?"

"Midwinters are usually only seven days, but this is a once-in-ten-years event, the decennial. We will have many important guests we don't see otherwise. Most of the other Calyx will have the luxury of not having to report for duty until after lunch, to make sure they get adequate rest. But you…" Ilishec sighed. "I don't know what he'll have you doing, but the crofter is not known for coddling his charges. Please guard your health."

"Worried I'll embarrass you?"

Ilishec's cheeks flushed. "No."

She raised an eyebrow.

He looked sheepish, like he'd been caught scratching himself in public. "Not on purpose, anyway. But the Calyx have put Solana on the map. You're why people love to come here. Everyone expects our best, but I also want you to benefit personally from this opportunity. Perfect your raw materials and work on building stock. Once the Festival starts you won't have time for sweat sessions and if there's demand for your *lonicera*—which there will be—it'll be better to have produced as much as you can beforehand so it can get through the refinery and bottling process."

"Thank you for the advice." She refrained from pointing out the mixed messages she was receiving. Take care of herself because she was going to be under more stress than the other Calyx, and with less free time, but also do as many workout sessions as she could manage, to increase her inventory so they would make money.

"What about the other… stuff." She couldn't bring herself to say poison here among her gentler, sweeter friends.

Ilishec gave her a grim smile. "I understand there is interest from as far away as Tryske."

Jess's jaw dropped halfway before she remembered herself and closed her mouth, pasting on a pleasant smile. "I don't understand how people even know of the… product."

"It's not part of my business, Jess. There is a dark market and the regional manager is faceless. My contact hasn't told me much other than business is on an upswing."

As the music began its denouement, and the Calyx executed the closing steps of the dance, Jess asked under her breath, "Any chance I could meet the faceless contact?"

"Why?"

"I want to know what they're looking for. Understand how it works. Is that okay?"

She expected him to say no, but he inclined his head. The look he gave her was touched with a new respect. "Let me ask. She's secretive, understandably."

"I'll bet." Jess smiled as the music finished and they released their hands. "So am I."

Part Two

Chapter Thirteen

Jessamine

Jess stood in front of the mirrors in the tailors' den, staring at herself in the glass. Olinya's couturières milled about her, giving final touches to the embroidery in Jess's gown. The costume she had worn for the inspection had been elaborate—in a way meant to obscure and distract from Jess's true appearance—but this, this was something else. Jess felt glorified, exalted, her every beauty enhanced and lionized. She looked so transcendent and celestial it was almost frightening.

Olinya floated in to cast her shrewd gaze over Jess. Gaby came in behind her mother, her expression studious.

Jess gazed at her reflection, touching the delicate embroidery on her bodice. She half-expected it to melt from the warmth of her fingers, like it had been conjured from minuscule veins of ice, or spider's silk.

"Do you like it?" Olinya

stood back, looking thoughtfully, as though considering that there might actually be something wrong with her incredible concoction.

"Like it? Olinya, surely, you've outdone yourself. It's a masterpiece."

Olinya smiled. "My dear I have lived through four Decennials. You are free to look through the sketches of my previous work to test your hypothesis. There is nothing wrong with my imagination, but my eyes are not what they once were. I suspect that Gabriela will be required to take on the burden of design soon."

If this frightened Gaby, she didn't show it as she crouched for a closer look at the hem.

"Gaby, do I see a problem with the trim at the wrist?"

Gaby straightened to check Jessamine's wrist. She frowned as her sharp eyes found what her mother had spotted from so far away. "Clearly, time has not diminished your powers, as you like to claim. The wrong thread was used on this motif."

Jess stood patiently as a seamstress was summoned, then held her wrist out for the minuscule flaw to be fixed. Olinya slipped away to do other things, promising she'd be back. While Jess waited, she admired her costume. She thought she would never tire of looking at it. The black satin bodice had a neckline that plunged nearly to Jessamine's waist, but a snug layer of dove-gray mesh that matched her eyes covered her entire upper half. This fabric—more net than anything else—had been embroidered with silver thread in the shapes of *lonicera* leaves and branches. The silver embroidery poured its artful curls and vines over the skirt, thickening until it coalesced into a thick cluster that encircled the hem. Whiskery honeysuckle blossoms in reflective white thread winked from within the folds of the gown like tiny fae. Images of Beazle and Greta had been embroidered into the gown, too. Beazle had been placed halfway down the skirt, tiny—his actual size—and caught in mid-flight. Greta had been embroidered among the lonicera leaves, added so discreetly that many would not even notice her, a subtle homage to her twin's familiar.

Gaby noticed Jess lovingly tracing Greta's form. Her fingers paused at their work.

"Do you like it? All the Calyx have their familiars represented somewhere in their costume. Yours is the only one with two."

"I love it," Jess whispered.

Gaby smiled and spoke softly. "We want you to know that we'll never forget Greta."

Jess hoped her gratitude shone through her eyes because she couldn't trust her voice, and the last thing she wanted to do was let tears fall on this creation.

Finally the seamstress and Gaby were finished. They stepped back to admire her with sappy looks on their faces.

Olinya came in to cast her gaze over Jess one last time. "Is there anything else we can do for you? Are the slippers comfortable?"

"Very."

Jess and the rest of the Calyx had rehearsed their performance for the opening of the Midwinter Festival for weeks. The choreography and every demand of the show was ingrained in Jess's body. She no longer had to think, she only had to allow the music to take her away. Now in her costume, she couldn't wait to share their hard work with the courtiers and guests. She longed to make Ilishec, Esha and Agir proud, and in such a dress, she felt she couldn't fail. She fully embodied the Calyx.

The trill of the flutes put everyone into a flurry. Jess couldn't see the rest of the tailors' den, enclosed by mirrors the way she was, but she could hear the excitement as the time to perform drew near. Gaby put a final touch to Jess's hair and helped Jess put in the earrings that Olinya had commissioned the palace jewelers to make: *lonicera* leaves wrought in white gold.

Jess emerged as Aster came out of her cubicle. She wore a voluminous gown of pale pink velvet. Tiny feathers had been used to make clusters of aster blossoms across the skirt. A pink belt cinched in Aster's waist, and a rigid strapless bodice drew the eye upward to the lacework hugging one shoulder. Trea sat on top of her dark curls like a tiara, flexing his wings.

"Jess! You look exquisite. Let's find Rose."

Aster and Jess were asked to wait outside Rose's enclosure, until the couturières were finished with her. But Aster couldn't wait. "Do you like it?"

Rose answered, "Olinya is a genius. Do you like yours?"

"Love it. And you should see Jess!" Aster reached out and clutched Jess's hand.

"Is she there?"

Jess squeezed Aster's hand. "I'm here, Rose."

"Be out in a second."

Rose emerged in a form-fitting column dress of red satin with a slit in the fabric that allowed Rose's long leg to sweep through. The dress covered Rose up to the neck, yet peekaboo windows in the shape of roses had been strategically placed across her body, showing hints of creamy skin. Blood-red roses adorned her hair, matching her satin dancing shoes.

"You're a vision," breathed Aster.

"If this is how the Calyx dress for the Midwinter," Jess mused, "how do they distinguish the king and queen?"

"With crowns, silly," replied Rose as Bombini buzzed around her, a little confused, until he found a real rose to crawl into. "We are the reason Solana is so wealthy, the reason people come from faraway kingdoms. We're meant to be the most beautiful creatures at the Festival. It's the way Queen Esha wants it."

"Besides," Aster added, "our beauty will fade along with our magic. The Calyx represent the fragility and seasonal beauty of nature. This will be the only decennial Midwinter Festival for the majority of us—many Calyx never even see one. We have to give guests something to remember."

They waited while more Calyx gathered, admiring one another as they emerged, finished and ready to show off. Olinya's skills for the female outfits had been exercised in other ways for the males': colorful fabrics and textiles with patterns deployed strategically across jacket panels, structured coats and cleverly tailored trousers. Every creation highlighted the botanicals the Calyx commanded, while also complementing their masculine beauty.

Thrumming with excitement, the Calyx made their way through the halls to the ballroom. As the final flutes trilled and the doors swept open, Jess let the music melt into her bones, allowing herself to be carried by the symphony as she swept into the room. Guests packed the outskirts and the three levels of balconies, crowding close together to catch a glimpse of Solana's most famous attraction.

The Decennial opening number was not a slow, lingering presentation. The music was upbeat, giving each Calyx a brief moment in which to show off. Perfume was not an overt part of it. There would be plenty of opportunity for guests to experience fragrances. There was no soil for the Calyx to fill either, as that also had a place at future balls. There were no mystic blossoms. Ilishec withheld this special magic for later. The costumes and the Calyx themselves were more than enough to impress new visitors to Solana. This was made apparent in the gasps and ahhs from the guests as all fifty Calyx moved through their choreography. They made shapes that could be admired from above, and moved gracefully about the room giving all guests a good view. These steps were simple and elegant, much less intricate than other performances. Though fragrance was not the point of this opening performance, their warm bodies sweetened the room, a mere promise of what they could deliver.

When they settled into their final tableau, the applause was robust and appreciative. The majority of the Calyx swept from the room, leaving a shift behind to dance and mingle. Ilishec rotated the Calyx fifteen at a time in two hour shifts.

Jessamine was among the first shift and was approached from all sides by bright-eyed, dazzled courtiers who admired her dress and gushed about the performance. She was asked to dance by two courtiers at the same time. To avoid making a choice, she waited until one backed away, promising him he'd be next. She moved into her partner's arms as the symphony struck the chords of a popular dance from a southern region. Her partner was clumsy but enthusiastic, and kept telling her how much he loved the smell of honeysuckle because it reminded him of his childhood.

Jess passed from partner to partner as her shift wore on, her feet were sore by the time the flutes signaled a changing of the Calyx. Grateful for the break, Jess gradually made her way out of the ballroom, being stopped and admired every few feet. With a deep inhale, she left the energy of the ballroom and followed the other Calyx to the kitchens where Mrs. Tierney had personalized elixirs waiting for them. After downing hers, Jess felt much better. She went to the tailors' den where the couturières examined her and fixed anything that had gone awry. After that she was allowed to carefully recline on a chaise longue with a book and a glass of lemon water. After the flutes trilled three more times, Jess made her way back to the ballroom to be swept up in the endless energy.

Near ten-thirty, Jess felt a gentle hand at her elbow as she took some water from the crystal fountain in an annex off the ballroom.

"Miss Fontana?"

She turned to see one of the senior staff members.

"Hob!" She smiled at him. She hadn't seen him since before Rahamlar. She was happy to have him see her looking beautiful and poised. He was beneath her in the court's hierarchy, but it mattered to her that he think well of her. Perhaps because she'd since learned that he had the ear of the queen, perhaps because he oozed a fatherly warmth that she was drawn to.

He gave a shallow bow and a polite smile. "You remember me?"

"Of course." Hob wore a distinctive blue bow around his low ponytail. "How can I help you?"

"I'm to escort you to Queen Esha's company for a private audience. I understand the matter is of some urgency." He held out his elbow. "Is now a good time?"

Jess's pulse sped up. The question about whether or not it was a good time was mere etiquette. When Queen Esha summoned, subjects obeyed. Jess downed the rest of her water, handed the glass to the fountain's attendant, and took Hob's arm.

Hob led Jess to a sumptuous and quiet hallway lined with huge mirrors and even larger paintings of idyllic scenes: fields of wildflowers, fae riding horses, grazing animals scattered across emerald green hills. He rapped twice with his knuckles on a set of double doors carved with calla lilies and foxgloves in full bloom.

A maid welcomed them into a sitting room with a

fireplace. Female courtiers dressed in beautiful gowns lounged on perfectly preserved antique furniture, reading or talking quietly and sipping from delicate glasses. Jessamine recognized some of the women from the ball, responding to their admiring gazes with a polite nod as she was led to an adjoining room containing an enormous four-poster bed. Queen Esha sat at a gigantic desk in the corner, scratching away on a piece of parchment with a pretty white quill.

"Miss Jessamine Fontana of the Calyx, Ma'am." Hob announced with a bow.

She put the quill into its holder. "Thank you, Hob. Leave us please."

He bowed a second time and backed out of the room.

Queen Esha pivoted to face Jess. "You look beautiful."

Jess rose from her deep curtsy, thighs clenched. "Thank you, Ma'am. As do you."

Beazle crawled to the hollow of her collarbone, knowing that an audience with the queen would always mean him too.

The queen tugged off her elbow-length white gloves and lay them over the back of her chair. Each finger held a ring made of a flexible line of tiny seed pearls that gleamed softly as she moved. A matching tiara encrusted with pearls shone from the queen's dark cap of curls. She held out a hand for Jess to take. Esha tugged her down, hooking an overstuffed stool from beneath her writing desk with her foot. The gesture was tomboyish and made Jess smile.

"Have a seat, Jessamine."

Jess sank onto the soft stool, her skirt puffing around her like a cloud. The queen turned her palm up and Beazle flapped over, plopping into her hand. He pressed against her fingertip as she stroked him softly down his spine from the top of his head. "I always loved bats, you know. Ever since I was little."

Jess dimpled. "Me too."

"Obviously," the queen laughed. She cuddled Beazle for a minute before returning him. Esha rested both hands in her lap. "How are you enjoying the ball?"

Jess folded her hands in her lap, mirroring the queen. "The ball is wonderful, Ma'am. And you? Are you enjoying it?"

The queen's eyes crinkled. "I find balls a little tiring these days. I have attended parties my whole life. As balls go, there are none more spectacular than a Decennial. I loved them when I was your age." To Jess's surprise, the queen reached out and touched her cheek bone, affection in her gaze. "I know you are working, but we are only young once. Remember also to enjoy it, my little Calyx."

Jess was touched. "I will. Thank you, Ma'am."

Esha withdrew her hand. "King Agir is aware we are having this conversation. It's important you know that I speak for both of us."

Jess went still. She associated Agir with the Fahyli side of her life, and Esha with the Calyx side. Was this about a Fahyli mission?

As if she could read Jess's thoughts, Esha said: "I am speaking to you in your capacity of Fahyli. Understood?"

"Yes, Ma'am."

"We received news today of King Osvitan's death."

The queen waited while Jess absorbed this. She had no feelings about the neighboring king. If anything, Osvitan had raised Faraçek, and Faraçek had killed Greta, so as far as Jess was concerned, the world was probably better off without the man who had nurtured such a son.

"I am… sorry," Jess replied, feeling like she was supposed to say something.

Esha took a deep breath. She tugged at a pearl on her gown. Jess thought she seemed nervous.

"Yes. Me too. King Osvitan was not quite a friend, but he was an ally and he was not a bad king, although his declining health meant that he could not serve his people as well as they deserved. It is sad not just because a decent man and ruler has passed away, but because the citizens of Rahamlar will be in turmoil, with their queen-in-waiting missing. Prince Faraçek is currently the only member of the royal family still in residence at the fortress."

Prince Faraçek's cruelly handsome features materialized in Jess's mind, making her skin prickle with contempt.

Esha continued: "The lawyers have confirmed that the custody of the kingdom of Rahamlar goes into the hands of a board of trustees for a period of five years, to give the missing queen time to be found, or turn up dead. Prince Faraçek cannot take the crown, at least not for the time being."

Jess let out a long breath. "That's good, right?"

The queen rubbed her forehead. "Yes and no. I am sorry to involve you in this Jessamine, but your new position makes you the most suitable candidate."

Jess's heart kindled. Candidate?

"We knew King Osvitan wasn't well enough to attend. Naturally, we sent him an invitation as a sign of respect and goodwill. The prince has accepted our invitation to the Midwinter Festival on his father's behalf. Prince Faraçek could be here as soon as tomorrow."

The queen's gaze lingered on Jess's face.

Jess was consumed by the memory of Greta's fragile little body lying on the table in front of the prince. It tore Jess's heart and she put a hand over her chest. Beazle scaled Jessamine's hair like a rope until he was buried inside her curls.

Esha brows knit together. "Are you alright?"

Jess nodded, but she didn't feel alright.

The prince. Greta's killer. Here at the ball. My territory. My court. My home.

"I have some idea of how you feel about him, Jessamine. What happened in Rahamlar was horrendous. Please believe me, we have not made this decision lightly. We suspect the prince of foul play in regards to his sisters, but we have no proof. You must spy on the prince while he is here and report back to us what you learn."

Jess absorbed this, her mind racing. Watch the prince. Follow. Eavesdrop. Spy.

"We do not believe he will remember you, but even if he does, it is of no consequence. You are to behave politely but impartially toward him. If he asks you to dance, you are to accept, just as you would any other guest. You are a professional. And dancing may provide an opportunity to get close, observe him, learn what kind of being he is, and perhaps of his plans." Queen Esha's eyes narrowed. "We will put him in a suite that will give you plenty of opportunity to watch him while he thinks he is in private, to listen in on his conversations and mark his movements. He may do nothing to give himself away, but then again, he may. You and Beazle are to be our eyes and ears. This assignment is important. I hope you can see that."

Jess nodded. "I can, Ma'am."

"The princesses are out there somewhere, dead or alive. Now that Osvitan has passed, we intend to put effort into finding them—and if need be—help them. We will not let the prince know of these intentions, because the truth is, we do not want the prince installed as king of Rahamlar. If Princess Serya, the true heir, is located alive, then we will protect her until she can be crowned. If she is not alive, then we will use whatever legal means are open to us..."—the pause seemed to add, *and illegal means as well*—"To have the youngest, Princess Isabey crowned, instead of Faraçek."

Jessamine let none of the storm inside of her leak out, gripping her calm exterior like a shield. "And if Princess Isabey is also dead?"

The queen frowned. "Then we will have a very difficult decision to make."

"Lady Çifta reported that Faraçek doesn't know where the princesses are, that he didn't have anything to do with their disappearance."

The queen knocked her head elegantly from side to side: maybe so, maybe not so. "Lady Çifta is a lovely young woman but we do not know her true character.

She is young, and therefore naive. I do not think she would willingly give us incorrect information; however, Faraçek may have misled her. He would be careful not to give away his true position to her, in case she repeated it to an enemy." Queen Esha gave her a look freighted with age and experience. "If he had anything to do with the disappearance of the princesses, then he is guilty of a very serious crime. If he hasn't, then he will want to discover what happened to them before we do. He may want to twist the situation to his advantage. Both the princesses, and we, will be better positioned if we find them first. Do you see?"

Jess felt like she was being drawn into a dangerous game. This was so much bigger than her, but she hated the idea of Faraçek ruling their neighboring nation far more than she disliked the idea of spying. With her communication with Beazle strengthening by the day, she had more confidence in their abilities than ever. Some part of her wanted a chance to impress Queen Esha and King Agir.

"We won't let you down, Ma'am."

The queen smiled. "Thank you. Do you have any questions?"

Jess shook her head.

"You are one of the least suspicious characters of the Scented Court, Jessamine. Remember to keep your thoughts off your face, and mind where your eyes go. They tend to wander in the same direction as our ears, but a good spy can bisect the two."

Jess blinked at the queen, surprised to hear her talking so specifically about the nature of spy work.

"Royalty makes use of similar tactics, Jess. We have more enemies than the average courtier. I've been partitioning my eyes from my ears since I was a little girl. It comes quite naturally to aristocrats. It has not come to you naturally given the nature of your childhood, but once you are used to it, you and Beazle will be twice as effective. I am certain Kite and Digit will have some good advice for you as well."

"They know Faraçek is coming?"

The queen waved a hand. "No, but they will. You can tell anyone you wish that Prince Faraçek will be here in a matter of days, as it will be widely known by noon tomorrow, but I'm sure I don't need to tell you to keep your assignment to yourself. However, don't hesitate to make use of Kite and Digit's experience."

"Yes, Ma'am." Jess got to her feet. "Is there anything else?"

Esha reached for her gloves. "Just, try not to be nervous. It makes a person sweat, and I'm told you're still working on that."

Jess flushed and tried to hide it by dipping into a curtsy. "Yes, Ma'am."

The queen turned back to her desk and picked up her quill. "I'll see you in the ballroom, Jessamine, where we cannot behave in quite so friendly a manner."

"Yes, Ma'am." Quietly, Jessamine slipped from the queen's chambers.

Chapter Fourteen

Çifta

"Has my lady attended many international balls?" Çifta's maid, Ann, made small talk as she tugged Çifta's gloves into place, lacing them up the insides of her forearms.

"There were always parties in Kirkik and I attended balls at the Royal Court of Boskaya, but never anything as big as this." Çifta gazed at her reflection. Her pale blue gown was overlaid with white crystals that brought out her eyes and contrasted beautifully with her hair. "I've never had a gown this fine, either. I hope my father doesn't have a fit when he gets the bill."

Ann stepped back, giving Çifta a satisfied once-over. "I believe you're ready, m'lady. Have a wonderful time. I'll be here when you return to help you undress. No matter how late."

"Thank you, Ann."

Çifta joined the flow of courtiers—a veritable parade

of glittering nobility dressed in their finest—making their way to the largest ballroom. Some wore elaborate masks, gravity-defying headdresses, or voluminous feathers in their hair. Still others coiffed their tresses into vertical sculptures—some so large and absurd that Çifta half expected birds to come flying out of them. Some men opted for hats, while others wore a warrior's tail, the way Laec did.

Çifta's heart tripped over thoughts of Laec. She hadn't seen him in days and no one she asked seemed to know if he was planning to attend the Decennial, or if he was even allowed. She gave up after casually asking three different courtiers. Any more and she'd start a fire of speculation that she wasn't interested in having to smother. Laec wouldn't appreciate being the target of court gossip either.

She joined a few of the ladies she had become acquainted with, sitting in plush chairs on a balcony, where they would have a good view of the Calyx performance. This was her first opportunity to witness the flora fae in their element, to see them do what they were trained to do and understand what made Solana so famous. Çifta intended to keep her father's stipulations out of her mind and enjoy the Midwinter the way it was meant to be enjoyed, free from the burdens and stressors of daily life.

Guests crowded the edges of the ballroom floor. Every balcony was full. Courtiers talked in excited whispers as they waited for the Midwinter Festival to officially begin. Çifta's gaze drifted up and up and up, taking in the decorative railings, the etherlight sconces and chandeliers, until she spotted a strange little alcove built above the third floor balcony, nearly at the ceiling. Using her binoculars for a better look, she giggled when she saw Mae's little bandit-face peek over the lip of this alcove.

Çifta nudged her neighbor, a popular fixture at the Scented Court nicknamed Lady Glimmer because she ran a jewelry shop in Solana City. "Look. Up there."

Lady Glimmer—true to her name, she was covered from head to toe in sparkly stones—peered through her own binoculars. She smiled. "Sy will be on the floor somewhere."

Çifta's heart lifted as if strung to a pair of doves. "So the Fahyli *will* attend?"

Lady Glimmer removed the binoculars and canted her head. "A Decennial is for everyone, Lady Çifta. Even the servants have a chance to attend at least one ball over the course of the twenty-one days. They do it on a rotation, of course. Solana is the only kingdom that does this, as far as I know. If you watch that alcove you spotted—excellent eye, by the way—you'll see other familiars. They've got little interest in parties, but they pop in now and then."

A trill of flutes sounded and a hush came over the room. The conductor raised his hands.

Lively music filled the air and the huge double doors swung wide. Calyx floated into the room, moving as elegantly as swans. Çifta hardly remembered to breathe, the sight was so exquisite. Each Calyx was uniquely dressed, some with costumes designed around obvious botanical themes, others with subtle details that inspired the use of binoculars. Çifta heard guests making a game out of trying to guess each performer's species, easily picking out Wisteria, Lily, Lotus, Rose, Proteas and Peony. The fifty Calyx swept around the dancefloor, choreography executed in perfect unison, showing off their beauty and filling the room with the fragrance of a summer garden, while outside a light sprinkle of rain was falling.

Çifta spotted Jessamine in an incredible gown overlaid with reflective embroidery, looking nothing like the young girl who had so bravely snuck into Rahamlar to rescue her. Here, fulfilling her true role, Jess looked like a living work of art. Çifta's heart ached with gratitude. She would love to talk to Jessamine again, but they seemed almost to never cross paths. The Calyx were the busiest citizens in the kingdom. Guests enjoyed the diversions of the Festival at their leisure, but Calyx had assignments. Çifta wasn't aware of the specifics, but ladies in the queen's parlor had talked about how demanding Calyx roles could be.

When the Calyx concluded the opening performance, the majority of them left the ballroom, leaving less than a third on the floor to welcome guests and begin the dancing. Jessamine was one of those who stayed. Eyeballing her position, Çifta headed for the steps.

Courtiers poured onto the dance floor and congregated at the refreshment stands. They stood at tall tables to drink and talk while watching the dancers. Some, Çifta was told, never left the floor until the clock struck one and the last song had been played.

As Çifta stepped down to the ballroom floor, Jessamine whirled by in some courtier's arms, smiling and chatting, holding her head like a queen. A young Calyx with bright red corkscrew curls materialized at her side. He bowed, his hand out in invitation.

"Would my lady like to dance?"

Çifta curtsied and stepped into his arms. The top of his head didn't quite reach her nose, but he smelled delightful, like blooming snapdragons.

From that moment on Çifta had barely a moment to breathe or even have a drink. She passed from one partner to the next, to the next. Her mind was a hurricane of names and faces, scents and smiles. Strange accents warmed her ears, rich fragrances filled her nose, and the diversity of conversations made her head spin. She laughed with Asclepias until her ribs ached, admired Proteas's silky hair as he floated her around the room, got tenacious hiccups after bouncing around to an upbeat waltz with Anthurium, and was even overcome by a fit of sneezing after a close dance with Heath, making her wonder if she was allergic to *erica*. And that was just her dances with the Calyx. She also circled the floor endlessly with courtiers from all over Ivryndi and even a few nobles she knew from Boskaya. She couldn't remember when she'd ever had so much fun, and lamented inwardly that her father had not found her a husband from Solana.

She had to politely decline when Asclepias asked her to dance for the fourth time, just to get some air. As she arrowed for an outdoor balcony, she combed the sea of heads for Laec's bright hair without success. She froze as she spotted an enormous black cat lounging against a wall, lime-green gaze following the guests as they gave her a very large berth.

Someone hissed and the cat shot her predator's gaze toward a dark head poking from a doorway. She chirped, her ribcage compressing, then got up and slipped through the door. A Fahyli Çifta recognized emerged, closing the door firmly behind the cat. He wore a finely tailored vest, close-fitting leggings and tall boots. He looked contrite.

"Sorry if she startled you. She's not allowed down here, but where there's food, there's Tully. Even better if its court food. She especially loves cured meats and deviled eggs."

"She didn't frighten me," Çifta lied smoothly. "She's beautiful. You're a friend of Laec's, aren't you?"

"I'm Panther." He bowed, not quite as gracefully as the male Calyx. "At your service. At least for the next three hours. That's all I have to put in. Not one for balls."

Çifta hid a smile. "You don't say. I was going to get some air. Would you like to join me?"

He brightened. "I'm up for anything that doesn't involve dancing. Perfect timing too because the rain has finally stopped." He turned and swung an elbow out for her to hold.

The night was cool and fresh but the balcony was warmed by etherlights.

Panther's eye snagged on a bar, where palace staff were mixing drinks. "May I get you a drink?"

"Absolutely. I'm parched. I don't know what to have, though. Make a suggestion for me?"

Panther introduced Çifta to a rose-tinted champagne. He had an odorless, colorless liquid that he said was a southern specialty. They circled the damp balcony, making small talk and sipping their drinks. By the time their drinks were refilled, she felt warm and relaxed. Panther made Çifta snort with laughter and cover her face in embarrassment. They returned to the ball, arms linked like old friends. They watched the couples swirling about the floor, and giggled at the collection of bees and butterflies drawn to a very tall feather headdress worn by a woman so short that her head could barely be seen.

"Are you going to dance with the lady, Pan? Or shall I show you how it's done?"

Laec's voice crashed over Çifta like a warm wave. Her stomach spiraled as she looked up into his face.

"You dance?" Panther looked genuinely shocked. "Why is it so hard to picture that?"

Laec was mock-affronted. "All Stavarjakians dance, you dimwitted simpleton."

Panther stepped back, palms up in surrender. "She's certainly not safe with me. I'm pure mayhem on a dance floor."

Laec led Çifta onto the floor as the music began. She recognized the song as a spin-off from a Boskayan waltz, which she'd danced in the living room of the Unya manor when she was still too young for balls. Nostalgia rolled over her as she performed her curtsy, but when she stepped into Laec's arms and his hand cupped her back, only the present mattered. The music and the blur of one hundred conversations enveloped them, cocooning them within their own little bubble.

Her artist's eye devoured the planes of Laec's face,

the dynamism of his hair, the uptilted ageless eyes, the mischievous mouth.

"You look beautiful, Lady Çifta," he said.

Since he wanted to play it formal, she replied, "As do you, Mr. Fairijak."

"Have you had any letters from your father?"

Çifta's smile faltered. "Let's not talk of Kazery tonight."

Laec shocked her by kissing her temple. "As you wish."

Çifta kept her face impassive but felt short of breath. She had not expected such an intimate gesture after the formality. Did it mean anything?

Laec led expertly, without faltering, even when a butterfly fluttered between them.

"How do you know this dance so well?" she asked, as a honeybee droned past. "It's Boskayan, you know?"

He focused over her head. "I do know. Actually, I learned it from Ilishec when I was twelve or thirteen. He came back for a visit and taught Elphame's entire court. They're mad for new dances in Stavarjak. I guess it stuck."

"I would like to visit Stavarjak one day. Is your queen as beautiful as they say?"

Laec looked on the edge of a smile. "That depends on your taste, and the day of the week. Elphame can look however she chooses. She has purple eyes and she's partial to white hair. Everything else changes on a whim."

"So it's not real? Her beauty?"

Laec shrugged. "What's real anyway?"

When he didn't expand, Çifta felt disappointed. She wished they could just say what was on their minds, be honest. She squeezed his hand twice. "Is anything bothering you, Laec?"

She thought she could read relief in his expression. Perhaps she'd supplied the opening he'd been looking for.

"Not quite bothering, that's not how I'd frame it. But I do have news."

"Oh?" She said it casually, but her heart scurried around behind her ribs like a little mouse.

"It's something that may affect your… predicament."

Her gown brushed against Peony's as she floated by in the arms of an aging nobleman. "What do you mean?"

He cleared his throat and lowered his voice a fraction. "King Osvitan has… bit it."

Çifta blinked. "Pardon?"

"Uh. He's dead," Laec said flatly.

Çifta felt like she'd bumped against something solid and rebounded in a new direction entirely, one she had no control over. "Is it certain?"

He pulled her closer, his breath dusting against the hair at her temples. "It's spreading through the court on the swift lips of the gossips. I'm sure King Agir and Queen Esha will make a formal announcement, but I wanted to make sure you knew."

Çifta took several moments to absorb this news. Her gut felt tight, but the more she thought about it, the more hopeful she grew. "This could work in my favor. I'm sorry, that's a terrible thing to say when someone so important has just passed away. King Osvitan was frail and withdrawn, but he was only ever kind to me. I will send my regrets—" Send her regrets to whom? The princesses had been kidnapped or run away, and she had no intention of having contact with Faraçek ever again. She'd rather eat her own toenail clippings. In fact she'd rather eat her own toes. "To the nobles and servants that I knew when I was there."

Laec said good-naturedly, "You don't have to pretend to mourn for my sake, Çifta. I have no feelings about Osvitan whatsoever. I only care about what becomes of you."

There was that breathlessness again, the struggling to fully inhale, a feeling of being wrapped in a breeze that caressed her face, and tugged oxygen away from her mouth, as though playing a game. Perhaps Laec could shore up his heart against her, but she could not shore hers against him. Fear lanced through her, fear that she struggled to keep off her face, squished down deep inside. Laec had the power to break her heart, utterly and thoroughly. He didn't know it, but he carried her heart with him wherever he went, and the emotional danger took her breath away. If he turned his gaze away from her, cut her out of his life, left the Scented Court to return to his own land… he would leave her in pieces, forever changed.

She knew he could see something on her face.

His bottomless gaze threatened to swallow her. "Are you alright?"

She tugged her mind and heart back into their yoke and tethered them, hard. "Princess Serya is the queen-in-waiting. She is whom my father must negotiate with now."

"Only… she is missing."

"Yes, so there is only one course of action."

He cocked a brow. "Find her?"

"Precisely. I must find her."

Whatever Laec thought about this, he hid it, but Çifta suspected a storm behind his eyes.

"I really hope that she is alive," Çifta added weakly, assuming that might also be part of what Laec was concerned about.

They executed their final steps and drew apart for the final bow and curtsy.

As they straightened, he said: "Drink?"

She nodded, grateful for the suggestion—she needed one now more than ever—and grateful that he didn't immediately abandon her. Arm in arm, they approached a refreshment stand where a flock of servants were using fresh squeezed juices to make botanical themed cocktails.

Çifta spotted Jessamine at the side of the bar chatting with a lady in a canary-yellow dress and matching hat.

Çifta caught Jessamine's eye and the Calyx tilted her head in an elegant nod of acknowledgment. She lifted a finger, a subtle gesture asking Çifta to wait a moment.

Taking their drinks and shuffling out of the way as thirsty courtiers rushed in for refreshment between songs, Çifta and Laec waited until Jessamine drifted over. Etherlight flashed against the embroidery on her gown, as though it were covered in tiny fae, winking in and out of view. Çifta fought off a wave of jealousy as Jessamine's luminous pale gray gaze went to Laec. They shared a smile that hinted at a relationship the nature of which was known only to them. Jessamine and Çifta exchanged kisses and the sweet smell of honeysuckle filled Çifta's senses.

"I was hoping to see you, Lady Çifta," Jess said. "May I have a private word?"

Jess drew Çifta away from the dance floor as a boisterous song began. Already dancers were laughing, their shoes scuffling across the floor. Laec remained within hearing distance.

"I have news. I'm afraid its not good news, but you should know as soon as possible."

"I already know." Çifta lay a hand on Jess's arm, the embroidery tickling her palm. "But thank you for seeking me out, I appreciate that more than I can say."

Jessamine's brows hiked up. "You already know? The queen said the news would travel fast, but I underestimated how quickly. What are you going to do? Will you stay at court? If there is anything I can do to… help you, please let me know. Although I'm sure Laec is already scheming."

"Thank you. As for what I am going to do, it's simple. I'm going to have to find Princess Serya. I really have no other option in the matter."

Now Jess looked confused. "Princess Serya?"

Jessamine's bewilderment now confused Çifta. "Yes… she is missing."

"I know she is missing. I was asked to find her, in my own way, but I failed." She shook her head, befuddled. "But, I don't understand how finding the princess will help."

The Calyx had been asked to find Serya? Jessamine was a permanent fixture at court. Why would anyone ask her to search for the missing heir? Çifta's mouth dropped open, then snapped closed. As her sisters would have said, she was utterly stumped.

"Well… I… uh," Çifta latched on to the one important fact that anchored her in this situation. "King Osvitan is dead, so I must now ask my father to negotiate with the new monarch. Hopefully, that will be Queen Serya. She and I developed a kind of friendship, and, although she did not witness all my ill-treatment, I cannot imagine she will not be open to making a deal with my father that does not involve me having to marry her brother."

Jess still looked bewildered. "I understand that and I hope it works out for you, but what about when Prince Faraçek arrives?"

Çifta felt like someone had thrown cold water into her face. "A-arrives?"

"Yes. When he arrives at court for the Midwinter Festival." Jessamine watched Çifta's face closely. "What news did you think I was delivering?"

"King Osvitan's death."

Jess let out a big exhale. "Oh. I see now. No, I wanted to warn you that Prince Faraçek could be here as early as tomorrow."

Çifta pressed a hand to her bosom, beneath which her heart was racing in fits and starts. The music distorted in Çifta's ears, the laughter of the dancers decayed into dissonant, evil-sounding cackles. The ballroom tilted one way, then the other. Çifta could see Faraçek's face, smell his strange mulchy breath, feel his iron grip on her upper arms… her feet dangling.

Laec was at her side, taking one of her hands. "Çifta?"

She mumbled some kind of thank you to Jessamine and headed for the door with Laec trying to keep up. She clung to shreds of decorum as she fought her way through the crowd. She couldn't bear to think about what they saw on her face.

Laec put his hand under her elbow as she took a corner too quickly and almost mowed Hazel down, who squeaked and backpedalled. Pulling Çifta against his side, Laec put his lips near her temple as they walked. "I won't let anything happen to you."

Her head felt hot and pounded with blood. She put her fingertips to her temples. "I can't be here if he is. I just cannot. No more balls, no more parties. Not while he is under this roof."

Laec slipped an arm about her waist, helping her dodge a group of Calyx and courtiers.

"Why is he coming?" she whispered. "Can he not be satisfied that he tortured me enough? He has to chase me to a foreign court? Is he coming to insist that Kazery force me to marry him?" She gasped, horrified. "What if my father is also on his way? What if I am almost out of time?"

Laec drew her toward a plush lounge chair tucked into a quiet alcove. "Just breathe. Listen to me."

She sank into soft cushions then put her elbows on her knees and her head in her hands. "Please, tell me something good."

"What is most likely," Laec said quietly, his voice a ballast in a storm. "Is that the prince is coming to the Decennial because his father just died. He needs to establish himself in the eyes of Queen Esha and King Agir. It's a test, a way to learn whether he can trust them to ally with him, when and if its needed. This type of thing is common, Çifta."

Çifta lifted her head, her gaze hopeful. "I didn't think of that. You're saying it might not have anything to do with me at all?"

He crouched in front of her, his face close to hers. "Exactly. Don't jump to conclusions. Try to think about the situation from his perspective. The prince knows he has lost you—not legally, yet, but emotionally—of that there is no doubt. He won't know the nature of the conversation you had with your father, but he likely expects that you told Kazery the truth—after which, he will not expect Kazery to uphold the betrothal. So, put that aside."

"Put that aside," she repeated, clinging to the lifeline of Laec's words.

He took her hands. "The king of Rahamlar has passed. The queen-in-waiting is missing. Prince Faraçek is not in line for the throne, remember, though I have no doubt he wants it. The crown must pass to the next human child, which is Serya."

"And?"

"And, the Decennial is not just the biggest *party* in all of Ivryndi, it's the biggest negotiating hall: alliances are forged here. The dancing and eating are just decoration. If I were Faraçek, I would attend too. No question. He will bring an entourage, as well. As many as he thinks he can get away with."

"Spies," Çifta groaned. "Even if I successfully avoid Faraçek, I won't be able to avoid his entourage. He'll have eyes everywhere."

Laec was quick to add: "But their first priority will be any news or clues about the missing heir… not you—a lady who was just a prisoner for a little while. Forgive my candor, but there are much larger pieces than you being moved across the chessboard of the midlands."

Çifta felt only slightly better. "I still can't be in the same room as him. I don't care how much fun the banquets and balls are. And I can't risk being seen by anyone from Rahamlar. They know my face, and they'll run straight to him."

Laec gave her a compassionate look. "No one will make you attend anything, but you'll miss one heck of a party."

She groaned again and dropped her forehead into her hands. So much for enjoying the Midwinter Festival.

Chapter Fifteen

Jessamine

Jess sat in the study adjoining Ilishec's workshop, nomenclature textbook open on the arm of an overstuffed chair. A merry fire crackled behind the wrought-iron grate, casting its warmth over her feet and legs, while the diamond-pane windows cast a murky light as rain slithered down the glass.

Outside, the garden was in hibernation, but spring and summer were still accessible in temperature and humidity-controlled hothouses. On a whim, guests could enjoy orchid displays, rosebushes in full bloom, and wisteria vines full of fragrant purple fronds. They could have tea among the well-stocked fish ponds, or visit the moss cave. Ilishec's gardeners had spent months preparing structures and beds to suit his vision. Then the Calyx blessed the project with their magic. Jess had loved every moment of the process.

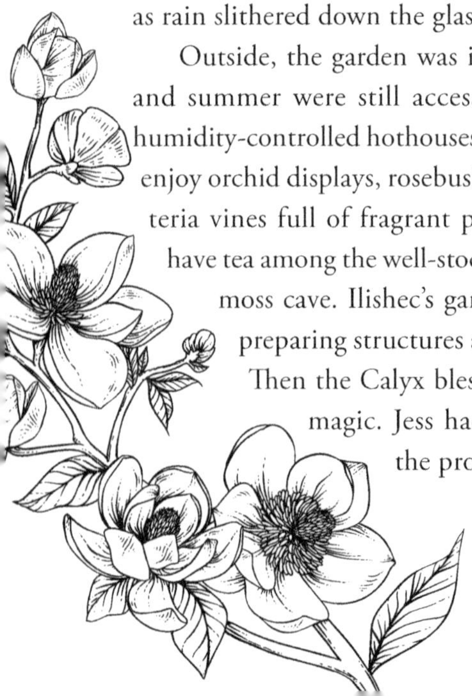

Because the feasting and

dancing happened every night in one form or another, and the Calyx were expected to be available for guests, they were on a strict rotation that would ensure everyone had adequate leisure time and sleep.

Every night the Calyx wore a different Olinya creation. At the end of the Decennial, Olinya would host a private auction where the costumes would be sold—unwashed and fragrant—and the money divided. Portions went to the villages for town infrastructure, servants and staff were bonused, and palace coffers were replenished. Precious bulbs could be purchased and taken abroad by visitors. And of course there were the lucrative perfumeries. It was all overseen by Olinya, Ilishec, and Queen Esha. Jess was starting to get used to the magnitude of the City's outputs, but it would strike her from time to time just how important the Calyx and Fahyli really were. The Calyx to generate wealth, and the Fahyli to protect it. The Decennial was one long and elaborate economic exercise.

Lectures had been paused for the duration of the Festival, and until Prince Faraçek arrived Jess had no Fahyli duties. But, now almost halfway through the Decennial and with no appearances from Rahamlar, Jessamine found her mundane nomenclature text a welcome distraction from the anticipation of her spy duties.

"There you are!"

Jess looked up with a start.

Ilishec plopped into the chair across from her. "I don't expect to find flora fae in the study during the Decennial. I've been looking for you everywhere. I had Indigo go all the way to the stables and the Perfume Shop."

Jess closed the textbook and set it on the low table beside her chair. "I'm sorry. I needed to be someplace quiet for a while."

Ilishec stroked a hand down his manicured beard. "I understand that. The Midwinter is fun but it's also a frenzy and quite exhausting. I came to talk with you about tonight, we have two foreign princes arriving, one of whom is our least favorite person of the decade."

Jess kept her expression neutral. "Finally."

"Yes, the queen mentioned that she had informed you. I am sorry, Jessamine. Sorry that you'll have to be in the same room as him again. Damn sorry his arrival didn't occur on one of your nights off. If I wasn't duty bound as a royal representative I could express some choice punishments I would like to see levied on Faraçek for what he did. Alas, he is a prince." Ilishec glowered. "A protected person."

Jess gave him a grim smile. "It's alright. I've been preparing myself for it."

"I could switch the roster if you need a little more time?"

Although he was kind to offer, Jess knew how complicated the schedule was.

"Thank you but there is no need to delay the inevitable." In a way, Jess was looking forward to testing herself. The queen's goals were much more important than Jess's personal feelings. There might be some pleasure in pretending respect toward Prince Faraçek, only to know in her heart that she was looking for ways to subvert him.

Ilishec's watchful gaze never left her face. "Are you sure?"

"I can't avoid my duties forever. Sometimes it's better just to get it over with."

"Good on you." He gave her an approving look as he got up. "He won't recognize you, you know. Arrogant unseelie like him think themselves above servants, and you were veiled and dressed in that horrid black mourning gown the last time he saw you."

"I've decided that it doesn't matter if he does. I won't remind him who I am, but if by chance he does recognize me, I will behave as the queen expects me to. I will never give him the satisfaction of letting him see how much he hurt me."

He nodded. "Good. I know you have good friends in Aster, and Rose, and Snap; they're all aware of who is coming tonight so they will be your silent supporters. But please know that if you feel overwhelmed or upset at any time, you shouldn't hesitate to find me. I would rather take care of you myself than hear about it later and wish I could have been there."

Jess thanked the gardener again and rose from her chair to return the text to the shelf. "I'd better get ready. Gaby is expecting me early to work out some details with something precipitous. Apparently, I'm wearing a head-dress tonight."

"Very good." Ilishec headed for the door, but stopped abruptly and turned back to face her. He hesitated, then spoke slowly. "If the prince should ask you to dance…"

Jess slid the textbook into place and gave the gardener

a flat smile. "I know. Don't poison him. I've made some stupid decisions in the past, but I'm not that stupid, and thanks to Peony, I'm not that sloppy either."

The gardener looked sheepish. "Of course. I'm sorry. Just had to make sure. See you tonight."

Ilishec disappeared into his workshop and Jess began the climb to the tailors' den.

Many hours later, waltz music filled the air and dancing couples occupied every square foot of the parquet floor. Jessamine was seated in the first balcony with a wealthy couple from Archelia who said she reminded them of their daughter back at home. They gave her a gift from their homeland, a small brooch in the shape of a sun with a glimmering orange precious stone that was found only along the shores of the South Ivryndian sea. It didn't go with Jessamine's costume—a frothy concoction of layers of powder-blue chiffon—but she was so charmed that she pinned it to her neckline.

When a waltz finished, Hob approached the conductor and whispered in his ear. The conductor nodded and the symphony blasted thematic chords reserved for important announcements.

Everyone moved to the balcony railing to see who had arrived, and Jess gripped the balustrade as the room fell silent. The crowd had parted away from the double doors that only opened for royal guests. A Solanan herald strode importantly into the room. Taking a deep inhale, he belted: "Announcing to the Scented Court…"

Jess blinked rapidly and sucked in a breath, bracing herself to lay eyes on her enemy, and to look happy about it—or at the very least, not look like she wanted to throw up.

"His Royal Highness, Prince Ruskin of Silverfall." The herald stepped aside and an entourage of a half-dozen fae came into the room as the lords, ladies, courtiers, servants and Calyx sank into bows and curtsies. Jess curtsied along with the rest of the women on the balcony.

Prince Ruskin of Silverfall, not Prince Faraçek of Rahamlar. Ilishec had said something about two important princes arriving, but she'd been so distracted thinking about how she would react to Faraçek that she'd forgotten to ask the gardener who the other prince was.

The conductor had the orchestra play a soft background phrase as Prince Ruskin approached the dais where Agir and Esha stood to welcome him. His hair was an icy shade with a hint of pale green, but unlike the majority of courtiers in the ballroom with white hair, there was nothing elderly about him. His mostly-male entourage were similar in their paleness and glacial coloring. With no more than tints of color among them, they stood out with their own unique beauty. The crowd closed in behind the Silverfall retinue, after which the dancing resumed. Jess blew out a breath and smiled at the kind noblewoman from Archelia who was murmuring with her husband.

The lady returned her smile. "Isn't it exciting?"

"Oh yes," Jess replied, uncertain what she was referring to. "Very exciting."

"No Silverfae royal has been out of Silverfall since the war of the silver queens."

"The war of…" She'd never heard of such an event. "When was that?"

"Long before you were born, my dear. I was just a young woman myself, and Silverfall is so very far away from Archelia, but even we heard the rumors. It must have been…" She looked to her husband for help. "What my darling, forty-five years ago?"

He seesawed a dry, wrinkled hand. "Not quite that long, I don't think. Perhaps thirty-five, but ancient history now. One wonders what has been going on up there to keep the Silverfall nobility sequestered. I suppose they never were the type to travel widely, I suspect they dislike foreign climates, but I remember the days when the royals would appear in foreign courts, just to show the world how beautiful and strong they still were. Quite incredible to see a Silverfae royal here, most remarkable. What did they say his name was?"

"Prince Ruskin," his wife peered through her binoculars, presumably scanning the room for his white hair. "He must be her son. What's her name? I always forget."

"Queen Sylifke."

Jess made a mental note to ask Laec about the war of the silver queens. Being Stavarjakian and a neighbor of Silverfall, maybe he'd know.

Jess descended to the first floor with the couple and stayed with them until a handsome young courtier she recognized from former parties asked her to dance. But as their energetic gambol finished, the orchestra announced another important arrival.

The herald slid to his place in front of the doors and announced, "His Royal Highness, Prince Faraçek of the Kingdom of Rahamlar."

The Rahamlarin entourage swept into the room with an energy that was entirely different from the Silverfae company.

Jessamine kept her gaze on the floor as she curtsied, only looking up after Prince Faraçek passed on his way to the dais. She rose slowly, her focus on his back. His head held high, his shoulders straight and broad, he was a sight even from the rear. He turned his head a little to acknowledge someone in the crowd and Jess saw his face. He was handsome, but like a barren terrain of jutting volcanic rock. His retinue were much the same: sharp features, grayish skin, strong faces and bodies, and a touch of menace.

Captain Yorin looked as he had when he'd inspected the Calyx, only more finely dressed. He looked like he wasn't keen on being here but had taken it on as a duty—not something to be enjoyed. Unlike the prince, who glided into the room with his eyes on the king and queen, Yorin's dark gaze swept over the guests, absorbing and discarding or filing information in his mind. Jess wondered what he was thinking.

Her dance partner put a hand under her elbow. "Are you alright, Miss Jessamine?"

The music had begun another dance, leaving Jessamine and her partner as the only still beings in the middle of colorful swirling gowns. Tearing her gaze from Yorin, she took her partner's hand. She let her mind wander as her partner chattered away happily, fumbling the steps only a little. Injecting an agreeable sound or smile was all that was required to keep him happy.

Beazle flapped over to her as she swung around the floor, satisfied with his night's hunt. Landing on her headdress, his satiation turned to dismay. He never liked when her head was covered.

When the dance concluded, Jessamine made her way around the floor to a table of refreshments near the dais where she could observe Prince Faraçek. She took a plate of sliced strawberries sprinkled with mint and topped with a dollop of whipped cream, camouflaging herself among the other hungry fae as they chatted and nibbled.

Faraçek was seated at Queen Esha's elbow, engaged in conversation. He looked so different when he smiled; gone was the manner of threat and suppressed rage. His sharp edges melted behind a charming grin as he talked animatedly. Even Esha gave the appearance of being utterly won over by the dashing unseelie prince. His cordiality increased Jess's unease. He was even more dangerous than she realized. He could act. No wonder Esha wanted to know what he said when alone with confidantes.

She was weaving her way toward the dais when an authoritative male voice caught her like a hook. "May I have this dance?"

Jess turned, remembering to plaster a smile on her face at the last second.

Prince Ruskin stood with one hand behind his back,

the other held out in invitation. His white eyes held hers fast.

"It would be my pleasure."

He led her to the dance floor, every bit a prince at home among courtiers. Jess received a shock when he cupped her back and cradled her other hand. His touch was cold, and she had to suppress a shudder.

Jess moved by muscle memory through the familiar group dance, her gaze on Prince Ruskin's. His eyes were disconcerting and difficult to read and his accent was not one that Sy had taught her to identify.

"Were you surprised to be asked to dance by a prince of Silverfall?" he asked, his gaze trailing from the top of her headdress down to her mouth. "There was surprise on your face."

They swayed close, palms coming to touch flat, then they swayed back.

"Yes, Your Highness."

Four steps forward, then a box step around the other. Another four steps back and he was in her view again. Now he was staring at Beazle, his eyes like little orbs of ice shot through with pins of piercing black. Distaste flickered across his features.

"Also," she added, "Maybe it was silly of me, but I didn't know that Silverfae were so… coldblooded."

The prince laughed heartily, though it didn't reach his eyes. Maybe Silverfae eyes were incapable of reflecting warmth. "We are as warm-blooded as you are, little Calyx. How naive you are."

Jess didn't contradict him by pointing out that his

touch made her wonder if he'd spent the last hour inside Mrs. Tierney's ice-box. "I don't know anything of your kingdom or your people. I have so many questions."

The prince executed the ball-changes the dance demanded with perfect technique. He guided her in a circle around him. She held her skirt out to the side and swept it back and forth—in time with all the other ladies in the room—so it fluttered with the music. The effect for those watching was delightful.

When they were done with the flourishes, he replied. "I would much rather ask you questions, starting with your name and your species. We do not have many flora fae in Silverfall, and those we do have are not part of our court. We have other… values."

"My name is Jessamine, Your Grace." She finished a more complicated step and then gave him the simplest answer. "My bat's name is Beazle, and my species is *lonicera*."

He looked thoughtful, his already thin lips pinched. "I'm not well versed in the names of plants, but I think that is a whiskery spring flower that smells like honey?"

"That's it exactly."

"And, I'm curious, do you know everyone here personally?"

She almost laughed at his idea that it was even possible for a Calyx—who met hundreds of new people in the course of a week, thousands during the Decennial—to know everyone personally. She managed to hold her polite smile in place. "No, Your Grace. I've met some, but there are many strangers who come for the Midwinter."

He looked disappointed in her answer, then peppered her with dozens more questions—as though her answer had been the opposite—about everyone in the room: the Calyx, the Fahyli, the courtiers, the nobility, the royals, even the servants. He wanted to know names and origins, even lineages—as if that were something she should know. She began to feel like she was failing a quiz. Did any Calyx know these answers? Even the veterans? She doubted it, but Ruskin was as insatiable as Jessamine was disappointing in her answers. He seemed more interested in females than males, perhaps understandable given the lack of a wedding ring on his finger. When they finished their dance she knew no more about Silverfall and the Silverfae that populated it than she had when they began, but her own mind had been plundered.

Prince Ruskin bowed and thanked her for the dance in a gentlemanly fashion, then turned his back and moved away through the crowd. Jessamine watched him go, bemused. Most courtiers chatted with her as they recovered their breath. If they were vigorous they might ask her to reserve them another dance. For Prince Ruskin she was instantly forgotten. His behavior wasn't rude, exactly, but it was strange.

She skimmed the floor and spotted Faraçek now dancing with Wisteria. Jess strode the perimeter, sneaking glances as they whirled gracefully across the floor. When they passed near, she caught a glimpse of Wisteria's familiar, Moony—a butterfly with white and pale-green wings—clinging to Wisteria's cheekbone. Prince Faraçek had a pleasant smile on his face, even laughed at something Wisteria said. Jess wondered what they were talking about.

When a courtier asked her to dance, she accepted, hoping the dance floor might afford a better opportunity to catch snippets of Faraçek's conversations, some dance formations set couples side by each for long stretches. But Jessamine's partner turned out to be a vigorous conversationalist and a lively dancer. It was too difficult for her to engage with her partner and also steer them close enough to Faraçek and Wisteria to eavesdrop. Jess had to give up and let her partner lead her wherever he wished. She comforted herself with the knowledge that it would be small talk only. Though she did make a mental note to ask Wisteria about her experience with the prince, because it appeared as though they were getting along.

Chapter Sixteen

Laec

Standing with Kite, Sy and Regalis in a corner of the ballroom, Laec watched Jessamine as she angled through the crowd toward Prince Faraçek, hoping she wouldn't do anything rash. He let out a sigh as Prince Ruskin intercepted her; but as the couple moved onto the floor and began to talk, Laec found himself intrigued for a new reason.

Queen Elphame had once told Laec about the days when Silverfae royals had attended international parties during the days of Queen Karinya of the Winter Kingdom. But when a new queen took the throne by violence, the Silverfae withdrew from court life. No one had seen a Silverfae royal outside of Silverfall in decades. Laec certainly never had in his lifetime. So why was Prince Ruskin here now? Why come out of hibernation after so long?

As Jessamine and Prince

Ruskin danced, Laec's gaze was drawn to another Silverfae male. Frost-colored hair, eyes like freshly fallen snow, tall and handsome, he surveyed the room with curious detachment. Most guests were enraptured by the food, the music, the Calyx, the costumes and flowers, pollinators and perfumes in the air. Not this noble. His intense and penetrating gaze went from courtier to courtier, seeking faces above all other details.

Laec strolled lazily toward the observant Silverfae guest, watching him watching everyone else, looking up briefly as he caught sight of Erasmus. The raptor peered down from a rafter, keeping an eye on his quarry at all times. You'd think after three months, there'd be a little bit of trust that Laec wouldn't bolt.

Returning his attention to the handsome young Silverfae, Laec saw a pattern emerge: he was far more interested in the female face than the male. So, seeking a relationship perhaps, or something more casual? The Scented Court was full of diverting females, fae and human. Laec couldn't blame him but wondered if he knew the rules about the Calyx.

Passing a waiter balancing a tray of drinks, Laec snagged two. They sloshed and tinkled with ice cubes shaped like bumblebees. Tiny purple violets and mint leaves floated on top. Laec wasn't sure what the drink was, but it didn't matter. He just needed an excuse to kick off a conversation. He approached the Silverfae male and offered one of the drinks.

Laec was tall, but he had to look up. "You look thirsty, friend."

The Silverfae turned those bright, otherworldly eyes on him and Laec was reminded abruptly of Çifta's, only hers were more glacial than fallen snow, with a tint of palest blue.

The Silverfae took the proffered glass. "Thank you… friend."

They sipped together. His companion smacked his lips and gave Laec a quizzical look. "What is this?"

Laec peeled a wet violet blossom off his upper lip and flicked it back into the glass. "Damned if I know. Everything tastes like flowers around here. You're out of luck if you want anything manly."

The fae laughed, eyes twinkling. "I'm Sasha."

"Laec Fairijak."

"You're from Stavarjak," observed Sasha. "If I couldn't tell from your name, I can certainly tell from your accent."

Laec tipped his glass. "Guilty, and you're from Silverfall. I can tell from your everything. You look like a well-dressed ice-sculpture."

Sasha chuckled, his attention returned to watching the pretty females.

Laec pretended to watch the pretty females too. "Met many Stavarjakians, have you?"

Sasha kept his gaze on the dancers. "One or two. Met many Silverfae?"

Laec took another sip, this time wrestling with a mint leaf. He chewed it up and swallowed it. "Not many. I'm surprised to see you so far south. In fact, I'm surprised to see your kind at all. May I ask what brings you to the Scented Court?"

Sasha swept out the hand holding the cup, his almost untouched drink sloshing over the rim. "What else but this? The spectacle, the finery, the beauty."

Laec wasn't convinced. He kept his tone casual. "When was the last time a Silverfae attended the Midwinter, I wonder?"

"Not since Queen Karinya," murmured Sasha, his gaze stuck on someone in the crowd.

"Is that right? Hmm. That would be before either of us was born… unless you're one of those fae that lives for centuries without showing their age." Laec didn't say the word sorcerer.

Sasha slid him a sideways look. "No. I'm not one of those."

Laec's skin prickled as Sasha's strange irises pierced his own. He said under his breath: "Could have fooled me."

Sasha did not indicate he'd heard anything.

Laec wasn't about to give up. "Have you ever been to Stavarjak?"

Sasha didn't miss a beat. "No. Have you ever been to Silverfall?"

Laec had to stifle a snort, wishing he knew whether the question was meant ironically or sincerely. Queen Elphame did not allow her courtiers to visit Silverfall. He assumed Sasha would know this, but maybe he didn't. He was unreadable, and Laec didn't like not being able to read people.

"No," Laec said. "I've heard Silverfall is beautiful. All that sunshine glinting off ice. Frozen waterfalls, snowdrop trees, evergreens covered with icing. I would like to see it one day."

Sasha seemed momentarily confounded by this comment. He took a long time to respond and when he finally did it was very quiet, thoughtful even. "I seem to remember that it was… once, when I was very young. We have not seen the way snow and ice looks under sunlight in a long time. I cannot even recall it clearly."

Laec had seen paintings of Silverfall among Queen Elphame's collection. The glare of them was not easy on the eyes. Someone had told him once, when he was quite young, that Silverfae had to wear dark glasses during some months otherwise they went snow-blind. He couldn't remember who'd told him such a thing, and he supposed they could just as easily have been kidding. But those paintings… they were real.

Sasha and Laec stood in silence for a time, watching the crowd. Laec put his half empty glass down on a nearby table, taking the opportunity to sneak another look at Sasha. He really was quite fixed on someone in the crowd. Following his gaze, Laec spotted Prince Ruskin still dancing with Jessamine. He couldn't tell which of the two was getting the lion's share of Sasha's scrutiny.

Laec said, "Your friend the prince seems enamored with my friend the Calyx."

For a brief moment, Laec thought Sasha's eyes flared with something ugly. It was gone, like a fish flashing at the surface of a pond. However, Sasha did not add any comment.

Laec changed subjects. "So… why now?"

Sasha's white gaze was nailed to the dancing pair. "What?"

"Why after so many years away do Silverfae make the long journey down to the Scented Court? What's changed?"

Sasha deposited his own almost untouched glass on a table. "Nothing has changed. We're here for the party."

"There have been other festivals. Why this one?"

Sasha finally shifted his gaze back to Laec. "Our queen wants products. Perfumes, dresses, cosmetics, all manner of queenly trivialities. We're fetching them for her."

"But, they could be shipped. If not directly to the heart of your palace, to the nearest Solana perfume store in Stavarjak where they could be picked up. Why send a prince to do the job of an errand boy?"

Sasha's eyes narrowed. "Why do you care so much?"

Laec shrugged. "I'm just making conversation, and I think it's strange. You cut yourselves out of Ivryndian affairs for… what? Forty-odd years? Suddenly its important that your prince attend this year's Midwinter to bring back perfumes? It's just… odd. You don't think it's odd?"

"No. I don't." Sasha's tone changed. "What's her name?"

Laec blinked. "Who?"

"The Calyx dancing with Prince Ruskin."

Prince Ruskin and Jess parted as they finished their dance. He bowed deeply, and she curtsied with such feminine decorum that Laec had a difficult time equating her with the young woman who had bumped along on the back of a horse in Rahamlar. "Her name is Jessamine."

"The world's smallest bat just landed on her shoulder. Shouldn't someone tell her?"

Laec laughed. "That's Beazle. Her familiar."

Sasha's brows arched high. "A Calyx with a mammalian familiar?"

"It happens."

As Prince Ruskin moved away from Jess, Sasha moved across the floor without excusing himself, leaving Laec bemused. After a few steps, Sasha turned back to give a hurried bow. "Thank you for your company. It was nice meeting you."

"You too," Laec murmured.

Laec watched Sasha ask Jessamine to dance and harrumphed in annoyance. Maybe there was nothing special behind the attendance of Silverfae, maybe it was as Sasha said. Queen Sylifke wanted perfumes and sent her son to make an appearance. Laec chewed his lip. Maybe. But he doubted it.

A flash of dark hair at an upper balcony drew his eye, but there was no one visible except an elderly couple watching the dancers and talking. Laec ascended the staircase to the balconies. Erasmus zipped after him, slicing through the air over Laec's head. Smiling to the elderly couple, Laec wove through empty seats and out the rear door that led into a quiet hallway.

Çifta stood gazing at a portrait of a young fae woman in a wispy lavender colored dress, one delicate hand reaching for a butterfly among the blossoms. A hundred more portraits like this one lined the walls. Erasmus planted himself on a marble sculpture of a fawn sleeping in grass.

Çifta brightened when she saw Laec. "Having a nice time?"

Laec put an arm around her waist, looking down at her. "No. It's miserable without you. Are you sure you won't come down? There aren't many dances left."

She wrinkled her nose. "Is *he* down there? I went to look but got paranoid he'd see me."

"Last I saw he was talking with Rose."

"Then, no. I won't go down." She let out a sigh so deep it seemed to come up from her toes. "Does anyone know how long he plans to stay? I hope he gets his business over with and leaves quickly. He never attended parties at Rahamlar, he doesn't even like them." She glowered and crossed her arms over her narrow chest. "That's not the world we live in though, is it? Princes can do what they like in this world."

As the strains of a waltz drifted from the balcony, Laec stepped away from Çifta, then bowed. "May I have this dance?"

Çifta's eyes sparkled as she dropped into a curtsy. "It would be my pleasure."

They came together to waltz soundlessly on the thick carpet runner, with no one to witness them except Erasmus.

Chapter Seventeen

Jessamine

It was silly for Jess to feel like she was being watched. Ilishec continuously reminded them that if they were out in public they were being observed. But this feeling was different. Someone was not simply admiring her, they were studying her. Intensely. When she found the owner of a gaze so penetrating she could feel it, she ripped hers away from him, only to have it traitorously snap back and then stick, like an ant trapped in glue. She'd seen him earlier, but she hadn't really looked at him. Now, she did.

As she took the stranger in, she felt Beazle take off in search of a quieter place to perch.

Eyes like silver coins set in a strong, angular face, he wore a dark blue jacket with two rows of buttons running to a stand-up collar. The contrast of his frost-colored hair against his uniform was so stark it was shocking, and though his eyes were the color of ice, they were so full of heat that she felt scalded. No one had ever looked at her like this before, like she was his destiny. And he was coming straight for her. For a heart-pounding moment, Jess understood what it felt like to be prey. Torn between the urge to bolt and the urge to rise to the challenge—to match his energy—she inhaled deeply through her nose. Calyx weren't allowed to bolt from courtiers, so she had to do the latter. Summoning all her courage, she met him on a square of parquet and went—as the orchestra struck up a waltz—straight into his arms without a hitch, no time wasted on the etiquette of a bow and a curtsy. Before she had a chance to fully appreciate the feel of his touch, of sharing the same air as him, they were halfway around the floor.

His ghostly gaze held hers, the small dark pupils missing no aspect of her face. "It's a pleasure to meet you, Jessamine."

To her horror, she blushed. Why did the way he said her name make her blush? Aster would say she'd gone soft in the head. She cleared her throat in the most delicate way she could manage. "You've caught me at a disadvantage, I'm afraid. You know my name. I feel like I should know yours. Sadly, I've not been given the honor…"

"I'm Sasha."

It was a good thing he was accomplished at leading. She had no idea where they were in the room anymore, and frankly, didn't care. She wanted to take in every detail of his features, read every emotion there. Everything about him was so different from Prince Ruskin. Sasha was more than a novelty, he was a revelation.

She had to say something, so she said the only thing in her mind. "I've never met any Silverfae before tonight."

"Is that why you are staring?"

She sputtered with sudden outrage and mis-stepped, almost tripping. "I beg your pardon! It was you who was staring at me!"

A roguish grin lit his features and his entire being seemed to transform. "I'm caught. But how could I not stare? You're the most beautiful creature in the room."

Ah, so he was a flirt, like so many others.

Jess had thought him somber and intimidating. She'd been wrong to be daunted. Now she could see how young he was, how easily laughter came to him, how lightness of being was his natural state, not gravitas. The tightness in her chest relaxed a little, which only let her feel the huge butterflies of attraction buffeting the inside of her ribcage. She swallowed. She was not allowed to feel this way about a guest. After this dance, she should politely thank him and remove herself from his company. She should. But she wouldn't. Appallingly, the thought of dancing with anyone else had suddenly become the most insipid proposition in the world.

Jess rooted deep into her training and dug up a friendly smile—as she would have done for any other guest who complimented her so cavalierly—and resisted the urge to explore her disconcerting reaction to him any further. "You obviously haven't met Rose yet, or Aster, or—"

The names of Calyx females—including her own—vanished from her memory as he pulled her close to keep her clear of another dancing couple. Jess had to remind herself to breathe as his body came near enough for her chest to brush his. She had to tilt her head back to keep her headdress from getting in his face, which put her nose under his chin. He smelled of evergreens, crisp and fresh as a brisk winter morning. She felt the soft puff of his exhale on her forehead. Her eyes drifted closed and time suspended. She imagined them dancing like this, only alone, and free of their formal dress. She gulped as they swayed apart again, averting her eyes to hide her desire. She had to get herself under control.

Sasha glanced at her coyly. "Where did Beazle go?"

"Hunting." She blinked. "How do you know his name?"

"A friend of yours told me." He flashed a look down. "I'm fauna fae."

Jess took in a breath, delighted. "A Silver-fauna-fae?"

He chuckled at her cobbled-together description. "We are not nearly so revered in Silverfall as here."

"What is she, your familiar?"

He narrowed his eyes and smiled playfully. "I'll introduce you sometime."

A plume of curiosity made Jess's heart flutter. "I would love that."

Over Sasha's shoulder, she noticed Prince Ruskin talking with Vanda, admiring her butterfly. The prince looked at Jess and Sasha, as if making a note of where his comrade was. Sasha swept her away, across the floor in another direction. Was she imagining it, or didn't he like the feeling of being so near his prince?

"Were you born here? In Solana City?" Sasha asked when they were once again lost in the throng.

"No, in a village less than a day's journey west of here."

"What's it called?"

"Dagevli. It's more like a hamlet. It has only one little school, but a lot of farm animals."

"And is it as sunny there as it is here in the city?"

"I suppose." She cocked her head. "Why?"

"I've just never seen so much sunshine. You're very lucky." He pulled her in again, his cheek briefly touching her temple. She heard and felt him inhale. "Is that where your family is? Dagevli?"

"My family—" With him so close, Jess felt dizzy. It was impossible to think straight. The truth came out before she had the wits to stop it. "I have no family, except for Beazle."

She blinked, horrified. It was like she'd had no training at all.

He looked down, through her. Into her. "No family? You are so young. No parents?"

Helplessly, as if her brain and voice box were acting separately, she heard herself say: "No, no family. I mean. I don't know for sure. My mother passed away and left me with a lot of questions. I had a twin."

His eyes shimmered with compassion. "I'm sorry about your mother."

She had to regain her self-restraint. "What about your family?"

But he was not dissuaded. "What happened to her? Your twin, I mean."

His eyes peeled back her decorum, penetrated her good manners, opened her ribcage, laid bare her person. The best she could do was keep her tone even.

"My twin was a him, and I don't know. He died when we were less than a year old, or so the records say."

"So the records say…" He watched her face. "Do you not believe the record?"

Jess gave up on her fight for distance—she'd already lost it anyway. Besides, it felt good, really good, to talk to Sasha honestly and about something real. And she had been asking herself exactly that question since the visit to the Registry.

"I know. It's stupid."

"Not necessarily. What reason do you have to doubt?"

Reluctantly, she thought about her old life. It felt like sifting through ashes. "After my mother's funeral, a friend told me that she believed Julian was alive… because his familiar stayed alive even after he was taken from us."

Sasha looked intrigued. "Is she alive today?"

"No, but she was until three months ago, and she didn't come to the end of her life naturally. On top of that, Julian's death certificate was signed with an X, so I don't know who submitted the information."

Sasha sucked in a breath, caught by the mystery. "Trying to hide their identity, or illiterate?"

"There are not many illiterate in Solana," she murmured.

Several bars of music expired as he mulled this over. His hand tightened gently around hers. "I can see why you doubt."

Jess had hardly allowed herself to hope that the death certificate might be a lie, but in her heart of hearts, it was what she yearned for. To have Sasha vindicate her doubt made her sinuses tingle. She looked away to give herself a moment to leash her emotions, realized that she didn't want to see the others in the room, and returned her gaze to his.

Sasha's eyes melted into hers. "I hope you find the truth."

Were her hands shaking? She wasn't sure, maybe his were keeping hers steady. "Thank you."

He swept her along the outer edge of the dance floor, skimming past the orchestra and a hundred dancing couples. Jess paid attention to nothing outside of the little circle she and Sasha made together. When the waltz ended, she felt desperate to make sure he stayed near her.

He released his grip on her waist, but kept a hold of her hand, turning his shoulders toward her. "Thirsty?"

She smiled and nodded.

Sasha took two glasses of pink champagne from a server.

Sasha took a sip, his gaze flicking around. He spoke a little louder than appropriate. "How delicious. We will bring some of your delightful products back to Queen Sylifke."

Jess was confused until she spotted Prince Ruskin in her periphery, and not far away. The pale prince had an ear cocked in their direction.

"Come." Sasha put a hand on the small of her back. "Show me the gardens."

"With pleasure, Sasha," she replied, feeling his name in her mouth for the first time. She decided she'd never liked a name more than this one.

They slipped through the party and took the hall leading out to the main garden of the East Keep. Jessamine grabbed a shawl from the stack of folded ones kept in a basket on the terrace and wrapped it around herself. There was one other couple standing on the terrace, chatting and too wrapped up in one another to notice Jess and Sasha.

As they walked toward the railing, Sasha twined his fingers through hers. She should pull away, put distance between them, but his delicious heat drenched her palm and it felt too good to deprive herself of it.

She was reminded of an earlier observation and turned to him with surprise on her face. "Your hands are warm."

He shot her a quizzical glance. "Yes?"

"Aren't Silverfae cold? Your kingdom is in perpetual winter, isn't it?"

He laughed and it warmed her all over. Who needed a shawl with Sasha beside her?

"What's funny?"

"We are the Winter Court, but our blood is just as hot as yours." He gave her a look that stopped her heart. "Right this second, I think mine is hotter."

She looked away, lost for words and staggered by his daring. She could feel his eyes on her, weighing her reaction. The other couple had gone back inside. They were alone now.

She floundered for a safe reply, one that wouldn't

incite further flirting, but might get him to talk about himself. "That's what Prince Ruskin said, but his hands were cold. Shows how much I know."

He dodged the topic of Ruskin smoothly. "I don't know anything about the Calyx, but I do know that Solana City is one of the most beautiful places I've ever seen, and without question, you are the most beautiful thing I have ever smelled."

She touched the brooch the couple from Archelia had given her, just to give herself something to do. "Thank you."

They walked down the wide steps leading to the garden paths. Though everything was protected for winter, the etherlights along the trails were lit. In the shade between lamps he stopped her.

"How is it done? Your scent?"

"It's magic. We just do it." It was a lame answer, but Jess couldn't come up with a better one, not with the way he was staring at her.

He leaned closer. "May I?"

Jess remained still as he closed the distance between them. His cheek touched her temple as he inhaled her scent. Could he hear her heart going crazy?

"Magic," he murmured, looking down at her. The light caught the tips of his pale lashes, they seemed almost to glow.

She forced herself to turn away, Ilishec's warning about always being watched ringing loud in her mind. She was pushing it even lingering out here alone with him. A cold breeze picked up a curl and it wrapped across her face. She pulled it away and offered what she was sometimes asked for by courtiers. It would give them a perfectly reasonable excuse for being out in the gardens, alone, on a cold evening.

"Would you like me to show you my magic?"

His expression was answer enough.

She crouched in the walkway and raised a honeysuckle shrub until it sprouted fragrant flowers. He ran a hand over its leaves, almost reverently.

She straightened. "Do Silverfae have magic?"

He plucked a stem from her *lonicera*. "Some of us do, but it is very hard won. Would you like to see?"

Jess could only nod.

Holding the stem gently in one hand, his other hand cupped the blossom. A pale wispy magic drifted from Sasha's fingers, creeping over the flower like fog. Frost formed on the petals, then spread up the branches and consumed the leaves. Sasha's magic built layer upon layer until the whole thing was coated with ice. He held it out to her.

Jess took the flower and held it up in the light. It had become an icy jewel that glimmered in her hand. She was afraid to breathe on it, it was so delicate and beautiful. "How long will it last?"

"Back home it might last years. Here, it is already beginning to melt. Your midwinter is warmer than our summer."

She looked up. "You have a summer?"

His lips twisted wryly. "You wouldn't think of it as such."

"Sasha!" A voice bellowed.

They looked toward the palace. Prince Ruskin stood on the top step. He beckoned sharply, then stalked away without waiting.

Annoyance crossed Sasha's face. He looked at her with regret. "I have to go."

Disappointment swept over her but she mustered the appropriate response: "Of course."

He kissed her hand. "It was such a pleasure, Jessamine."

"It really was… Sasha."

"We are here until"—he paused, uncertain—"for a while. At least for all of the rest of the Festival, perhaps longer. May I see you again?"

She picked her words slowly. "If you come to another ball, I will likely be there."

He was not deterred by her distant response. "I mean, let's talk on our own one day. Not at a party with hundreds of others."

She could hear Rose's voice during orientation warning her not to get romantically involved with guests.

While her mind whispered, *too late*, she heard herself answer: "I'd like that."

He squeezed her hand then let her go. She was unable to tear her eyes from his broad back until he'd ascended the steps and disappeared from view. She stood there until Beazle landed on her shoulder.

What are you doing out here? It's freezing.

She shivered, clutching the shawl around herself. It really was freezing. How could she not have noticed that her breath was hanging in the air and the tip of her nose was numb? She scampered up the stairs and back to the warmth of the palace.

When Jessamine returned to the ballroom, she was disappointed to find that the Silverfae retinue had retired for the night. Not a single ghostly head of hair remained to brighten the room. Either Prince Ruskin had a powerful grip over his retinue's schedule, or Silverfae found it preferable to miss the last dance of the night. She spent the last waltz in the arms of a courtier who couldn't stop yawning, which made her fight not to yawn herself. When the last bows and curtsies were made, Jessamine and the final shift of Calyx, exhausted and glowing with fragrant sweat, made their way to the quiet parlor where the Calyx rested their feet and took a nighttime tonic before going to bed. Jessamine retrieved her drink and followed Wisteria, where they collapsed on a bench seat full of pillows. Other Calyx draped themselves across the furniture while they drank, kicking off their shoes and scratching themselves. A few lay sprawled on the floor with legs in the air, letting their blood go the other way for a little while.

Moony was perched on the top of Wisteria's auburn curls, flexing his pearly wings.

Jessamine gestured to the butterfly. "He is very beautiful. What kind is he?"

Wisteria licked elixir off her top lip. "Thanks. He's a Moon Dust butterfly. Don't you love his coloring?"

"Very much." Her heart gave a pang of longing for Greta.

As though he could sense the ache in her heart, Moony fluttered from Wisteria's hair toward Jess, landing on the back of her hand.

"He likes you. He doesn't usually go to strangers."

"I'm not a stranger, am I?" Jess admired Moony's finely feathered wings and long graceful antennae.

"Apparently not." Wisteria laughed as Moony crawled up Jess's arm to her shoulder, then around to Jessamine's back. He crawled across her shoulders and to her collarbone, his little feet tickling her skin, then fluttered into the air, circling their heads before landing on the window.

Jess tried to sound casual. "How was your dance with the prince?"

Wisteria cocked an eyebrow. "How was *your* dance with the prince? I would much rather have danced with the Silverfall prince."

"Prince Ruskin asked a lot of questions."

"He is very handsome, in the way those Silverfae are… so pale. Kind of like Moony, I guess. maybe that's why I'm drawn to them. Prince Faraçek is handsome too, but in a dangerous way, you know? And after what he did… well, I kind of hope he knows that the Calyx are only being polite because we have to be. None of us will ever forgive him. Every one of us has imagined something similar happening to our own familiars." She held her hand out to Moony and he fluttered to her, perching on a knuckle.

Jessamine didn't know what to say. The Calyx didn't speak about Greta, probably not wanting to cause her further pain. Jess appreciated Wisteria's solidarity, her empathy.

Wisteria put a hand on Jessamine's arm. "We might have to dance with him, laugh at his jokes, smell his strange breath, and pretend his conversation is more diverting and entertaining than any other guest of the Midwinter. It's all fake." Wisteria's expression revealed the true extent of her dislike for the prince. "Letting him touch me made my skin crawl."

Jess was amazed. "You are an incredible actress, Wisteria. I saw you with him. I could not tell you felt that way."

Wisteria looked smug as she took another sip of her elixir, lifting her tonic with the hand Moony was clinging to. It looked like she was wearing a stunning butterfly ring. "I've been Calyx for seven years, I should be good at it. I've danced with all kinds of strange partners. Faraçek was the ultimate test. I'm a true connoisseur of our art now." She giggled then stopped as Moony rotated on the back of her wrist, spinning in a slow circle. The little butterfly's head twisted back and forth, then he spun back the other way. He stopped and flexed his wings a few times.

"He's tired." Wisteria let out a long exhale. "As am I. I'm going straight to bed. Nice chatting with you, Jessamine."

"You too, Wisteria."

Jess watched her return her empty glass to the tray and then head for the door, walking a little off balance. When she reached the doorway, she put her hand on the jamb and paused, her other hand going to her head. Moony still clung to her wrist. He made another clumsy circle then stilled. Wisteria disappeared and Jess looked over at Gardenia to see if she'd noticed anything peculiar. Gardenia had been watching over the edge of her book.

"That was odd," said Jessamine. "Wasn't it?"

Gardenia shrugged, the movement so graceful it could bring tears to an artist's eye. "Not so much. She's been dancing for hours. Earlier today she did three sweat sessions. They're both exhausted, poor things."

Jess took her own empty glass back to the table, a little off balance herself. Now that she was upright again, she really felt ready to topple over. Grateful to have reached the end of another night, she went to her room to prepare for bed. As she heard Beazle rustle himself into position from her headboard, she crawled beneath the coverlet with a smile. Maybe she'd get lucky and have beautiful dreams about a certain male with frosted eyes.

Chapter Eighteen

Jessamine

Jessamine's chance to spy came the following day, when Faraçek returned from the daily ride. Unless the weather was poor, a party of aristocrats—accompanied by Fahyli, servants, and two or three Calyx—rode out from the palace stables shortly before noon. They journeyed to different parts of the pretty foothills and forests at the base of Mount Vargon, where they were fed a sumptuous picnic and spent time playing games or reading and napping in the sun, before returning to the palace.

Jess's shift on the daily ride was scheduled for a few days hence. Jess assumed Faraçek would take part, but she didn't want to wait to have something to report back to Queen Esha. So when she learned from Aster that Prince Faraçek would join the ride on a day Jess had no Calyx duties, she sought Regalis to find out when the party would be expected back at the palace. Before the prince returned to his suite to wash and change for that evening's banquet, she and Beazle were sequestered in the walls.

The dark and musty corridor was too narrow for her to sit with her legs stretched out, so she leaned against a cold stone wall, scratching at what felt like spiders crawling in her hair and along her arms. A little light filtered in through a small opening in an outer wall around the corner from her, but it was hardly enough to make out the details of her own hands, so Jess had brought a candle—more for comfort than from any real need for illumination. She wished she had brought something soft to sit on, but somehow a pillow seemed very un-spy-like.

Beazle was delighted with their afternoon activity. He hunted for bugs in the cracks while Jess shifted her position every few minutes in a fruitless effort to get comfortable. When they finally heard voices she was on the edge of dozing off, her head tilted to one side. Rubbing the kinks out of her neck, Jess quietly got to her feet and brought her ear to the wall. She had positioned herself near the anteroom leading into his parlor. She counted four male voices as Faraçek moved further into the suite.

Beazle stopped sniffling in the dust and emerged from a crack. Jess crept along the passage, following the voices and straining her ears. Everything was muffled. She caught snatches of words but there were two conversations going on simultaneously, making it impossible to make any sense of either of them. What did reach her ears were scraps of phrases that had little relevance.

"…hot water…"

"…increase the land tax…"

"Don't interfere, there is more…"

"…rich with resources…"

"It's impossible to…"

"…bloody blister. I should have him hung."

Jess blew out a frustrated huff. If they moved into the next room she might have better eavesdropping, but the men seemed content to stay where they were.

Beazle landed on her shoulder and crawled to her neck, where he bumped his nose against her skin. Absently, she put a hand up and he crawled into her palm, wrapping around her thumb. He shook like a dog, his tiny warm body tickling her palm. When he squeaked, she shushed him.

"…there's not enough room… understand the neutrality…"

"…thick fog and snow… like it, nothing…"

"…be able to wear proper boots for a week…"

Beazle squeaked again and Jess shushed him with more force. He nipped her thumb hard enough to get her attention.

Quit ignoring me!

She gestured to the sound of the voices with an *I'm a little busy at the moment* look.

Send me. This is why they chose us.

He was right of course, but her heart balked. She'd already lost Greta. How could she send Beazle into danger? Straight into the suite of the prince who had killed their family member? She closed her fingers protectively around him, feeling his softness, his vibrancy, his life force. She shook her head. Beazle crawled through the gap between her index finger and her thumb to peer out at her.

You don't trust me?

I don't trust him.

He won't even see me. Beazle stretched his mouth wide, showing fierce little teeth. *I am silent. I am shadow. I am mist.*

Jess smiled. *You're a poet.*

He licked his lips like a cat. *I can spend all day in the walls. You can't. Do you want to have something to report, or not?*

She sighed in defeat and lifted Beazle to the stones. He hopped off and crawled into a crack. She put a hand over her heart and took a steadying breath. Turning her back to the wall, she slid into a seated position and closed her eyes, tuning in to her familiar.

The cold from the wall soaking through her tunic receded. The smell of dirt and minerals and dust grew strong. The hair on her body felt like it was standing on end, bringing a new level of sensitivity to her skin as Beazle nosed his way through to the other side.

The sound of running water, a bathtub being filled. Rustles of clothing or towels, and the sound of someone undressing. A squeak of wet porcelain and a sigh of pleasure as he lowered himself into the bath. More squeaks as he settled against the back of the tub.

"Shall I lay out the black leather and velvet, m'lord?"

Jessamine eyes flew open. He sounded like he was right next to her. The only sign that it was Beazle's ears at work, not hers, was a faint echo. She closed her eyes again. She'd missed the prince's response. It hadn't been important but next time, it might be. Jess relaxed, ignoring the desire to scratch the back of her thigh.

"—will do."

"Very good, m'lord."

A shuffle of footsteps against the floor, rustling fabric, sloshing water, a door being closed. Then everything went quiet. Silent, but not still. Beazle sniffed: warm wet skin, soap. Steady breathing. Fingernails were picked and cleaned, a head was dunked, hair was lathered, skin was shaved… but only a little. Rinsing, more lathering, more rinsing. Finally the bathing was finished; falling water cascading off a body, the rasp of a towel against skin, the rubbing of wet hair. The scent in the room changed, although only an animal would detect it—cypress and white spruce oils, the smell of a forest in the autumn after a rain—damp, earthy, mulchy.

The servant returned and helped his prince dress: fabric rustled, snaps closed, a belt buckled, a brush with stiff bristles. The room was crossed many times.

Distantly, the outer door opened and closed. Someone waited quietly in the anteroom. Beazle was too far away to smell them.

His clawed feet grasped at the rough wooden rafters as he scurried to the corner where the shadows congealed. As the prince passed out of the washroom and into the sitting room where a fireplace crackled, Beazle swooped to the doorjamb.

"My prince."

A deep, authoritative voice Jess recognized: Captain Yorin.

Prince Faraçek went directly to the fireplace. "Any news?"

"We are greatly hindered, m'lord. If you could secure permission—"

"I'm working on it," snapped the prince. "Honestly, you're a worse nag than Ander ever was… rest his soul. These things require delicacy, flair, charm, not to mention impeccable timing. Traits you know nothing about."

"Yes, m'lord." The captain sounded unaffected by the prince's rebuke, almost like he heard it every day. "We continue to seek answers. You can appreciate, I am sure, that my men are not accustomed to a court such as this. They are excellent soldiers, but out of their depth in a ballroom."

"That sounds like an excuse." Faraçek's voice was cold.

The captain carried on in that same unaffected tone. "Not at all, m'lord. Merely a fact. Perhaps if you—pardon me—perhaps if *we* had asked a few of Rahamlar's finer nobility to accompany us—"

"You know we can't trust that lot. One of them may even be responsible."

A pause.

"They are not on her side either, my prince. Perhaps you underestimate the kind of support you would—"

"I said no. It's too risky. We keep the group who are aware of what we seek as small as possible. Too much hangs in the balance."

"As you say, m'lord. It makes our task that much

more challenging, but I understand." The soles of Captain Yorin's boots scuffed the floor.

"What say the men?" Faraçek murmured.

"It was as you thought, my prince. They do not want a crippled queen."

Prince Faraçek muttered. "I know unseelie. The hand that removed the relic from my grasp was not a gray one. They want me to have it. They want a return to the days of old. Centuries of mingling has made us weak—the opposite of what my father always claimed, the old fool."

If the captain agreed with this, he did not say. His silence was thick with weary patience.

Jess's felt like she'd taken hold of something meaty but slippery. What relic? A relic was something from the distant past, so perhaps it was tied to the kingdom's former strength?

While the retinue were being prepared to perform in Rahamlar, Ilishec had told them that King Osvitan claimed that the source of his kingdom's strength lay in the mixing of unseelie and humans, a partnership, a uniting of strengths. So what did a return to the times of old mean?

"If I may venture an opinion," the captain said. "I do not believe you will alert suspicions if you ask Agir for help. In fact… I believe you might attract misgivings if you do not ask."

Faraçek scoffed. "My father already did. Remember? They do not appear to care."

"Oh, they care." Captain Yorin dropped his unattached tone. His voice grew dangerous. "If you ask face-to-face, not via some impartial scrap of parchment, they will be forced to make a move."

"But in what direction?"

"It doesn't matter, not as long as we find her first. What's important is that they reveal their hand, so we need them to mobilize. From there it should be easy for us to tell if they are as faultless as they appear to be."

"You already said that it wasn't likely someone of their court who helped her."

Jess tugged on her bottom lip. Were they talking about Princess Serya or Lady Çifta? Or had they started with one and switched to the other?

"Not quite. I said that I no longer suspected it was Calyx. They are… like fine crystal. Beautiful and fragile, weak. But there are others who may have been given the information second-hand and acted on it. Queen Esha was right. Anyone in Solana—citizen or guest—can access any fragrance they want as long as they have money. It would be the perfect cover. Someone wanted us to think it was a member of the Calyx. It was clever. I admit they had me fooled, at first."

Jess couldn't stop a smile from creeping cross her face. *We still have you fooled, Captain.*

The prince snorted derisively. "They still have you fooled, Yorin."

Jess covered her mouth to stifle a laugh at Faraçek's direct echo of her thought.

Faraçek sounded disgusted. "You're no closer to uncovering their identity than you were the night you found the sleeve. They are probably not even here any longer, if they ever were."

"The fact remains, we need their permission to move about freely. I have overstepped my bounds far enough. If my prince would only ask—"

"You harp like an old woman, but fine. I'll consider it." The prince moved away from the fireplace. "I'm expected downstairs. Have you spoken with the crofter?"

Captain Yorin paused before answering. "Not yet. I shall. It must come about naturally."

"Well don't wait too long, Yorin. I grow impatient. Every day that passes is a day that it could be further from me. For all we know it could be in Archelia by now."

"I doubt that, my prince. Its value is known only to us."

"All the more reason for an enemy to put distance between me and it."

They moved toward the anteroom together, then out into the hall. Jess opened her eyes. So the prince was looking for something in addition to his sisters, although it sounded like he wasn't too concerned about Isabey.

Dust fell on Jess's head as Beazle squeezed through a crack in the mortar and dropped to her shoulder.

"Good job, Beaze," she whispered, putting a hand up to him.

It was easy. He hopped into her palm.

She smiled grimly as she made her way along the passage to the nearest exit. So easy that she hadn't needed to hide in the walls at all. She could have let Beazle do the sneaking and just tuned in from a nearby alcove—same result, without all the dust and spiders.

The soldiers at the queen's door let Jessamine in immediately. She strode in with Beazle sitting on her shoulder. The parlor was eerily quiet, the alcoves empty. The faint scent of woodsmoke permeated the room, as the fire smoldered low. Queen Esha reclined on a plush chaise with a small long-haired dog asleep in her lap. She gestured to the empty sofa across from her.

"I'm delighted to see you, Miss Fontana. The crofter told me of your plans. I complained of a headache I do not have and sent away all my ladies in the hopes that you would appear, and here you are. What have you come to tell me?"

The queen listened—her hand moving steadily over the dog's back, her dark gaze on Jess's face—as Jess relayed everything she and Beazle had overheard. A crease marred Esha's forehead.

When Jess finished, the queen did not reply, only stroked her dog thoughtfully.

"Does any of it surprise you?" Jess ventured.

The queen braced her forearms on the arms of her chair and shifted herself into a more upright position, slowly, so the dog wouldn't wake. "It does not sound as though Faraçek had anything to do with the disappearance of his sisters, either directly or through orders. That does surprise me. If not him, then who?"

Beazle looked back and forth between them as they spoke.

"But Lady Çifta did say that Princess Serya believed he made an attempt on her life."

"Someone did, anyway."

"So if the prince doesn't know where she is, isn't the most likely scenario that she ran away?"

The queen templed her fingers, where a collection of pretty rings sparkled in the etherlight. "Strange thing for a queen-in-waiting to do. The throne is rightfully hers."

"Perhaps she's not planning to be gone long. And what of the relic? He sounds more concerned about that than he does about his sisters. Do you know what he is referring to?"

The queen let her head fall back on the chaise. "The world is full of relics. Every kingdom has valuable artifacts. It could be anything: a sword, a painting, jewelry, article of clothing… It sounds like an item that gives the bearer some kind of authority."

"Like a seal?"

"If that were the case, why call it a relic? The king's seal is a modern item, forged anew every year, not some antique thing."

"Perhaps it's an old seal he is after?"

"Perhaps." But the queen looked unconvinced. "You have done well. I will discuss this with my husband. You're sure you left nothing out?"

"Nothing, Ma'am."

Esha's eyes drifted closed. "It sounds as though the

good prince may approach us soon with a request. Thank you for your service. I will prepare myself."

Jess left the queen to her thoughts.

Chapter Nineteen

Laec

Laec slowed as he approached the training yard. Laughter and boisterous talk drifted over the walls. A small crowd of human soldiers had gathered just inside the gate. Laec had to press through them to reach Panther, Regalis and another Fahyli standing at the crest of the hill in the yard. The crofter's bear dozed in the sun with three dogs sprawled against her side, while Erasmus and Ferrugin wheeled overhead, screaming.

It was easy to see what was so amusing: Tully and a huge white wolf tussled playfully in the grass. The sight of the big black cat and a big white wolf with a thick ruff rolling over one another in the dirt, nipping and barking, was so entertaining that it had interrupted the daily training schedule.

The wolf bolted from beneath Tully's paws as if electrocuted, yipping as she steamed across the yard with her tail tucked and her long pink tongue lolling out. Tully gave chase, her sleek glimmering hide a blue-black blur. Muscles bulging and lantern-eyes aglow, she sped after the wolf, only to backpedal hilariously, coming up on her hind legs and pawing at the air as the wolf skidded to a halt and turned the tables. They clashed and rolled again, a tumble of contrasting fur and flashing teeth.

The crowd laughed, some wiping moisture from their eyes, as the two huge animals capered about, in what looked like the pure joy of being alive and finding a worthy opponent for a day of rough and tumble.

Laec stepped closer to Kite, his eyes on the wolf. "Who is she? It is a she, right?"

"That's Rialta. Gorgeous, isn't she?"

In typical Kite fashion, she offered no additional information. Laec was about to prod her when he spied a head of bright white hair. Sasha knelt in front of Panther, a long stalk of grass clamped between his teeth. His gaze followed Rialta with a look that only meant one thing: a deep familial connection.

Laec felt poleaxed. "She is Sasha's?"

Kite nodded, giggling at the antics. "Yep. He's fauna fae, and what a pair."

He wasn't sure why he was so surprised. Sasha had had no reason to introduce his nature along with his citizenry, and big foreign mammal familiars didn't attend balls—even the big Fahyli familiars didn't attend.

Sasha stood, stretching his long legs. He leaned closer to Panther, angling his head as the shorter Fahyli said something. They talked with their hands, engaged in the kind of conversation that could be had only between Fahyli about their familiars. Laec felt a stab of jealousy. He'd begun to feel accepted by the Fahyli. Sasha had just arrived but already he was like one of them.

Rialta and Tully came barreling toward the crowd, which scattered like a flock of panicked chickens. Rialta knocked into Sasha's legs as Tully took a leap straight at Panther's chest, like the two had planned an ambush. Panther dove aside just in time to avoid being hammered. With Panther and Sasha dragged into the fray, the crowd's enthusiasm surged. Laec overheard Sy challenge Regalis to a bet, with the odds in Tully and Panther's favor.

Laec watched for a while longer then quietly withdrew, leaving the Fahyli to their games. His thoughts had turned to another foreigner: Çifta.

He snuck up on her as she stood with her back to the door of the artists' tower, in front of an easel placed near a window. A portrait of a young man in dark shadow was emerging on the canvas beneath her deft touch. Normally the artists in the tower captured Calyx portraits from life, but Çifta was doing this painting from memory. However, the lad's features weren't fae, and Laec couldn't recall having seen the subject's face around the palace either. There was enough of the young man's clothing to suggest rough homespun fabric and the neckline of a uniform that looked vaguely familiar. He appeared to be in his early twenties, with dark blond hair, kind eyes, and a nicely curved jaw. Çifta had drawn him in a dim indoor setting, lighting his features with some off-canvas source that Laec guessed was a torch. The lad's expression was of earnest concern, like he was about to say something important.

Laec had to give up trying to place him. "Who is that?"

Çifta whirled with a gasp, wet paintbrush bearing brown paint in her hand. She smacked him softly, flat on the chest with the palm of her free hand, a ladylike gesture of reproach. "Don't sneak up on me when I'm painting! In fact, don't sneak up on me. Ever!"

On a reflex, Laec trapped her hand against his chest. The heat of her palm soaked into him. Quickly, before he thought too much about how nice it felt, he let her go, forcing his gaze away from hers and onto her work. "It's very good."

Çifta turned back to the portrait. "Thank you. There's something not quite right about the mouth. It's been bothering me for days."

"I don't recognize him."

"You wouldn't. He's someone I met in Rahamlar." Çifta cocked her head, squinted, then added a few strokes to the jawline. "Not formally, and he never told me his name. He's the one who delivered Princess Serya's message—that I should break the betrothal—and I owe him a debt of gratitude. They tried to get me to leave before I got in worse trouble."

Laec recalled Çifta mentioning the messenger. He was clearly emblazoned in her memory.

"I thought they hired you to draw Calyx?" Laec said casually, trying—and failing—not to sound jealous.

Çifta shot him a look of suppressed amusement, a

look that suggested that she could hear the jealousy in his voice but was too gallant to mention it. "They did. But the Calyx are so busy with the Midwinter Festival that we have more downtime than usual. I've been thinking about my time in Rahamlar a lot lately, and about the princesses. I hoped that this exercise might bring back some detail that would be helpful. They were kind to me."

"He came to your room late at night, right?"

She shot him a look of strained patience. "Yes, it was late. And if you say it was improper then I'll shove this brush straight up your nose."

Laec laughed. "I was just wondering how you knew it was Princess Serya who sent him. It could have been someone else."

She turned her bright eyes on him. "Why would I doubt his word?"

"Because the next morning you wrote a letter to your father and Prince Faraçek caught you with it. You said he read it there on the steps and got angry. Did it ever occur to you that this young man might have been sent by the prince to test you?"

Çifta's eyes widened a fraction as she took this possibility in, but she dismissed it a moment later with a shake of her head. "He had Princess Serya's seal."

The punishment for stealing the seal of a royal was harsh in every kingdom. In Stavarjak it involved—a favorite of Queen Elphame's—the chopping off of limbs; in Silverfall it meant a whipping to the edge of death; and in Rahamlar… Laec wasn't sure what the punishment was, but felt certain it would be severe.

"Did you ever see him again after that night?"

"No, because after that I was imprisoned. The only people I saw were courtiers when I was escorted to the dining room, the guards, and—when I was lucky—a lady's maid."

Laec was hardly listening, as an idea formed at the edge of his mind. "What did Serya's seal look like? Do you remember?"

"Of course. Hers had the Rahamlar cowbird on it, with its wings out in mid-flight. Around the edge of the seal was a circlet, a lady's crown. All the Rahamlar seals have that bird, in one form or another. Isabey's had it perched on a branch among leaves."

"Could you draw it in detail?"

Lady Çifta withdrew her brush, eyeing the painting. "Naturally. Faces from memory are difficult. A ring is not. Why?"

"Would you?"

She looked at him in surprise. "Now?"

"If you don't mind. I'm getting an idea, something that should help your situation." Her expression brightened but he put up a hand. "Don't get excited yet, I don't know if it will work. I need a drawing of the seal, a good one. As detailed as you can manage."

Dropping her paintbrush in a cup of water, Çifta went to a nearby art table and plucked a small square of textured sketching paper from a box. Selecting a pencil with a very sharp tip, she applied light strokes to the page. The shape of a man's clenched fist took form, and on his index finger, a fine ring with a flat surface. Homing in on the seal, Çifta darkened its hollows and brightened its raised surfaces. An image stood proud against the gold, just the way Çifta had described it.

Laec watched the image take form, amazed. Çifta's talent seemed more magical to him than the mystic blossoms spun by the Calyx.

Çifta glanced up. "Shall I add color? It was gold."

He nodded.

She placed the drawing beside a tray of watercolors. With delicate strokes she added hues of gold, yellow, brown and ochre to bring the seal to colorful life.

"Why a cowbird?" Laec wondered as she made the final touches. "They're not beautiful or memorable."

"I wondered that too." Çifta flashed him a sly glance. "So I looked it up in Ilishec's library. He has an amazing collection of reference encyclopedia about the natural world, as you'd expect. Cowbirds are not pretty, but they're very clever and opportunistic. They lay their eggs in other birds' nests. If the other bird notices and ejects the parasitic egg, the female cowbird has been observed destroying the remaining eggs as punishment—to discourage other birds from fighting back. But most of the time, the other birds don't notice the extra egg and raise the chick alongside their own. However, cowbird chicks are larger than most other chicks and they eat a lot. Most of the time, the smaller chicks die or get pushed out of the nest."

Such behavior would be expected of fae species, but coming from a non-fae bird, Laec was appalled. "That's insidious."

Çifta looked appropriately scandalized as she nodded. "And do you know what Rahamlar's motto is?"

"I can't recall seeing any motto when I was there."

She shot him a grim smile. "Perhaps because they don't really want outsiders to know it. *Quae providentia initiat, promovemus*. In English: *What providence initiates, we advance.*"

Laec mulled this over. "So, they're opportunistic, like the cowbird."

"Exactly. The motto might sound pretty, but the corresponding behavior certainly is not. One could even suggest that it is without honor." She drew back and they studied the drawing. "How's that? Detailed enough?"

Laec thought it looked amazing. "If it's true to your memory then it's perfect."

She blew gently on it to dry the color then handed it to him. "What are you going to do with it?"

He took it, leaning in to kiss her cheek. "Just trust me."

She smiled into his eyes. "I do."

Chapter Twenty

Jessamine

Morning sun glistened off the hides and shining hooves of many prettily saddled horses. Doves cooed and fae starlings filled the air with ribbons of diving, swooping birds.

The courtyard was abuzz with preparations. Stable hands held excited horses, nickering and pawing at the cobbles, eager to depart. Dogs followed servants around as they bustled about with supplies and tack. Courtiers chatted as they waited for other party members to arrive. Jess and Rose exited the palace together, but all eyes went to Rose as she descended the steps like a princess.

She wore a small navy top hat pinned at a jaunty angle, and white netting loosely covered her eyes. A tight-fitting navy bodice accentuated her bosom while a belt of rosebuds cinched in her tiny waist. Bombini had buzzed off elsewhere, uninterested in chasing horses all morning.

Jess scanned the crowd for Sasha, only half-listening to Rose describe her evening. Jess had told him covertly that she'd be going. At first she couldn't see him and her heart fell. Perhaps something came up. Or—perish the thought—he'd decided not to come. They had not found an opportunity to be alone together and she was hoping this ride might provide one.

When his bright head appeared not far away—he'd been checking a hoof—butterflies filled Jess stomach. They locked eyes. When he winked, she smiled so wide that her cheeks ached.

"What are you grinning about?" Rose followed Jess's gaze. "Oh." Which she followed with a warning look. "Don't overdo it, Jessamine. Not in public."

Jess felt annoyed but what could she expect?

"I won't." Jess tore her gaze from Sasha, her cheeks heating. It took a moment for Rose's words to properly sink in. "Wait, what do you mean 'not in pub—'"

"Hello, lady fae!" Snap grinned from atop his mount, a gray gelding with dappled hindquarters. Olinya had put Snap in a burgundy vest with matching leggings, and high black boots. He wore neat lines of kohl under his eyes to help keep squinting to a minimum. A newsboy cap perched on his red curls. His magic had exaggerated his impishness, deepened his dimples, and brightened the red of his hair to near blazing. The courtiers found him charming and cute, but he still lacked the devastatingly handsome features of the mature male Calyx.

They murmured hello as Rose was helped into her

side-saddle by a stable hand. Settling her knee around the pommel, she fluffed her skirts so they draped fetchingly.

"Does Olinya ever run out of ideas?" Snap wondered aloud as he stared from Rose to Jessamine and back again. "You two look amazing."

Jess took her turn being helped into her saddle, a leg-on-either-side kind, happy for the riding costume Olinya had put her into—a combination that Jess could have kissed her for—black leggings, golden riding boots and a button-up blouse with snug cuffs. Her hair was pinned half-back and cascaded between her shoulder blades. A cap similar to Snap's kept the sun's glare out of her eyes.

When the courtiers and Calyx were mounted and the horses were on the edge of rebellion, the party were led from the courtyard by a few of the more popular nobles of Solana and a selection of impeccably dressed guards. At each of the Calyx's knees, fastened to their saddles, were pockets containing money, little wrapped gifts, and flowers. The outings attracted locals to the main throughway where the Calyx tossed items to the crowd. The king and queen rewarded citizens who made an effort to support royal events, as it impressed visitors to see well-dressed citizens lining the streets, cheering and waving as the courtiers paraded past. The visitors would tell stories of the Decennial, driving more tourists to the city to buy perfumes and other wares—an endless circuit.

Jess was so preoccupied by the distributing of every last gift in her saddle's pockets that she didn't realize Sasha had maneuvered his mount close to hers. As the riders passed through the city gates, he was right behind her.

His horse fell in step with hers as the riders spread out. He was like a cool drink on a hot day, dressed in simple riding gear of grey trousers and jacket. He wore no hat and his hair glistened like spun silk under the sun. He squinted and held a hand up to his brow to fend off the glare that was made worse by the snow that had fallen overnight. It would all be melted away by mid-afternoon, but right now it lay over everything like a thin blanket.

"You've no hat," she observed. "It's a bright day. Won't you suffer from the light?"

"I haven't an appropriate one. In Silverfall, we wear hats to keep our heads warm, they don't have brims."

Jess searched in a bag and withdrew a small pot, another of Olinya's clever tricks. "Put a little of this under each eye."

He squinted at the pot. "Ink?"

"Kohl. It will make it easier to see."

He gave her a look that suggested he suspected she was teasing him.

She laughed at his expression. "Look at Snap."

Sasha looked enlightened. "Does it actually work?"

"Try it."

Jess watched, amused, as Sasha took off a glove, unscrewed the cap and dipped a finger in the kohl. He applied a thick line beneath his right eye. "Like this?"

"Exactly." Jess bit off a smile. Sasha looked like he'd had an accident with an inkpot.

He applied the same beneath the other eye, screwed on the lid and handed it back. "Thanks. It does help. I can already tell."

Jess dropped the pot into its pocket. "You have a white landscape in Silverfall, right? All that snow and ice. How do you deal with the sun's glare? It must be even worse than here."

"We don't have sunshine in Silverfall."

"No sun? Wait, so, it's always dark?" Jess gaped. She couldn't imagine it.

Sasha nudged his mount around a lumpy tussock, weaving closer to Jessamine. "It's dark because it snows a lot."

"Oh. Right." Jess felt dumb. It was a winter kingdom, of course it snowed a lot.

"But even when it's not snowing, the clouds are always there: purple, blue and gray, they hang thick and low over Silverfall. They're pretty in their own way as they move across the sky quickly. But this scenery…" He gestured to the rolling pastureland, the mountains and forests in the distance. "I don't know what I was expecting, but I never imagined a world like this. It is all so… alive. There are so many beautiful birds. We have birds in Silverfall, but they sound angry. Yours sound happy, like little angels." He looked wistful. "No one told me."

Seeing Solana through Sasha's eyes made Jess appreciate her kingdom in a way she hadn't before. "I guess we take it a bit for granted. So, is this your first time out of Silverfall then? I was told that Silverfae don't venture far from their borders, but I thought… well, you seem like one of the well-traveled ones."

"This is my first time." Sasha looked like he wanted to say more, but didn't.

Whatever he was thinking, Jess didn't like how it was making him feel, and said the first pleasant thing that came into her mind. "I'm really glad that you came."

He dimpled. "Me too. Did you not bring Beazle? I'd like to meet him."

"He's sleeping in my room." She straightened eagerly. "Where is your familiar? Will she join us at some point?"

He shook his head. "She frightens the horses."

"How intriguing! She must be a big predator?" Jess remembered the thrill she had had when she saw Tully for the first time.

He shrugged and gave her a cryptic smile.

Her shoulders dropped. "Don't make me wait too long. A person can expire from anticipation, you know."

He laughed. "But it's so much fun making you wait."

"Beast!" She pouted. "At least tell me her name."

He considered it, and decided he could part with that much. "Her name is Rialta."

"That's beautiful. I love it and can't wait to meet her. Maybe, one day, I can also see your kingdom." She was intrigued by the idea of visiting the land that this handsome Silverfae was from. Would she be as drawn to the Winter Court as she was to him? If so, she might never leave. She looked away, afraid he might read her secret thoughts. But when he was quiet, she glanced at him again and saw he'd lost his smile. For a moment she thought she'd overstepped.

He said, "It's not like this, Jess."

Perhaps he was worried she'd be offended by the weather. "I wouldn't expect it to be," she said quickly.

"But a land of perpetual winter has its own charms. Doesn't it?"

He cocked a silver brow. "Have you ever been outside of Solana?"

"Only to Rahamlar."

"Right. Your closest neighbor. It's so near that it's probably not that different. Your seasons, terrain, flora and fauna would basically be the same."

"I guess. It's wetter, but otherwise, it's pretty similar."

"What do you imagine the charms of Silverfall might be?"

Jess hadn't thought about it all that hard, but she had lived through a couple of cold winters in Dagevli, winters that blanketed everything in snow and made the air sharp. "The way snow makes everything look like its covered with icing. Frost makes pretty shapes on glass. We bundle up in warm clothing to go outside, and wear hats and mittens and boots that lace up. We light our wood stoves and fireplaces and make hot, comforting food. Darkness comes sooner and there's nothing to do in the garden, so we can sleep in longer and go to bed earlier, like the animals. Winter is peaceful and quiet. I always read more in the winter."

"And if it was always winter? Would you like it as much then?"

"I guess not."

The horse's hooves thudded against hardpacked earth as they trailed the chattering party, letting more and more distance grow between them. Sasha glanced at the backs of the riders. Was he worried about being too far from the party, or concerned about something else? He made no move to speed his mount.

The implication of what he had said finally struck her. "Are you saying you don't like it in Silverfall?"

"It's not Silverfall I don't like," Sasha said. "I never knew… I mean, I *knew*, but I didn't *know* the way you know something you've lived through. You see?" He looked at her earnestly.

She felt lost, but she really wanted to understand. "Can you describe it another way?"

He raked a hand though his white tresses, mussing them. The look of naked emotion on his face went through Jess's heart like a needle. He was frustrated. He wanted her to understand but struggled to find the words. She waited patiently.

"Sometimes, I'm not good with words."

She smiled. "You're fine, Sasha. Better than fine." There had certainly been nothing wrong with his words the night they'd met. Although Ilishec would beg to differ.

"That's sweet of you."

His gaze narrowed on a rider close to the front of the group ahead of them. Ruskin. The Silverfall prince rode alongside Prince Faraçek. They were mirror opposites: white hair versus black, bulky versus slim, pale complexion versus gray, round face versus a long one.

"You have benevolent rulers." Sasha paused. "No, it's deeper than that. You have *seelie* rulers. There are seelie and there are seelie, and your monarchs are the kind of fae that the ancients wrote about. Our ruler? She is strong, but she is not… she is nothing like them. Queen Sylifke is a lot like the kingdom she rules."

Jess offered the only adjective that came to mind. "Cold?"

He nodded. "But—as you pointed out earlier—there is nice cold. Cold that makes art on window panes. But there's also cold that cuts, cold that burns."

"You're saying she's the latter?"

Sasha seemed far away. "I guess I am. Only, I never knew it. Not fully." His gaze flicked to hers. "Not until I came here."

They swayed gently with the movement of their mounts as the party approached the end of the grassland and the start of treed foothills. The riders slipped between the trunks like water through stones. Conversation slowed as the atmosphere changed. Sunlight came through the canopy in shafts. Hoofbeats dulled against the cushion of dry needles and the spicy smell of the trees grew strong. A few ground-dwelling birds took off, squeaking their indignation.

Sasha pulled her attention away from the forest. "Were you told the old stories as a child? The ones about when the kingdoms were all fae, and the monarchs were different?"

Jess shook her head, touching the reins softly to her mare's neck to guide her palfrey closer to Sasha's gelding. The two touched noses companionably. Jess was close enough to see the many-pointed silver stars encircling Sasha's pupils.

"Are you talking about actual Ivryndian history," she asked, "or fables?"

"I'm not sure." Sasha chuckled. "Maybe both. But it's not a fable that Ivryndi was once divided into four kingdoms with seasons that never changed."

That was very old history and Jess's schoolteacher had only touched on it briefly. "The Autumn Court, Winter Court, Summer Court and Spring Court."

"Yes. Silverfall has always been the Winter Court and Stavarjak has always been the Spring. A long time ago, before Solana was established as its own separate kingdom, Rahamlar and Boskaya were autumn, while Tryske and Archelia were Summer. But as humans arrived and intermingled with the fae, it weakened the bloodlines… and the magic. Slowly, so slowly no one knew what was happening until it was already done, the monarchs of the Autumn and Summer courts lost their sovereignty and their seasons. They fell into the cycles that the majority of Ivryndi has now."

"But is that a bad thing?" Jess asked. "I like having distinct seasons. It seems more natural. Doesn't everything have a cycle? Even people. The Calyx certainly do."

Sasha shrugged. "Bad or good, I can't say. But Silverfall and Stavarjak kept their seasonal integrity, even if it was for different reasons."

"And those reasons are?"

"Stavarjak has had the same queen for so long that no one remembers anyone before her."

"Queen Elphame." Jess thought of Laec. She hadn't talked to him in a while.

"Yes. And while Silverfall has had many queens—"

"Never kings?"

"Very few. We've never taken kindly to kings—they seem to suffer short and violent reigns—while we've had many queens. We are a kingdom that keeps to itself. We tend to choose Silverfae partners and have Silverfae offspring; we don't stray far from home often enough to mix with other fae, or humans. So, Silverfall is still the Winter Court. But what I was trying to say earlier and failing at was this: while I knew that the season of our court was linked to our monarch, I never understood that the kind of winter we have has everything to do with our monarch too. Winter has positive and negative qualities."

Jess thought she was starting to follow the trail he was leaving her. "Summer is lovely because it's when everything is in full bloom and most days are sunny and warm, but there are also biting insects and sometimes too much heat."

"Right. Queen Sylifke is as Silverfae as they come, as Silverfae as any queen before her, but she's also unseelie. *Very* unseelie." Sasha gave her a look that said there was more to say but he hoped he didn't have to.

Jess thought about Prince Faraçek. Her heart dropped. "I've had my own unseelie experience, and I think I know what you're saying. I was sheltered from it as I was growing up, but I learned, eventually."

Sasha canted his head to avoid a branch. "What happened?"

Some mornings Jess still looked for Greta. "I lost someone close to me by an unseelie hand."

Sasha took in air. It was not quite a gasp, but it was audible. Her words had impacted him like a fist. "So you know what I mean. Even young as you are."

Jess smiled at him, thinking he wasn't much older than her, even if he seemed older at first glance.

"Elderly Silverfae have told me of a time when the sun shone in Silverfall, when it sparkled off the snow in exactly the way that you describe. I didn't believe them. Not then, but now… I catch glimpses in my mind of glittering ice, bright blue sky, and sunshine so strong that we had to protect our eyes. I haven't thought of those dreams—or memories, if that's what they are—in a long time. There is something about this place that has brought them back, unearthed them like buried treasure, like gold. But are they fool's gold, or genuine?"

Jess was afraid to interrupt his ruminating. She slid her mount closer. Their legs touched. He was too preoccupied to notice.

"I think those stories were real," he said. "They were given to me like contraband, something forbidden—which was why I didn't believe them—told as though the walls had ears. Now I know they were given that way, not for a child's wonder, but because they were afraid."

"Afraid?" echoed Jess. "Afraid of what?"

"Not what." Sasha gave her a look of deep unease, a look laced with sadness. "Who."

Jess didn't ask him to clarify, it was clear enough that he meant Queen Sylifke.

They came into a clearing as the last riders ahead disappeared into the forest on the other side, leaving Sasha and Jessamine alone. The glade was filled with slanted beams of sunlight, glistening off hillocks of snow.

Their conversation ceased as the horses waded in. Paths raked through the snow by riders who'd gone ahead of them were softened as the wind kicked up.

Sasha swung off his horse and walked into the glade. Looking back, he gave her a smile that made her heart ache. He bent to scoop up as much as he could hold, then tossed it into the sky. "This is good winter. Rialta must love this."

Jess dismounted and waded out to be with him. Their horses snuffled into the snow so deeply their heads disappeared, looking for grass. She scooped up an armful and tossed it skyward, tilting her face up as it floated down. They shoveled a huge pile together, then jumped into it, laughing and giggling like children. When they'd exhausted the novelty of it, they stood and dusted the flakes from one another.

He touched her face. When he brought his lips down to hers, she closed her eyes and forgot who she was. Pleasure rushed through her body as she reached up to touch the sides of his face, letting her fingers slip into his hair. She'd never felt softer, silkier locks.

When he withdrew, she opened her eyes. There was no one in the world but them. His hand curled around hers and he brought it down to his chest where he lay her palm flat against his heart. Jess was utterly lost. Was this what it felt like to fall in love? If this wasn't falling in love, then how could anyone bear it?

Something in their periphery floated in the air like bubbles.

A new spell took over as the air filled with transparent shapes of honeysuckle blossoms. As wispy as cat's ears, they caught the breeze and lifted. Sasha reached for one. It popped against his skin. He drew his hand to his nose and inhaled. His eyes drifted closed, pleasure softening the planes of his face.

Jess reached for one, amazed.

"Jess," Sasha whispered, opening his eyes to look at her. "You're a wonder."

Mystic blooms. She caught one against her wrist. It was as sweet and green as a spring morning. Her first chromatypes, and she hadn't even been trying.

"You made them." Sasha watched the honeysuckle blooms as they drifted up and away, out of reach.

"Actually…" she looked at him. When would she be able to look at him without feeling utterly bowled over? "I think *we* made them."

Abruptly, he looked at her, fully taking in her meaning. For as long as she lived, she'd never forget this moment.

He looked like he was going to kiss her again. Then someone called Sasha's name from very far away. Ruskin. Of course, Ruskin.

Jess and Sasha traded a look of guilt. Sasha uttered an oath.

They returned to their horses.

Rose called Jess, sounding a little closer than Prince Ruskin had.

They spurred their horses into a trot, leaving the glade behind. Jess looked regretfully over her shoulder as they passed beneath the canopy, catching the last of her mystic blooms as they were swept into the sky.

By the time the party returned to the palace, Jess was emotionally and physically exhausted.

In an effort not to encourage questions about why they'd fallen behind, Jess and Sasha had returned to the group and spent the rest of the day with other members of the party. Even the long ride back to the palace was spent at opposite ends of the group.

Jess hoped it was as agonizing for Sasha as it was for her. Her gaze had continually sought him out, as if drawn by a magnet, until Rose came over under a pretense of showing Jessamine something.

As she held her hand out to Jess, Rose whispered, "You need to stop looking at him."

Jess felt the blood drain from her cheeks, but Rose added, "There's always a way to be together… alone. Any more of those moony looks and Ilishec will hear of it and start asking questions—and he is very good at spotting a lie."

Jess had made a concerted effort to treat Sasha no differently than anyone else. It was torture. She longed to ride beside him, to talk with him, to look over and see those amazing features that had scored themselves on her heart in such a short time.

Later, she continually told herself. Later.

Rose had as much as given her permission to fall in love as long as she kept it a secret.

As the horses were stabled and the party dispersed to clean up, she and Sasha exchanged a polite but distant goodbye, which cleaved her heart in two. She made her way toward her room, intending to wash off the day and hoping that someone had told Sasha the Calyx had to appear not to have favorites.

Then she began to worry. What if someone had told him that the Calyx were actually forbidden to have relationships with courtiers? What if they'd used that word: *forbidden*. Wait. Was it forbidden, or was it just frowned upon? Now Jess couldn't remember. Frankly, she'd kind of dismissed it as unimportant at the time. Courtiers were, by and large, not the type Jess was attracted to. Jess was attracted to Fahyli types, males who smelled like the outdoors, who had skills that went way beyond dancing. Maybe she'd imagined she might fall in love with someone like Regalis or Panther, even Digit, and was in no danger of being attracted to a guest.

She'd never imagined someone like Sasha existed.

When someone grabbed her by the wrist and pulled her into a corner she almost screamed. Looking up into Laec's bright mischievous eyes calmed her a little. Whatever he wanted it could have nothing to do with Sasha.

"You scared me!" she hissed.

He pulled a face of outrage. "I was calling you from down the hall. Didn't you hear me?"

Jess had heard nothing. She flushed. "Sorry."

"Honestly, Jess. You need your ears candled. What's wrong with you?"

"Nothing, I—" Wait, it was Laec who'd snuck up

on her. She had no reason to feel guilty. "What are you doing here?"

He glanced down the hall, covert-like. "I need to talk to you. Can I… can we step into your room for a second?"

Her gaze narrowed. "Are you even allowed to be here?"

Laec rolled his eyes, took her by the shoulders and gave her a little shove toward her door. "Just get in. Before that bloody bird figures out where I've gone."

Jess wasn't sure which bird Laec was referring to, but she let him into her room. He shut the door and faced her, digging beneath his vest for something. Producing a small piece of folded paper, he handed it to her. She unfolded it to find a colored drawing of a ring on a fisted hand. The ring was engraved with a crown encircling the image of a flying bird.

"What's this?"

"Princess Serya's seal," Laec said. "Can you do that trick again, see if you can find it?"

The hair on her arms stood up. "Where did you get this?"

He was almost dancing in place. "Does it matter? Can you do it?"

Her jaw felt tight. An inanimate object that belonged to Princess Serya? It was exactly what King Agir and Queen Esha needed. "Where did you get it, Laec?"

He sighed. "Lady Çifta drew it from memory. Will it work?"

Jess studied the drawing, her stomach folding in on itself. A warning flag raised itself, filling her mind and growing larger by the second. In her hand she held the key. Esha would be incredulous, amazed, grateful. For Jess and Beazle it likely meant… danger, risk, a mission. A few days ago she would have leapt at the opportunity Laec had just presented. But now? A few days worth of heartbeats. A kiss in a glade, a heartfelt conversation, those silver eyes. Jessamine's entire outlook, her hopes and dreams, had all changed.

"This is bigger than us, Laec. I can't just… we can't just… do this. Not after what we've already done, and you're still under house arrest."

Far from appearing chagrined, Laec brightened. "So it'll work?"

Jess blinked. "That's… so not the point."

"Sure it is." He snatched the drawing back. "I didn't mean for you to do it right this second."

She put her hands on her hips. "Well good, because I won't. There are… problems."

The look he gave her was like a fox stalking prey. "Such as?

"I've only ever used *solidago* to find things that were close by. That seal could be anywhere. It could be in Rahamlar. We could be led straight into enemy territory."

Laec looked bored. "That didn't scare you before."

"Yes, but…" How could she express the fear she now held within her breast, not for herself, but for Beazle.

I'm not afraid, Beazle thought sleepily from the rafters.

"That's also not the point," she answered aloud.

"Sorry?" Laec looked around the room, spooked. "To whom are you speaking?"

She ignored his question. "If I use *solidago* to find this, Beazle communicates it to me."

"What an efficient system," Laec replied, not understanding her at all.

Jess shook her head, irritated. "Think for a second. What will happen if it does work."

He spoke slowly, like she was an idiot. "We find the princesses, we rescue them if they are in trouble. We get rewarded. Then, after Serya is crowned, Kazery renegotiates with the new monarch, leaving Lady Çifta out of things entirely. It's a perfect plan."

Jessamine paused. "Who is Kazery?'

"Çifta's father."

She'd lost the plot. "Renegotiate?"

Laec put his hands on her shoulders and gave her a little shake. "Keep up, Jess. Kazery hasn't let Çifta off the hook because she won't explain what really happened in Rahamlar. When we find Serya, everything basically solves itself. So will you do it?"

Jess scoffed, pointing at the drawing. "Do the king and queen know you have that?"

Laec took her hand, those fae eyes holding hers, suddenly serious, suddenly full of need. "Not yet. I wanted to talk to you first because if you're not willing, or able, to help then we don't have a blind man's chance in the dark of finding Serya. If I ask for their trust, enough to give me a chance, and we succeed, not only will I be back in their good graces, I'll be in Kazery's good graces too, *and* it'll solve Çifta's problem. Theoretically. But it all hinges on you, Jess."

It struck her like a mallet to the back of the head that Laec felt about Çifta the way she felt about Sasha. Her cheeks burned and she looked away as her heart filled with empathy. If he had experienced any level of the agony she'd gone through on the ride home…

"I didn't say I wasn't willing."

"So you'll do it?"

She exhaled. "You get their permission, and I'll do it. What choice would I have?"

Laec brightened, then looked troubled as her words sank in. "Don't you want to find them?"

"Sure, but—" Her reasons were purely selfish. She wanted to keep Beazle safe, she couldn't bear it if anything happened to him. And… and Sasha. She didn't want to miss a moment's possibility of his company, but she couldn't admit any of that aloud.

"Yes, of course I do," she said, waving him away. "Now go."

"Good." Laec headed for the door. "You need a bath, by the way. You smell like honeysuckle and horses. It's a very weird blend."

She rolled her eyes. "I spent the afternoon riding. What a shock."

Laec closed the door and Jess went into the bathroom to fill the tub.

In spite of the nerves she felt about what Laec wanted her to do, she couldn't prevent a smile from creeping across her face. She hadn't just spent the afternoon riding, she'd spent it falling in love.

Chapter Twenty-One

Laec

Laec approached the queen's parlor; sounds of delighted laughter drifted from her rooms. The tall male servant stationed by the door put a hand up as Laec went to open it.

"State your business, please."

"I have an audience with the queen," Laec lied.

The servant lifted his nose, skeptical. "I wasn't told."

Laec put his hands behind his back and swung forward on his toes, looking smug and confident. "There must be some mistake then. Check with her yourself."

The servant looked positively huffy. "I do not check with the queen to ensure a mistake has not been made."

"Well, who do you check with? Because I'm telling you, your information is bad." Laec tapped his toe. "Go on. I'll wait."

"I'll not be taking your word," the servant replied coldly. "I know who you are and—"

The door opened and three Calyx emerged on a fragrant puff of air. Laec caught a glimpse of the fireplace where Esha usually sat and saw orange skirts draped over delicate knees, one slippered foot peeking from under the hem. Keeping the Calyx between him and the servant barring his entry, Laec slipped inside.

"Hey!" The servant followed Laec, hooking him by the elbow.

Queen Esha looked up from the book in her lap to see Laec straining toward her, a pleading look on his face.

"It's alright, Emory." The queen put her book aside. "He has an appointment. I forgot to tell you. I'm sorry."

Emory let go of Laec immediately. "Beg your pardon, Ma'am."

"No need. It is I who must beg yours." The queen gave Emory a smile that lit the room and the servant visibly melted.

Laec couldn't help shooting Emory another smug grin as the man retreated, closing the door with a final glare.

The queen gestured to the overstuffed cushion beside her. "I wondered when I would see you again. I am sorry about the awful business of your house arrest. I didn't expect Agir to keep it in place so long, but we have appearances to keep—at least through Midwinter. I hope you understand."

He sank down beside Esha. "Believe me I understand all about appearances. I never had an opportunity to properly thank you for your… guidance. Without it, Lady Çifta…"

"Psht." The queen's gaze slipped around the room, then she winked.

Laec made his eyes as big as possible. "I came to ask if you might be willing to give me an opportunity to redeem myself."

"It's not me you need to redeem yourself to," the queen replied. "King Agir is still rather irritated with you."

"If I locate the missing princesses, might it alter his feelings?"

Queen Esha gaped. "What do you know?"

Laec pinched his lips together.

"You can't tell me," she said flatly, not looking surprised, which surprised Laec.

"It's best if I don't, Ma'am."

Laec was once again amazed by the differences between his own queen and this one. Asking Queen Elphame to trust him by allowing him to keep information from her was akin to stepping in front of a stampeding herd. She'd insist on knowing, even if it jeopardized the kingdom. Laec's fondness for Queen Esha grew. She trusted him—wise or not, she trusted him. He hoped he didn't let her down.

Queen Esha ran a finger along the textured spine of the book in her lap, never withdrawing her eldritch gaze. "You want to ask a certain Calyx to use a certain gift that you have been the beneficiary of once before. You should know that we already asked her. She's not able to use her gift on people."

Laec took a breath. He had to be careful. He didn't want to lie to the queen, but he had to steer her away without outright denying that Jessamine had anything to do with his plan. "I am aware that her magic doesn't work on people."

Her curiosity piqued but she didn't push him. "So, you simply wish me to ask my husband if he'll release you from your arrest for long enough to execute your plan?"

"Yes, Ma'am." Laec tried not to fidget. He reminded himself that he was not trying to fool the queen, merely get her help without involving her in the details. His intentions were true.

The queen looked into the fire thoughtfully before answering. "I know my husband well, Mr. Fairijak. If he agrees—and that is a big *if*—he will feel duty bound to send guards along with you. Not to help, but to ensure you return to the palace to serve out the rest of your punishment."

Laec nodded, noting her use of his surname, a way of distancing them. Esha couldn't guarantee Agir's response.

"I would expect no less. The king's word and judgment must be upheld."

"Do nothing until you hear from me. Agreed?" The queen held out her hand.

"Agreed, Ma'am." He kissed her hand.

Now he just had the most difficult task in the world: waiting.

Chapter Twenty-Two

Jessamine

ALMOST ANOTHER WEEK of the Midwinter Festival passed, with Sasha never far from Jess's thoughts. The Festival went from being a novel and extremely busy period of work to something entirely different. Just knowing that he was there—at the banquets and balls, walking through the hothouses, socializing in the parlors while the winter winds blew past the chimneys, making the fires flare—meant the world to her. She longed for chances to dance with him, to talk with him, even if she had to share his company with others. To lay her eyes on his glacial beauty made her heart feel light and happy, almost giddy. She refused to think about him going home. Refused. Because she couldn't bear to taint the new and exciting things happening within her heart with the knowledge that it would end.

Even Jessamine's sweat sessions with Peony changed. The prolific Calyx repeatedly asked Jess what she

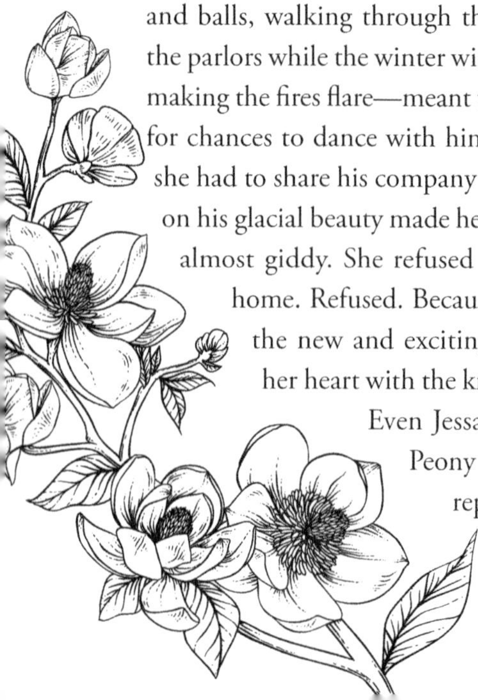

was doing differently. Jess gave vague answers with very little truthful content: she was well rested, she was practicing on her own time, Mrs. Tierney had added something potent to her elixirs to stimulate her magic. The truth was that the glow of falling in love had somehow helped her to "get out of the way" of her magic. Was it because her thoughts were elsewhere? His bright gaze, broad shoulders, and beautiful hands filled her daytime imagination and her nighttime dreams. Chromatypes spiraled from her body with hardly any effort at all.

Peony had been elated and gone straight to Ilishec to claim credit. Jess didn't care—it kept their attention off the truth. When Ilishec asked her to show him her *lonicera* chromatypes, she did so, easily and prolifically. He was thrilled. Ilishec had asked her if it had been Peony's tutelage and Jessamine shrugged, supposing it must be. She'd give Peony all the credit if it made the Calyx less prickly, and as long as Jess could go on dancing with Sasha. She was deeply afraid that Ilishec would see through her and tell her to stay clear of the Silverfae, but so far, those fears were unfounded.

Sasha had come across the information—he'd confirmed—that Calyx were warm and hospitable but never intimate with courtiers. Jess was glad he knew they had to be careful without having to explain it. So they danced and talked with others as well. It was a coordinated and strategic effort with great treasure at the end of it. Sasha cast his glorious smile and divine gaze over a great many Calyx and courtiers. Jess did the same. But when they came together it was sunlight and raindrops, it was petals on the wind, it was beating hearts, fluttering stomachs and stolen kisses. It was a new kind of magic that made flora magic look banal.

It was love.

So when Jessamine was abruptly herded sideways into a small room and the door shut behind her, it took her far too long to realize it wasn't a tryst.

The someone who had herded her from the hall had done so without hurting her, but the force this being could wield if he wanted to was not lost on Jessamine. He nodded at someone else across the room. Jess whirled to face a woman she'd never seen before. Human; older than the queen, but younger than Hazel. She wore a basic black dress with a ring of keys dangling from her belt. She had short curly blond hair going mostly gray. Even in the dim light of the small room, her eyes were vivid green.

"Jessamine Fontana?" The woman's voice was calm and deep. Clearly, she was accustomed to commanding attention and respect.

Jess was immediately contrite. She was in trouble. She had to be. "That's me."

"I am sorry to interrupt your day so rudely, please forgive me. My method is a little unorthodox, but I don't do appointments. Shortly, you'll understand why. My name is Vivian, and this conversation is not happening."

Jess swallowed and took a moment to breathe. Her thoughts went to Beazle, then to Sasha, and back again. Her bat was asleep in the rafters of her bedroom. She wished he was with her, to witness whatever this was about.

"Does Ilishec know about this meeting?"

Vivian smiled. "He said you asked for it."

"I asked…?"

Vivian moved around the small table to the front, where she perched a hip on the edge. She waited patiently for Jess to clue in.

"You're the faceless manager!"

"Is that what he called me? Not very flattering." Vivian rubbed a thumb into a palm, then enfolded her fingers. "I won't take up too much of your time; but however brief, our time together is important, so please listen. I am a… liaison for Solana."

"A liaison…" Jess parroted. "Like… a go-between?"

Vivian gave a little bow. "That's right. I am an important part of palace business, and you, my dear, are rapidly becoming important yourself."

The man behind Jess made her feel uneasy. She stepped away from him.

Vivian's eyes crinkled. "He won't hurt you, dear. Quite the opposite. If you were ever in trouble, Mr. Strolight here would sacrifice a limb to save you. Isn't that right, Mr. Strolight?"

Jess looked at the big man, who only gazed back at Jess with watchful knowing eyes. He had a scar running from one eyebrow that skipped over his eye and resumed on his cheekbone, nearly reaching his upper lip. It was a lucky thing that he hadn't lost his eye from whatever steel had left that mark.

"I've been following your progress. Documenting would be a better choice of words. I, with a few select chemists, have been monitoring your profiles, and sharing samples with some of our clientele. Your mastery of your raw materials has improved by leaps and bounds. Your profiles have grown steadily more impressive, and more potent. Your *lonicera* isolate is lovely, to be sure. But I am interested in your other substances. You, my dear, are what we refer to in the business as a fount. There is, in fact, only one other being under this immense roof who comes anywhere near your ability. If you're willing—we operate with full consent—I would like to offer your materials officially on the market. They will fetch ten times what your *lonicera* perfume will fetch."

Jess couldn't stop a gasp. Ten times? Even Rose's perfumes, some of which were so valuable they sold in volumes no larger than a half ounce, were not nearly so dear. She could leave Solana more wealthy than she ever dreamed possible after all. "For… poison?"

Vivian shifted to her feet. "Not necessarily. Are your substances toxic? Yes, many of them can be, but they are more than that. Your essences can heal, too. Atropine, for example, can be used to treat certain heart conditions. The other Calyx make perfumes that bring pleasure and joy to a customer, but yours will have much more profound impacts upon people's lives."

The memory of the unseelie soldier toppling over in the road with vomit on his chin breached in Jess's imagination like a huge sea-creature. "But… they can still be used to kill."

Vivian was patient. "A knife can be purchased by a hunter or a chef, what they do with it is their business. Your extracts are powerful, Miss Fontana. Best of all there is a lively market for them. Talk to Ilishec about it, if you like, but I suggest that you bring up our conversation with no others." It was a directive.

"I think I will." She didn't wish to talk it over with Ilishec so much as give herself time to think.

"Suit yourself. Just remember that customers are waiting."

Vivian retrieved something from the pocket of her skirt. She looked Jess directly in the eyes. They were the same height. The maternal kindness in those eyes was unexpected. She anticipated that someone who operated in the shadows—selling substances that could just as easily topple nations as defend them—to be colder, harder. Vivian pressed something smooth and round into Jessamine's hand, warm with body-heat.

"You earned this from one quarter of a batch of *atropa* you produced four weeks ago. It was refined, bottled, and introduced to the market as samples."

Jess lifted the coin and it glimmered in the light of the window. Pure gold, stamped with a wreathed lion's head. Such a coin could purchase three Dagevli cottages or a large section of farmland. Jess had never seen so much money before, let alone held it. She turned as Strolight was opening the door for Vivian.

"How do I contact you?"

"You don't. I'll be in touch." Vivian and her bodyguard swept from the room.

Jess was still mulling over the conversation with Vivian as she walked back to her room. When she heard footsteps approaching she dropped the coin into her pocket.

Snap appeared beside her, his brow furrowed. "Have you seen Moony?"

"Wisteria's familiar?"

Snap nodded.

"Not lately. Why?"

He raked a hand through his curls, then twisted and pulled them, leaving them as a rope on his forehead. "Wisteria can't find him. He's not in any of the hothouses, or any of his usual favorite places, and it's too cold for him to be outside."

Jess's gut tightened. A familiar never stayed far from their fae for very long. "When did she last see him?"

"Last night at the ball. He wasn't with her when she went to bed, she says, but she assumed he'd be there when she woke up this morning. He wasn't. Now everyone is worried."

"He'll turn up," Jess told him. "I'm due at the tailors' den shortly but I should have a little time after I'm dressed. I'll help look."

He nodded. "Thanks, Jess. I'll tell her."

Jessamine raced through her bathing routine and arrived at the den early. Rushing the couturières wasn't well received, until Jess told Olinya why she was in a hurry. The master tailor transformed into a drill sergeant and Jess was costumed in record time. She left the den in a deep red column dress, hair arranged in a tall structure draped with *gelsemium* blossoms. Dangly earrings brushed at the sides of her neck as she rushed toward Ilishec's workroom.

She found Wisteria hunched together with her best

friend Dianthus, their backs to the door. Snap, Heath and Iris stood in a concerned little clump, Iris chewing her thumbnail and looking like she wanted to cry. Heath and Snap were talking quietly.

"Did they find him?" Jess asked.

"Yes, but something's wrong," said Snap. "He's sick and can't seem to fly. He was stuck high up in the drapes on the third terrace overlooking the main ballroom. I guess he got up there and couldn't come down. The cleaning staff found him, but only because they were changing those drapes for tonight's decor. If they hadn't, I don't think we'd have found him in time."

Jess observed the way the Calyx were slouched forward with worry. "Ilishec will be able to help him. He can fix anything."

Snap nodded. "I'm sure he'll be ok."

Since Wisteria had told Jess that she was very firmly on Jess's side, Jessamine wanted to do the same for Wisteria. She approached the end of the table where Wisteria and Dianthus were huddled, their shoulders pressed together. Nearby, Ilishec paged through an encyclopedic text with the glasses he so rarely wore perched on the end of his nose.

Jess touched Wisteria on the arm. When she saw Jess, her face crumpled. "Moony is sick."

The look on Wisteria's face went straight to Jess's heart. "I know. I'm so sorry."

She pulled the fae into her arms, exchanging a concerned look with Dianthus. Dianthus moved so Jessamine could see Moony.

She had to stifle her horror.

The little white and green butterfly was curled in on himself, nearly touching his own abdomen with his proboscis, and twitching as if in pain. His antennae ran down the length of his forelegs over and over, as his head twisted from side to side. Wisteria gave a sob and Jess held her closer, stroking her back.

Jess soothed her with a gentle, confident tone. "He'll be alright. Ilishec won't let anything bad happen to him."

Ilishec glanced up with a glazed, troubled look then went back to his text.

Jess released Wisteria, kissing her cheek. She pulled a stray hair away from Wisteria's mouth and wiped her wet cheeks.

"Use your magic," Jess suggested, "to bring him out of this."

Wisteria hiccupped. "How?"

"Can you communicate with him?" She touched Wisteria's forehead. "In here?"

Dianthus said, "I know what you're getting at, Jess. But insects aren't so good at telepathy."

Wisteria sniffed, looking hopeful. "I can try."

Jess squeezed Wisteria's hands. "I'm on duty. I'll come back as soon as I can, okay?"

Wisteria nodded again, already staring at Moony with a look of intense concentration.

Jess looked at Ilishec, hoping for something encouraging from him, but he was too absorbed in his search to even notice when she left the room.

Chapter Twenty-Three

Jessamine

Jess was wrapped up in a dark-green oversized scarf and hat, playing a chilly game of croquet in the courtiers' garden with a group of nobles. She was half-listening to a handsome courtier with explosively curly hair named Colin Prattle as he—true to his name—prattled on about technique, and watching as Rose allowed herself to be "taught" how to properly swing the mallet. The scene edged on the ridiculous. Calyx often played the game themselves and Rose was usually the victor, but while the Calyx worked, every gesture and word was oriented to delight the guests. At times, that meant faking being bad at something—croquet or fencing, for instance—anything except dancing and active listening, those two skills had to be as honed as the blade of an axe.

When Jessamine saw a blur of white hair out of the corner of her eye, she looked up in hope. Prince

Ruskin had joined a small group of ladies in pastel gowns beneath a trellis choked with leafless wisteria vines. Disappointed, Jess had turned back to the courtier, who was telling her a story—something about another kind of game—when Sasha emerged from the shadows near the palace. He was arm in arm with Lady Lecta, a stately older lady Jess had seen at balls or seated at the head table. She was a distinguished woman, with a calculating gaze and a kind smile. Her ear was lifted to Sasha, and he was laughing as he talked. His smile made Jess's knees watery, even when it was directed at someone else.

"…turn." A voice penetrated her daze.

"Hmm?" She looked at her companion, whose name she had forgotten.

"It's your turn, Miss Jessamine. Unless you'd like me to take it for you? You seem distracted today." The handsome courtier held out their shared mallet, pursing his lips in a way that was probably meant to be flirtatious. Jessamine thought he looked prissy.

"Sorry." She took the mallet, tossed the end of her scarf over her shoulder, and focused where she needed to aim.

Rose moved close. "Make sure your weight is spread evenly. I just learned this from Master Peabody." She lowered her voice. "Is Moony any better? I slept in and didn't have time to check on them this morning."

Jess shook her head. The night before, she'd returned to Ilishec's workshop on a break to find that Wisteria had been excused from the evening's duties. She'd taken Moony, and a powder Ilishec had ground for him, and gone to bed. When she didn't show for breakfast, Jess had taken some fruit up to her room. There had been no change in Moony, and Wisteria was in no mood for eating. She'd taken to holding a pool of nectar in a spoon with the medicine dissolved into it, keeping it steady for her butterfly, who seemed as uninterested in food as Wisteria was. It was a sad sight.

Rose stepped back to give Jess room to take her shot. The ball skirted the wicket and rolled down a soft grade to settle in a grassy divot. The party applauded politely. Jess pinched the bridge of her nose, feigning distress at her lack of skill.

"A respectable shot," said her companion with a patronizing grin as he took the mallet back. "A little less spin and you might have had it."

"Of course. Less spin." Jess gave him a saccharine smile, batting her eyelashes.

She tugged her knitted hat down over her ears and snuck another look at Sasha. He was seated on a bench near the lotus-spackled pond with his back to the game. Lady Lecta had gone. Jess's heart surged out of her chest toward him.

At the sound of applause, Jess pulled herself back to the game. Whoever thought that the Calyx had it easy was only right when the Calyx weren't in love with someone they weren't supposed to be in love with. Jess wondered how many of her fellow flora fae had a similar problem.

Across the garden, near a dogwood tree, Peony strolled with an older gentleman in a pale blue jacket. She gazed up at him with sparkling eyes out of a sumptuous fur-lined hood, flashing those white teeth in perfectly timed smiles, the ultimate companion. Courtiers played chess on a huge chessboard, directed by a nobleman from Boskaya Jess had danced with many times. Everyone looked like they had no desire to be anywhere else.

When Ilishec came into the garden, Jess pasted on a smile with the gusto of a carpenter determined to drive a round peg into a square hole. If the gardener noticed that Jess was struggling, he didn't show it. She took that as a triumph, but by the end of the game, she felt exhausted. She was less drained from her self-defense lessons than after a few hours pretending she was having a marvelous time.

When the courtiers broke for refreshments, Jess took a cup of hot chocolate from the refreshments stand and left the garden in search of Sasha. She had a half hour before she needed to be in the tailors' den. She passed through the stone archway dividing the courtiers' garden from another that was undergoing some landscaping. When an arm snaked around Jess's waist and pulled her into the shadows, she knew his touch instantly. He drew her in for a covert kiss, then quickly released her as they heard laughing voices nearby.

"I've been waiting forever for you to finish that game." He looked at her with besotted eyes. "Next time, remind me to sign up. At least then I won't have to watch a popinjay with absurd hair fawn over you. I could do the fawning."

She grinned.

He looked around. "There are no leaves on these bloody trees. I'll be spotted for sure," he said in a low voice. "You look like a topiary. If you stand still, people won't notice you. But I look like an ice-cream cone."

In answer, she pulled him behind a trunk and lifted her face to his in invitation.

"Then again, I'm not one to shirk a job that needs doing," he murmured, and kissed her so thoroughly that her head whirled and her stomach seesawed like a bird in a high wind. All of her exhaustion fell away.

He drew back, a little out of breath. "Jess."

Only the whisper of her name, but so much was said. He longed to be with her as much as she longed to be with him. He was falling. He was nervous about getting her into trouble, but his desire to be with her was impossible to ignore. There was concern, too. She withdrew from it like a sensitive fern. She didn't want to think about what was worrying him, because then she'd have to think about it too.

Getting themselves under control, they emerged from the shadows and walked calmly toward the palace—although the color was high in Sasha's cheeks. They were simply guest and Calyx, making easy conversation as they headed for the warmth of a parlor. Jess pulled off her scarf and hat. They found private seats behind a large potted plant.

"Where is Rialta today?" Jess asked casually. She was still eager to meet Sasha's familiar, but she was nervous, too. She'd fallen for Sasha. What if his familiar didn't like her?

Sasha's smile was sad. "She went to Mount Vargon to hunt."

His expression kept her from teasing or pressuring

him. He could have introduced them many times by now. Something was making him hesitate. Jess swallowed hard as she wondered what his reasons could be. She covered her unease by shucking her wrist warmers.

The moment they were off, Sasha took both her hands. A lick of fear ran up Jess's spine at the earnestness in his face. He looked like he had something serious to say, and she was sure she didn't want to hear it. What she was trying so hard to not think about, slipped through like an icy wind through a crack. The idea of Sasha leaving was like a fist around her throat.

"How do I go back to life…" she murmured. "After you?"

She didn't realize she'd spoken out loud until his eyes softened.

The pads of his thumbs traced circles on the backs of her hands. "Jess… I-I'm sorry…"

"Sorry?"

He squeezed his eyes shut and shook his head. "In Silverfall, they make fun of Solana. I was given the wrong idea about what it would be like here. I had no idea I would meet you. You've bewitched me, Jess. I'm in trouble. There's no other word for it. Heart trouble."

"Heart trouble." She seemed unable to do anything but parrot him.

He shifted forward on his seat, closer to her. "I wouldn't trade being in heart trouble over you for anything, Jess. Nothing in the world. I'd take trouble that leaves my heart scarred, over a lifetime of not knowing that these feelings exist."

His words pierced her like a hot blade. It sounded like he was preparing to say goodbye. She felt the same as him, yet putting his fear into words only made her own fear come alive. His words woke something that was pretending to sleep. She didn't want to know the answer, but she was even more afraid not to ask.

"When do you have to go back?"

Some of the urgency in his expression softened. "Luckily, we are failing in our mission so far, which means our stay keeps getting extended."

"Your… mission?" Jess blinked at his phrasing. "You're not here for the Midwinter, and the perfumes?"

Regret flashed across his face. Then he seemed to accept something. He waited as a chatting couple passed by on the other side of the plant. When they'd gone, he said, "We—Prince Ruskin, to be more specific—is looking for someone."

"Who?"

He scoffed, letting go of one of her hands to tug on his hair. "I can't tell you because I don't know. Not really. We're chasing a myth, as far as I'm concerned. It's private Silverfall business. No one else is supposed to know. Don't say anything to anyone, please."

If he'd asked her to lie down on the floor so he could step on her to reach the light fixture, she'd have done it.

"Of course I won't say anything. But maybe I can help. I'm quite good at finding… well… not people, but things." She thought about Laec's approach to finding Serya. "Are there any objects associated with this person that you seek?"

He was mystified. "You're good at finding things?"

"It's part of my flora magic. It happens when I conjure *solidago*, which in fables is supposed to help find lost objects. I've only used it twice—it worked differently each time, but it worked."

His expression became serious. "You shouldn't tell people this, Jess. It's dangerous for anyone outside your trusted circle to know this about you."

"It *is* a secret," she replied. "My friends know, and of course Ilishec and a few others, but they would never spread it around."

He held out his hands. "You just told me."

"But you're trustworthy." She was lost in his bright eyes, his strong jaw, the set of his mouth, so serious but waiting for a something to come along and give it a reason to smile. "You're… Sasha. You're different. You're… almost as inside my circle as someone can get." She flushed. "Is it wrong to admit that?"

He touched her chin, sadness moving over his face like a passing cloud. His lips parted, but his eyes flicked to someone behind her. He withdrew his hand and straightened.

Laec came around the potted plant. "I've been looking for you all over the place." He shot a calculating look at Sasha, one that Jess couldn't quite read. Then he gave her a deep, mocking bow. "You're required at court, Miss Jessamine."

"But its hours until the banquet. I'm due at the tailors' den in… now." She surged to her feet, grabbing her scarf, hat and wrist warmers. "In fact I'm late."

"Your costume will have to wait." Laec curled a hand under her elbow. "I was trying to be diplomatic. You're not required at court, you're being summoned by the king. Best not to keep him waiting."

She threw an apologetic look at Sasha. He stood, concern in his silver eyes.

"It was lovely chatting with you," she said, hoping she sounded formal.

Sasha held up a hand.

"Yes, lovely chatting with you," Laec parroted, sending Sasha a pasted-on smile.

Jess glared at him. "That was rude."

As they passed through the parlor doors, Laec muttered, "You need to be careful around him."

Jess's heart felt like it stopped. She put a hand on her chest to make sure it was still beating.

Breezily, she asked, "Why do you say that?"

Laec picked up his pace, tugging Jess along with him. "Because he came with Ruskin, and there's a snake if I ever saw one."

So, Laec had a problem with Ruskin, not Sasha. Jess relaxed a little, but tugged her elbow out of his grip with a look of reproach.

"Guilt by association? I expected better from you."

He sniffed. "Well, don't. Pick up the pace, and quit looking at me like I shaved your bat."

Jessamine was so curious about what the king might want that she didn't notice when Laec didn't take her to the lion's pride room, or anywhere near it. They emerged from a side door of the West Keep before Jess finally asked him where they were going.

Laec led her toward the training yards. "The king doesn't want to see you. That was just a ruse. I had to get you to come without asking questions."

"Laec!" She punched him in the shoulder a little too hard, then shook her hand out, resorting to shooting daggers at him with her eyes.

He didn't seem to notice her punch. "What? Was what you were doing so important? Flirting with a courtier? You need to set your priorities straight, little Calyx. You can thank me later."

Jessamine couldn't decide what piqued her more: her lack of witty comeback or Laec's cavalier attitude toward the Calyx.

"Flirting *is* a priority when you're a Calyx, you numpty."

"Yes, but you're also Fahyli."

Jessamine came up short. "How do you know that?"

Laec tugged on her wrist to keep her moving. "Like it was hard to figure out. Even if Ilishec hadn't told me, I could tell from this." He lifted her hand, gripped in his.

She was starting to sweat. "What *this*?"

"Your hands. They're calloused. I even saw bruises on your back a couple of weeks ago, at the ball where Olinya made you wear a dress the size of a napkin. She should do a better job covering those. Even a fool could figure it out."

Jessamine made a sound of feminine outrage. "A

napkin? You little hedgepig! Olinya is a genius. You try designing hundreds of unique costumes for fifty different fae, each with their own theme."

Laec shot her a grin. "I know. I'm just playing with you. It's fun to watch you get red-faced and disgruntled. It's cute. And isn't that a funny word?"

"Which word? Cute?"

"Disgruntled. It means vexed or displeased."

"I know what it means."

"Right, so if I was happy, could I say that I was gruntled?"

"A gruntled moron, maybe." But she laughed as she followed Laec through the wooden gate.

She drew up short and abruptly stopped laughing.

In the yard was a small group of Fahyli and their familiars: the crofter, Regalis, Kite, Sy, Digit and Panther. They looked over as Jess entered. Tully lifted her head as Laec and Jessamine approached, eyes half-hooded and gleaming. Mae was trying to catch Tully's tail, swiping at it with her tiny black claws. Ferrugin and Erasmus swooped in to land on their respective fae as Laec drew Jessamine over to the group.

The presence of the crofter made Jess bite back questions. He looked as grumpy and annoyed as ever: arms crossed over his dark-green boiled leather and brown leggings.

A huge furry brown shape moved near the fence. Jess suppressed a squeak of fright as a bear waddled over to the group, snuffing in the grass. She lifted her head and gazed at Jessamine with bright black eyes, then collapsed in the grass and rolled onto her back, paws flailing.

"That's Kashmir," Laec told her. "Ian's familiar."

It took Jess a second to remember that Ian was the crofters name. "Oh."

She felt painfully self-conscious in her pretty winter costume. She pulled the scarf away from her face and tried to smile. They all looked so fierce. Kite in particular, who wore her hair severely pulled back into knots that ran down the center of her skull to the nape of her neck.

Sy popped something into his mouth and chewed, hooded eyes sparkling with good humor and confidence. His inky black hair stood up in spikes. He looked as much the bandit as his familiar did.

The crofter spoke to Jessamine. "We've orders to follow you and your bat wherever your magic says we must go. The objective is to retrieve Princess Serya; hopefully her sister as well."

Laec handed Jess a familiar piece of paper: Çifta's drawing of the seal.

She gulped. "Now? *Right now?*"

The crofter tugged on his wrist guard. "We'll wait for you to change, of course."

Jess's pulse bolted like a frightened barn cat. "But, I have duties. I'm expected at court."

"You're not expected anywhere. All arrangements have been made. I have a written and stamped decree. Do you need to see it?" The crofter made a move for a pocket.

"No, I believe you," Jess replied weakly. "I just...

a little warning would have been nice." She aimed this at Laec.

"Sorry. I've been busy." He didn't look sorry, pushing the drawing at her.

Kite added, "We just got the order a half hour ago. None of us has had time to prepare."

Jess gazed at the drawing of the seal, her mind racing ahead to what might happen when she used the *solidago* magic to find it. She could stall, but only for a short time. She looked at the crofter. "Beazle isn't with me. I'll go get him, change, and be back as fast as I can."

Ian nodded. "We'll be waiting."

Jess turned to go. When Laec made to follow her, she spun on him. "I can change on my own, thanks."

Someone snickered, maybe Sy. Jessamine didn't look back. Her mind was a storm. Find the seal. A Fahyli mission, and an important one. It would help the kingdom, possibly foil Faraçek's plans, and it could help Lady Çifta.

But Jessamine didn't want to go anywhere, not with Sasha still there.

She sped straight to the parlor where she'd last been with Sasha. She couldn't get away with running—she looked like she was still on duty. She nodded politely at everyone she passed, saying hello to those she knew. But her stomach was in knots.

Sasha wasn't in the parlor any longer. When she thought about leaving without being able to say goodbye to Sasha, it made her feel ill. What if he left before she got back?

Growing frantic, Jessamine wasted valuable time

checking libraries and parlors. When she finally found him reading a book in an alcove beside the Koi Library, she almost burst into tears. He grinned, then immediately lost it when he saw her face.

He lay his book on the bench as she slid onto the seat next to him. "What's wrong?"

She took his hand beneath the table. "I have to go away for a while."

His eyes widened. "What's happened?"

"I-I…" She stammered, wondering how much she could say. She wished she could spill everything to him, but even if she was allowed, there wasn't time. What came out was edged with her fears that she'd not see him again. "I have a mission. It's important, and its secret."

"Mission? Hey, slow down." He put his arm around her with a glance at the thick curtains. "Maybe close those?"

Jess undid the ropes, letting the curtains fall. Only the light from the small window behind Sasha lit their faces. Somehow, it made her feel a little better, being with him in the dimness. She touched his face. "It's part of my atonement. I owe the king and queen for something I did. Something bad."

"I can't believe you would ever do anything bad," he whispered.

"I did it without permission. Part of my penance is… I have to go. Today. Right now."

"For how long?"

"I don't know. We… we're looking for someone." She tugged at a strand of hair. Minutes were ticking by. The others were waiting. But she couldn't bear to leave Sasha. "I guess we're both looking for someone."

She put her hands on his shoulders. She couldn't ask him to wait for her, but she wanted to ask him to do whatever he could to prevent leaving. He could read what she wanted in her face. He brushed back a lock of her hair, his gaze going from her eyes to her lips.

"I hope we are still here when you return, but if we're not… I'll invent a reason to come back. I will."

Her heart ballooned with hope. He kissed her, pulling her against him, almost crushing her. She kissed him back with everything she felt burgeoning inside her, everything that frightened and filled her: passion and desire, fear, hope, excitement, and expectations she was afraid to admit were already full-grown.

Leaving the alcove was the most difficult thing she'd had to do since standing beside her mother's casket. She couldn't look back, but she felt his eyes on her until she rounded a corner.

On the edge of tears, she burst into her rooms, calling Beazle. He was so startled that he fell from the rafters, plopping on her bed. He shot her a baleful look, yawning.

You don't have to yell. You don't even have to use your voice.

Sorry.

As she ripped off her costume, tearing an underarm in the process, she relayed in broken images what was expected of them. She scrambled for her leathers. After pulling the pins out of her hair, she fixed her brown locks into a tail. She took a second to look at herself in the mirror. Her hair was frazzled, her eyes glassy and red. She looked desperate.

Fully awake now, Beazle landed on her shoulder.

I don't like him. Look what he's doing to you. You're a mess.

A tear slipped down her cheek. She brushed it away so hard it hurt. She could hide her feelings from Ilishec and the Calyx. She couldn't entirely fool Rose, but she could keep the extent of her heart's desires veiled. Rose thought she had a crush, but what she was feeling went way beyond a crush. She felt on the edge of a precipice, one she was both terrified to fall from but somehow also wanted to take a flying leap over the edge of.

She couldn't hide her feelings from her familiar, though.

"Oh, Beazle," she sobbed.

She lifted a hand and he crawled into her palm. He looked up at her, annoyance and compassion swimming in his shining black eyes.

"I am a mess, and I'm sorry, but it's too late. There's no going back. I love him and I don't know what to do. It all happened so fast. I didn't know it could happen so easily. It's dangerous, this love business."

I don't know about love. Beazle wrapped his limbs around her thumb. *But don't think so much. You're giving me a headache. You say we must find that seal. Let's find the seal. Then see.*

She rubbed her nose and sniffed. Taking things in bite-sized chunks made a lot of sense. If she thought about all life had placed before her she wouldn't take any bite at all.

"Find the seal, then see. You're very wise for such a tiny being."

He cocked his head. *Not wise. This is a bat's way. Why think past a moment? Pointless. Pointless headache.*

"Right. Pointless headache."

She kissed Beazle and put him on her shoulder while she pulled on her boots. With a final look at her stricken features, she pressed a thumb into the worry lines between her eyebrows, trying to press them away. When she'd got her face somewhat under control, she left her suite.

Part Three

Chapter Twenty-Four

Laec

Jessamine returned to the yard in her Fahyli leathers and boots, with Beazle clinging to her ponytail. Wisps of hair and curls she'd neglected floated about her flushed face. It took Laec a moment to adjust to the vast difference between her two personas, Calyx-Jess and Fahyli-Jess hardly looked like the same person.

"Ready?" He gave what he hoped was a reassuring smile. Her answering expression was a grimace.

Jess chose a patch of earth in the middle of the yard, a place that had been rubbed nearly bald by years of wrestling and fencing practice. The Fahyli gathered around, curious. Laec was curious too. He knew this remarkable magic worked but wondered how they did it.

"A little space, please." Jess knelt with the drawing of the seal in her hand.

The Fahyli shuffled back a few feet. Kite dropped cross-legged to the ground and Laec joined her.

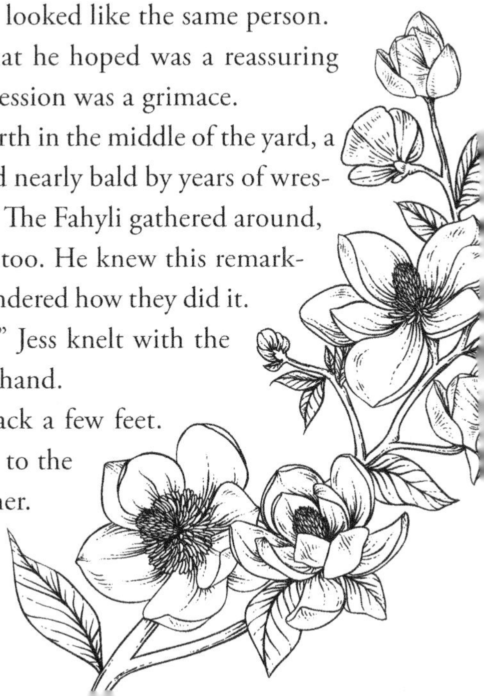

A moment later, they were all seated in a rough circle around Jessamine and Beazle.

Jess stared at the sketch, considering its details. Then she reached a hand over the soil and closed her eyes. Stems of tender seedlings curled out of the ground. Beazle squeaked and jumped from Jess's shoulder to the dirt. He curled into a ball, tucking his head between his wings. Like that, he was smaller than a pecan in the shell.

Solidago twisted upward, reaching for sun and sky, maturing, spreading branches lined with little yellow blossoms. Jess's eyes remained closed, but Beazle unwrapped himself and pushed his nose into the earth, overcome by what appeared to be a desire to dig a tunnel.

Jess opened her eyes as Beazle's back became covered in dirt. "Beaze! What are you—"

She leaned forward as if to grab him, but Laec had seen plenty of magical behavior in his life. Beazle was caught up in the *solidago's* spell.

"Just wait, Jess," he said. "Beazle isn't in danger."

Tensely, they watched Beazle disappear entirely into the dirt. Jess's eyes drifted closed again. She twitched, her eyelids tightening, her face turning this way and that. Her visions—Laec assumed she was having visions—went on for some time before her eyes popped open.

At the same time Beazle's head popped out of the earth at the base of the *solidago.* He looked up at Jess with a chuffing sound.

"Due east of here." Jess looked at Laec, then around the circle of the Fahyli, before settling on the crofter. "In a thick wood."

"How far?" Ian asked.

She looked pained, rubbing at her temple. "I don't know. Not exactly. It's through a mountain range, straight east and beyond, a dense green forest full of very old trees. After that, there's a… a swamp. A very wet place with… strange green lights? Sound familiar?"

The Fahyli exchanged bemused glances, but the crofter produced a parchment from a small satchel. He lay it flat on the ground and the group drew into a tighter circle to study the map.

"This is Solana City." Ian put a blunt finger on the marking of the lion's head, where the palace was. "Straight east, you said. Then?" He ran his finger slowly across the page.

"Past those mountains." Jess pointed out the range. "The river I saw must have been the Tadylat."

Ian nodded. "The Tadylat runs not far from Nasyk."

Jess recoiled as if punched, shooting the crofter a haunted look. "Nasyk?"

"It's a small agricultural town in the foothills. Past it is Syrgana Forest." He pointed to a large patch of green. "This must be where you were shown. Right?"

Jess nodded, pale. "I guess so."

Laec watched her face, not sure he liked the expressions there. Whatever had been bothering her when she'd arrived, it appeared to be growing in concern.

"What's the matter, Jess?" he asked.

Her luminous gray eyes flicked from the crofter to Laec. She lowered her voice. "Just… someone told me once they thought my mother might have been from Nasyk."

"Ah," Laec said, at a loss for any other response.

The crofter was watching them closely, Laec felt his measuring gaze taking in everything, weighing and marking.

He said: "Your mother passed away recently."

Jess nodded.

"And you never knew where she was from?"

"No sir."

"Who was it that thought she might have been from Nasyk?"

Laec watched the interaction between Jess and the crofter, fascinated. Ian had never struck him as someone who might be even remotely interested in the private lives of his Fahyli. They were on the brink of pinning down a location—even if it was a vague one—for the princesses, but Ian seemed caught by Jess's family mystery.

"My neighbor, Tad," Jess explained. "He said that my mother sometimes talked the way they do in Nasyk. I want to visit, but I haven't had time."

Ian grunted. He stroked the shadow of a beard on his chin as Kashmir gave an echoing grunt.

"I know Nasyk well. They do talk in a way of their own. Perhaps, if we are successful in finding the princesses, you can take the time to visit Nasyk on our return. The village is off the main road, but we pass the crossroads. If you're quick, we might make it work."

Jess stared at the crofter as though finding it difficult to understand him. Laec shared her surprise, but they didn't have time to ruminate further. He touched Jessamine's shoulder. "I've been through Syrgana. It's an easy place to get lost. Did you see anything else that might help us pinpoint the seal better?"

"The seal… I saw it, but things weren't clear. The other times, Beazle actually flew away and showed me what he was seeing in real time. It wasn't like that this time. Probably because the seal is so far away—it could take Beazle days to get there."

Ian leaned back on his haunches. "Which is why he tunneled."

Jess scooped up her bat. She stroked him, cleaning some of the dirt from his fur. "I didn't know what he was doing at first, but he says he needed to get close to the roots. He showed me a place that was swampy."

"With green lights," Kite added.

Jess nodded. "There were doors, and shallow water, and mangrove trees, and… and… voices. I got the impression that this part of the forest has a kind of magic. It felt like it didn't want to be seen, didn't have a name. Maybe that sounds crazy. It was just a feeling I got."

Laec looked over at Ian. "There is a section of forest beside Syrgana that defies being named. Someone I met on the road told me that every time they try to put it on a map, the name disappears. And whenever they try to erect a sign, it disappears too."

The crofter frowned. "Definitely an enchantment. We'll have to be careful." He cast his cool gaze back to Jess. "Be prepared to do this again, perhaps a number of times."

Jess replied, "Of course."

"Syrgana is a two day ride. If we ride hard, we might

get there in a day and a half." Ian looked around the group. "Make preparations. We leave in three hours."

Laec was checking Grex's tack as the stallion watched him with soft black eyes. Horses for the party of Fahyli, the crofter, and one Stavarjakian fae had been outfitted and geared up.

Kite and Panther stood holding their bridles, stroking their horses' noses and chatting quietly. Regalis was digging at something in his horse's hoof, while Digit and Sy peered over the crofter's shoulder at a map. The group was ready to leave, only Jessamine had yet to arrive. A stable hand held a spotted mare for her.

A silhouette materialized from the darkness at the edge of the courtyard, where an archway led into the kitchen gardens, but it wasn't Jess. It took Laec a moment to recognize Ilishec's shape. His uncle was moving like a criminal, a little stooped, like he didn't want to be seen. His head was down, but lifted as he neared the horses. The gardener had something tucked in his hand, held near his body. Laec put up a hand to show his uncle he'd seen him.

Ilishec lifted a finger requesting a minute, then arrowed for the crofter. His expression was now illuminated by the etherlights of the courtyard. He looked upset. Maybe even angry.

The gardener didn't spare so much as a greeting for the crofter. He leaned up into the taller man's face and spat: "If you do not bring her back wholly unharmed, I will see to it that you are shunned by the Scented Court until the day you die. There won't be a restaurant in the city that will welcome you, a merchant that will make a deal with you, or a carpenter that will fix your front step. Do not underestimate my ability to ruin your life, Ian."

The Fahyli watched the gardener with wide, shocked eyes.

"Ilishec, wait—" The crofter, who looked as surprised as Laec felt, put out a hand.

The gardener had already turned his back and was heading toward his nephew.

The look on Ilishec's face drove a spike of worry into Laec's heart. "What was that about?"

Ilishec gripped Laec's forearm, pulling him away from the Fahyli. "I need a private word."

Laec followed his uncle across the courtyard to the corner of the stables. He could feel Kite watching them.

"You should know uncle, I've had eyes on me ever since I got back from Rahamlar. Whatever you're about to say might be overheard by a certain wily raptor."

Ilishec's gaze darted skyward and skimmed the tops of the stable and the stone wall encircling the courtyard. "I don't see him."

Laec had been half jesting. He hadn't expected Ilishec to care. "Well, now you're really scaring me."

Ilishec pulled Laec close by his forearm, speaking just above a whisper. His uncle's brow was dewy with perspiration. "First, promise me that you won't let anything happen to her."

"Jessamine?" Laec almost laughed. "Uncle, that little Calyx is probably the deadliest of all of us. She'll be fine."

Ilishec's grip tightened, almost painfully so. "Just because she's deadly doesn't mean she has the wits to keep herself alive. I was against her joining the Fahyli from the start, she doesn't have the character for it, even if she has the mammal. She's young, she's naive, and she needs to be protected. Understand?"

"I'm surprised you think you have to ask. Is this what's got you tied up in knots? Trust me, she's with a very competent group—"

"Listen! This is important. Critical. I need you to take this." He shoved a sack of what felt like coins, and a small wooden box into Laec's hand. "You're going to Syrgana, yes? There is an unnamed village. It must be where the princesses are hiding. As far as I'm concerned, Jess and Beazle have as good as confirmed it. When you get there, ask for Calvatia. Show her what is inside this box and ask her for help. She'll know what to do. Whatever she gives you for me, deliver it as quickly as you can. Lives may depend upon it."

Laec looked down at the sack and the box. "What's in it?"

Ilishec looked harassed. "It's better you don't know. Ride swift and good luck. As soon as you are back, find me immediately. It may be already too late." He shook his head and muttered, "I don't know. I just don't know."

Laec tucked the things his uncle had given him into his messenger bag. He and Ilishec exchanged a hug and he watched the gardener go before returning to the Fahyli and Grex.

Jessamine came jogging down the steps. Laec

thought she might have been crying, but she could just as easily be tired. She redirected when she saw Ilishec, her brow furrowed.

"How is he?"

Ilishec took Jessamine's hands. "Don't you worry, Jessamine. Don't you worry about a thing. I'll take good care of them. You concentrate on getting back in once piece, as swiftly as you can. Yes?"

Jess threw her arms around the gardener. He kissed the top of her head as she clung to him. Laec thought they looked like a father and a beloved daughter.

After a lengthy moment, Ilishec said with a smile in his voice: "I do have to go, Jessamine. I'm needed."

She released him and stepped away, sniffing. "Of course."

Ilishec touched her cheek and then strode back the way he had come.

Laec walked Jessamine to where her horse was waiting. "How is who?"

She hooked her foot in the stirrup and swung up into the saddle, looking more comfortable there than the last time he'd seen her on horseback. "Moony. Wisteria's butterfly. He's ill."

"Oh. And where is Beazle?"

Jess waved a hand dismissively. "This is dinner time. He'll follow." Jess looked around at everyone. "Sorry to keep you waiting."

Laec thought that Ian just seemed relieved that she'd shown up.

The crofter spoke from atop his horse. "We'll arrive

in Linke by midnight, sleep, then get an early start. Stay together, we ride fast."

Laec and Grex brought up the rear as they passed the palace gates. Tully would be somewhere near and Erasmus and Ferrugin were probably observing the party from great heights. Laec assumed that Kashmir—bears could be fast over short distances, but they couldn't keep up with galloping horses over many miles—was not coming. Mae was on the saddle in front of Sy, cradled in her own specially made hollow, with a soft leather strap she could slide beneath. Laec thought the coon looked more comfortable on a horse's back than any rodent had a right to.

Outside the city, the road became wide and flat where the horses settled into a trot they could maintain. The party steadily closed the distance between themselves and Syrgana.

Chapter Twenty-Five

Jessamine

On arrival at a local inn in the small village of Linke, they fed and watered the horses before sleeping on narrow lumpy cots in small rooms—the size of cleaning closets back at the palace. They rose early for breakfast, bought a packed lunch from the innkeeper, and were back on the road before most of the village was awake.

The crofter and Panther set a ground-eating pace, the rest followed in pairs: Sy and Digit, Regalis and Laec, Kite and Jessamine. They drew fascinated stares from passersby and peasants working in the fields. Though they wore nondescript boiled leather and leggings, not Solana livery, Jessamine suspected that most people knew who they were. Ferrugin and Erasmus hardly made themselves known, flying ahead, scouting, but how many raccoons did one see riding on the back of a horse? Plus there was some-

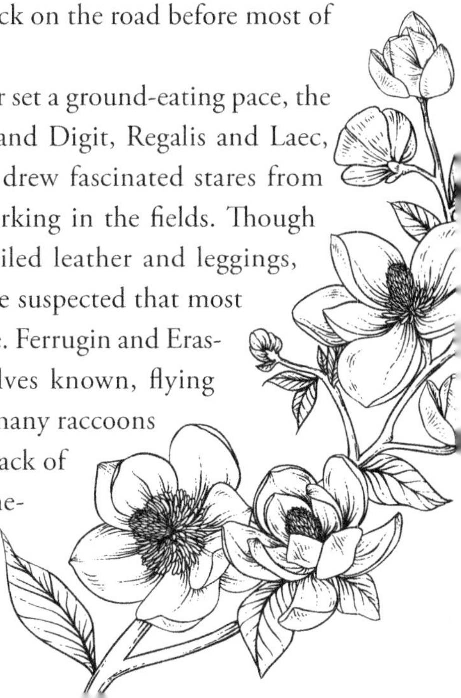

thing in the way the Fahyli carried themselves—a quiet confidence. Jessamine hoped she one day also embodied their self-assurance. She felt at home on horseback now, but the knife strapped to her thigh felt more like an unwelcome hitch-hiker than an extension of her person.

There were still plenty of sights to admire as they made their way from valley to valley, dotted with orchards full of gnarled snow-dusted trees. Fluffy gray clouds drifted overhead like fleecy ornaments and the mountaintops wore caps of pure white. Piles of hay and wrappings of burlap had been put around delicate fruit-bearing vines and trees, looking much the same as the orchards and gardens around the palace.

The group had to slow as they came to a busy crossroad, falling in with wagon traffic. Jess stared at the signpost pointing south. Nasyk was hand-painted in bright yellow letters. She felt Laec's eyes on her.

She drew her mare closer to Grex. "Did you come this way on your journey from Stavarjak?"

"I came from the Hashe estate, which is further south of Nasyk, so I never visited the village. I crossed the Tamyrat and passed through Syrgana too, but also further south of here. This is new territory for me."

After the crossroad, the traffic thinned, and Ian had them trotting as the wilderness between the mountains closed around them. The ground became rockier and rougher, farmland grew sparse, the trees thickened and the air cooled. Remote terrace farms could be seen up the mountain sides, long skinny orchards layered vertically like a cake.

They stopped in a quiet grove for lunch, where they could water the horses and rest. After lunch the road widened, though traffic was still minimal.

Jess heard a sound like a steady distant thunder, growing in volume. She asked whoever cared to answer, "Is there a storm coming?"

Regalis looked over his shoulder. "It's the whirlpool."

Jess's eyes widened. "Where the Tadylat and Tamyrat cross?"

"That's the one."

Jess had been told about this amazing natural wonder of Solana in school geography classes. Never did she expect she might one day see it for herself. The whirlpool was a unique feature that drew sightseers from all over Ivryndi. Both rivers were wide, deep, and fast-flowing. The Tamyrat was frigid while the Tadylat was merely cold. The two watery behemoths twisted and snaked their way across the geography of the continent before they, fatefully and violently, crossed paths. The resulting collision was described in books as having epic proportions—there were even stories of unfortunate villagers becoming mesmerized by the swirling water and falling in—as the waters became one, blending and churning and frothing, before carrying on through the channels gouged out over time.

The thunder of the whirlpool was a constant presence, steadily growing in intensity. The road led to a bridge with a low railing, over a deep scar in the earth carved by the rivers over thousands of years. Mist coated their hair and clothing and made the horses appear darker in color. The air was so thick with humidity that it was almost a fog.

A rotting sign had once displayed a map, but the image had become unreadable.

The crofter indicated they should dismount and let the horses graze. As one they moved to look over the edge. Far below was the whirlpool, more spectacular than Jessamine's textbooks had described. The rivers poured into the gorge and clashed into a swirling bowl of bright teal opaque water. The dimple in the center was large enough to suck down a ship, which was why—Laec explained—both rivers had sturdy and well-functioning docks built far up and downstream, so that these watery highways, used by traders and militaries alike, could continue to perform their critical duty: quickly carrying goods back and forth, connecting north Ivryndian kingdoms to south. Naturally, there were stories of inexperienced sailors, rafters, or bargemen who poorly timed their exit then had no choice but to face the whirlpool. It was said that there was a fortune's worth of treasure and goods snagged and smashed along the bottom of the gorge like so much jam, never to be retrieved again.

Along the sides of the gorge were rocky outcroppings and clusters of trees clinging to life. There appeared to be caves, too. That was another aspect of the whirlpool's mythology. Were the caves made by fae or men? Or were they natural, simply gouged out of the rock over time? Had they once been lived in by brave but foolhardy people? One thing was certain, any explorer who wished to visit them—unless they had wings or powerful magic—could not do so without risking their neck.

Ian let the Fahyli admire the whirlpool until the

horses were refreshed. They crossed the bridge, leading their nervous mounts rather than riding them. The bridge was a marvel of engineering, built of sturdy beams and metal braces. It formed an elegant arch over the whirlpool, with long ramps that extended well past the edges of the gorge.

"This is Syrgana," said Laec as they crossed. "See how the trees are different?"

Jess had been so preoccupied with the whirlpool that she hadn't noticed that the forest on the other side of the bridge was completely unlike the one they'd just left. The trees were fuller, shorter, fatter, and far more gnarled than the towering, creaking evergreens that had been part of the landscape for the last several hours. The ground was mossy and spongy, full of lumpy tussocks and dotted with little pools of greenish water. Vines and creepers twisted around every tree. In summer, in flower, they would add beauty, but right now they made the forest eerie.

"A word before we continue," said Ian, beckoning them closer before they remounted. "We're heading into a forest that is known to be home to outcasts. If we are approached, keep your weapons sheathed. This land belongs to Solana, but the monarchs don't interfere with the runaways and refugees who are drawn here."

Kite glowered. "Don't you mean brigands and thieves?"

The crofter ignored her, looking at Panther instead. "Keep Tully out of sight unless I signal otherwise. That goes for the rest of you, too. No duplicating." Ian shot a warning look at Kite. "I mean it, Kite. Keep that raptor of yours under control."

"Yes, Crofter," she murmured.

"We're here for information, not conflict. Don't invite trouble. We are not to give them reason to believe Solana has turned against them. We keep the peace. Understood?"

They said they understood, and Ian let them mount.

As the trees closed in around them, and they fell into pairs again, Jess caught snatches of conversation between Regalis and the crofter. She thought she heard them mention Rahamlar unseelie. She nudged her horse to ride a little closer. Digit and his gelding were behind Regalis. He shuffled his mount over to make room for Jessamine.

"Why would they be in those parts?" Regalis was asking. "Are they not trespassing?"

The crofter shook his head, his body swaying gently back and forth with the movement of his horse. "They have permission to look for the princesses. The king had to give it to the prince when he asked, otherwise it would appear we have something to hide."

Regalis ducked to the side to avoid a low hanging branch. "I don't like it."

Ian grunted. "Neither do I, but what can we do?"

Regalis looked up as though expecting to catch a glimpse of the sky, but the canopy was too thick. "Find the princesses first."

"Thanks to Jess and Beazle," Ian murmured, "we will hopefully do just that."

A warm flush of pride filled her chest. She'd be sure to relay Ian's subtle appreciation of their contribution to Beazle when he woke. She felt Digit's gaze, and looked over to see him smiling.

The deeper they pressed into the forest, the more arcane and enchanted the landscape grew. Trees became deformed things full of knots and lousy with plate-sized fungal growths stacking themselves around trunks like steps. Thick limbs crisscrossed over the double-track road, blocking out the remaining daylight with an impossible tangle. Conversation dwindled, then ceased, as the soundscape became rich with the songs of frogs, crickets, and other less easily identified creatures. The air grew heavy. The double-track narrowed to a single-track, then to a tacky trail that meandered back and forth in a nonsensical way. Mist gathered in ditches and moved between tree trunks like gently probing fingers. Before long, it seemed there was no trail at all, only vague overgrown paths going every direction.

The crofter pulled up and looked back at Jessamine. "Are we still going the right way?"

Everyone stopped and Jessamine dismounted, going to her knees on the moist, cool forest floor.

Calling Beazle from his hunting, she conjured a stem of *solidago*, thinking about Princess Serya's seal. Her own vision went blank as Beazle sent her images from the sky, looking down from above dense leaves. The vertigo had always passed quickly, but this time it lingered, bordering on nausea. Beazle's images swayed back and forth like a pendulum, blurring and fuzzing. Breaks in the canopy gaped like toothy mouths. Flashes of green light blinked from these gaps, still swaying back and forth, making it impossible for Jessamine to see the source. Mentally, she begged Beazle to stop. When her vision returned, she found she had sprawled on her side. Digit and Laec were standing over her, looking concerned.

She pushed herself up to sitting. "It's like it doesn't want to be found."

Laec handed her a waterskin. "I think that means we're headed in the right direction."

Jess took long swigs of water. They waited until Beazle returned before pushing on ahead. Beazle chirruped, sounding tired, and crawled into Jess's hair. She felt him relax against her skull and go to sleep. As the dim light grew dimmer still, the horses began to behave oddly. They kept wanting to steer left. Only Laec's stallion, Grex, didn't seem affected. Jessamine guessed that a stallion from Stavarjak had encountered more enchantments than other horses, which is what she suspected they were dealing with. Neither the crofter nor the Fahyli seemed to notice this behavior. Jess kept having to tell them to correct their path. The horses resisted, tossing their heads and nickering in annoyance. Regalis's horse turned in two full circles before he finally went in the direction he was told. Jessamine took the lead so she wouldn't have to keep getting their attention when they wandered off. Laec brought up the rear.

Suddenly Jess felt like her ears were full of water. She shook her head, trying to get rid of the feeling, but it only grew. When Laec spoke, she couldn't understand him, because now it sounded like she was underwater.

"I can't hear you," Jess replied as he pushed Grex alongside Jessamine's mare.

"I said, there's a spell or something," Laec told her in slow, enunciated phrases.

She stuck a finger in her ear. Panther was shaking his head, while Sy flexed his jaw to make his eardrums pop. Regalis had the heel of one hand against his temple, while Kite just looked irritated. The horses were shaking their heads and flicking their ears, and still trying to walk to the left.

When Jess's eardrums popped and her hearing cleared, she let out a huge sigh of relief.

Laec shook his head like a dog shaking off water. "That was awful. Looks like the horses are feeling better, too."

Jess nodded, flexing her jaw. Ahead she spotted something through the trees. A green glow. "We're on the right track, though. I saw those lights in the *solidago* vision." Jess directed Laec's attention to the glowing green things ahead of them. "What are they?"

The answer came to her as they drew close to a trunk decorated with whimsical little light sources. "They're mushrooms!"

"Head's up," shouted Panther from the back.

"Not alone!" called Sy, at the same time.

"What?" Jess turned in her saddle.

"Heeyaaaaaugh!"

A scream reverberated through the trees, followed by more screams. Jess's mare whinnied with fright as dozens of sturdy-looking people dropped from the canopy and popped out from under carpets of moss.

Jess's mare screamed again and reared up on her hind legs. Jess was getting better at riding but she was not ready for her mare to rise up. She flew off, landing hard on her back. From her vantage point, the world was full of people in earth-colored clothing and horses' legs. Men in hoods had climbed onto Grex's back and were in the process of pulling Laec from his saddle.

Hide, Beaze! Jess thought, as she scrambled away from the thundering hooves, catching glimpses of Ian and the Fahyli dealing with their own attackers.

I am hiding. I'm in your hair, remember?

Right.

They were vastly outnumbered. Panther was pulled to the ground and brought to his knees by two hooded men. Ian, roaring his displeasure, was already on the ground and engaged in a fistfight with a fellow who matched him for size. Another fellow, this one broader than he was tall, jumped on the crofter's back, wrapping a thick arm around his throat. Ian choked and his face turned red. Regalis had three smaller people draped from his neck and shoulders, he was swinging around trying to free himself. Legs flew outward, one of them clocking Kite in the side of the head. She went sprawling into a thick shrub.

Erasmus screamed from somewhere, followed by a human scream of pain.

Oh, oh, thought Beazle.

There was a burst of blue-gray raptors and hundreds of Erasmus duplicates zoomed around the forest, attacking the hooded men in a storm. Someone swung his club and connected with a duplicate, which exploded in a puff of feathers. His success seemed to stun him at first, then he screamed at his cohorts how the birds could be dealt with. Those who weren't wrestling with the Fahyli began to swing their clubs. Someone screamed as a bird flew at his face, ripping and clawing. A dog-sized duplicate of Erasmus ripped the hood off another, exposing short dark blond hair and a face that looked surprisingly sweet. He was lifted by his cape, gurgling, and strung up in a tree. Duplicates vaporized as they were clubbed down. The original was found, captured and wrapped up in a cloak, squawking and screeching.

Thanks to the crofter's earlier command, the Fahyli allowed themselves to be subdued and brought to their knees. Roughly, they were dragged into a semicircle and disarmed. The horses were corralled. Jessamine was dragged from the bushes and tossed unceremoniously in front of Panther, who was bleeding from his nose. She struggled to her knees, noticing that Kite was covered in mud, like she'd been shoved face first in the muck. She kept her eyes on the ground. Hiding rage, or shame? Jess couldn't tell.

The largest of the men pulled his hood back, revealing a misshapen, pock-marked countenance. His upper lip had a ridge of scarring that gave him a perpetual snarl. He was stooped, but big and muscular. A curved sword hung from his belt, a detail that gave Jess pause. These hoods hadn't used deadly weapons. At least, not yet.

"Who is in charge here?" the pock-marked one bellowed.

"I am," replied the crofter with a calm that impressed Jessamine. "What right have you to attack us?"

He laughed then spat, his hands on his hips. "You're in our territory. We have every right."

Ian replied with steely authority, even though he was on his knees. "This land belongs to King Agir and Queen Esha. It is not your territory."

The scarred man sneered. "You think so? He thinks this land doesn't belong to us, lads."

The hooded men responded with derisive laughter, spitting, and growls of displeasure.

Scarface bent at the waist and leered into Ian's face. "Point it out to us on a map. Show us the deed and titles. Prove they own it, and we'll leave. Won't we lads?"

More laughter, but it was silenced as the leader drew his scimitar from his belt, slowly, a deadly light glinting in his eyes. "I'll save you the trouble, since you can't prove anything, and dispatch you and your trespassing cohorts right here. Your blood will water the forest floor."

He brought the blade to beneath the crofter's chin. So much for not using deadly force.

The others seemed to take this as a signal. In a flash, there was a blade at every throat.

Ian lifted his chin a little, betraying no fear. "I am the crofter of Solana, and these are my Fahyli. We are not here to interfere, to steal, or to in any other way damage you or the forest. We are looking for two princesses from Rahamlar. If we do not find them, we will leave. You'll never know we were here."

"I don't care if your mother is Queen Elphame herself," spat the scarred man, pressing his blade into Ian's neck. A trickle of blood ran down the crofter's throat.

"I know you!" Laec said loudly, looking at the young man with dark blond hair who had been rescued from the tree and was now holding Grex by the bridle. "You warned Lady Çifta before she was imprisoned in Rahamlar. She made a portrait of you."

The young man's eyes widened. The scarred man looked at the young man, then at Laec. The hesitation was long enough that Laec was encouraged.

"Lady Çifta is grateful for what you did," he told the young man. "She would like to know that Princesses Serya and Isabey are alive and well."

The pock-marked one looked at the younger fellow with something like respect. Jessamine realized that the younger man had clout. Maybe he was a soldier, but Jessamine thought he looked more like a farmer's boy. He came closer to the group.

"You know Lady Çifta?" he asked Laec.

Remarkably, the scarred man did not interfere, though he did not remove his blade from Ian's neck, either. In fact, no blades were lowered.

Laec had a hand on the wrist of the hood guarding him, keeping the blade back from his jugular. "I helped her escape. So did the raptor you're suffocating under that cloak. We are friends of Lady Çifta's, and of the princesses as well. We've come to help. Will you take us to them?"

The young man considered Laec. He sent a signal to the men keeping the bird bound. They pulled away the cloak so Erasmus could breathe, keeping his wings pinned down. He screamed, which made many wince. Jess wondered what he and Kite were saying to one another. For that matter, she wondered how far away Tully was, and how she felt about her fae being bashed about. She hadn't interfered, which Jess thought showed incredible restraint. Jess hadn't been beaten up, she'd spent too much time scrambling around on the ground. But if she had been abused, Beazle would have reacted. That was certain.

Maybe, Beazle thought. *Maybe not. The crofter is smart. I trust his judgment.*

Jess cocked an eyebrow. *Are you sure? He has a blade at his neck.*

The crofter spoke. "We could have fought back. We had weapons, and the skill to use them. We have other animals, dangerous ones who scented you before you showed yourselves. This proves we wish you no harm."

The scarred leader sneered. "What animals? That sounds like a load of fish guts to me." He barked. "Don't you believe him! Its a ploy."

Ian said, "Pan."

On his knees near Jess, Panther bowed his head.

Tully screamed from not far away. The roar of the big cat made the hoods jump. Some swore, others shifted uncomfortably.

"She's a two-hundred-fifty-pound feline," Ian said. "So you know I'm not lying. Just one of four other familiars with their eyes on you right now."

Mae, Beazle, and Ferrugin. The hidden three were not nearly as scary as Tully, but the hoods didn't know that.

See? Smart, thought Beazle.

Having made them sufficiently uneasy, Ian repeated the original request. "If you know the whereabouts of Princesses Serya and Isabey of Rahamlar, we humbly ask that you take us to them. King Osvitan has died. Their kingdom is in great need of their presence."

"How did you get this far?" the scarred man replied, his tone gruff, his manner chastened but not contrite.

"We have a little magic of our own," Ian said, leaving things vague.

Jess was grateful that neither Laec nor Ian had brought her to their attention.

The young man said in an authoritative voice: "Let them go. We can execute them later if we discover they are lying. But if they're not…"

He didn't finish his sentence, but held out a hand to Laec. "I'm Shade. The irate one is Fixnix."

"I'm Laec, that's Ian—"

"Save your introductions," snarled Fixnix, sheathing his sword. He yanked Ian up, then shoved him forward. The crofter just caught himself from sprawling over a root. "Your names don't matter here. Move."

CHAPTER TWENTY-SIX

JESSAMINE

FIXNIX HAD SOME of his men lead the horses while the rest followed the Fahyli or melted away into the trees. In what seemed like a few minutes, the forest grew very dark. The glowing mushrooms increased in both number and variety as they traveled, and grew brighter as the last of the filtered daylight faded away.

I'm hungry, Beazle thought as Jess picked her way through the increasingly swampy terrain, keeping close to Laec. Her boots were soaked through. She was thankful the water wasn't too cold. Speaking of water, she was thirsty, and her waterskin was in her saddlebag.

Let me hunt. I won't be seen, I promise.

Jess didn't know how Beazle could make such a promise, but she didn't have the heart to make him wait. He was tiny and had very little fat on him, so not eating when he was hungry was dangerous, much more dangerous than these hoods. Even

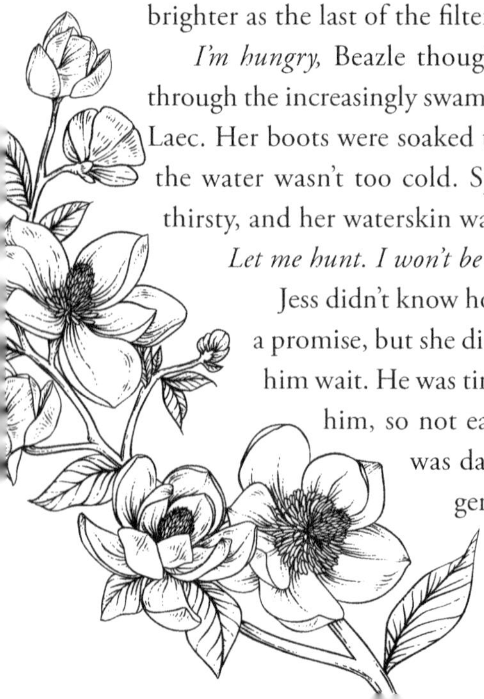

if he was spotted, the odds that the hoods would realize he was a familiar and not a wild bat were remote.

Go on, she returned. *Fill your belly, little love.*

He dropped into a fold in her collar then crawled down the front of her tunic to her waist. She needn't have been so concerned. It was so dark now that no human eye would detect him. He fluttered from her waist, dodging legs and headed straight for a cluster of slender-stemmed mushrooms casting a blue glow across the tree trunks. Beazle sniffed at the fungi, deciding that the mushrooms themselves were less interesting than the insects they attracted. He flitted around, entertained by their strange surroundings as he snatched his dinner out of the air. The mushrooms now included blue, orange and yellow ones. Some of these growths were as flat and wide as plates, other were fat-stemmed and looked like matrons in spotted dresses. Still others were tall and slender, like warped candles wearing little caps.

The Fahyli were led to the edge of an overgrown riverbank, where algae-coated rafts were lined up along a rotting dock.

"The horses will be stabled." Shade made a gesture, but Jess wasn't sure if it was an order to the hoods or an explanation to the crofter.

They were divided into groups and put aboard leaky, barely buoyant vessels. One after the next, the rafts were untethered and pushed out into the flow, steered by a hood with a bargepole. They slipped into deeper and wilder woods, carried along by a strong current. Frogs went silent while the rafts passed, taking up their music again moments later. Thick reeds shrouded the riverbanks while gnarled roots crawled through the soil, creeping down to the water like witchy fingers. The illuminated mushrooms had sprouted all over the place, and lit their surroundings with diffused multicolored patches of light that weren't quite sufficient to make out the hood's faces, shrouded in the shadows of their cloaks.

Jessamine pointed out a round door carved into a fat gnarled tree trunk to Laec. A little round window beside the door was lit from within. Soon these doors and windows were everywhere—on trees making islands in the middle of the river, and all along the banks. Wooden docks and walkways snaked through thick reeds. Trees with thick trunks had many windows stacked vertically, suggesting the interior of some of these homes were several stories high. A door opened and a figure in a dress emerged, wearing a shawl and holding a bucket. She froze as the rafts passed by, dark eyes reflecting the light from a cluster of blue mushrooms that lined her walkway. More tree-dwellers emerged, some had children with them, others stood alone or in pairs, backlit by the light inside their homes.

They drew up to the dock of a large island, slipping between the mangrove trunks encircling its edges. Fixnix and the hoods escorted them along a narrow mushy trail snaking its way between the trees. A woman in a ratty cloak materialized to talk with Shade. They talked quietly, gesturing to the Fahyli and the crofter. Shade pointed out Laec and she reacted with surprise, her spine straightening. She retreated into a tree, leaving the door open enough for Jessamine to see a set of narrow steps.

Beazle landed on Jess's vest and crawled up to her collar, then beneath it.

Tasty bugs. I like this swamp.

I'm glad you're pleased, Jess thought wryly. Her stomach gurgled—she hadn't eaten since the whirlpool.

They were made to wait, shifting from foot to foot on the spongy trail, until the woman reappeared. She spoke to Shade, who beckoned to Laec. The crofter made a move to follow but Fixnix put a hand on his chest.

"Have a seat," Fixnix rumbled.

Go with Laec, Jess thought. *Be my eyes and ears.*

Beazle didn't need to be asked twice. He landed on Laec's sleeve, and Laec lifted his cuff, letting the bat hide beneath it.

Jessamine found a stump to sit on. She pulled her legs up and sat cross-legged, looking down into her lap. She closed her eyes as Beazle relayed what he was seeing and hearing.

Ducking under the low doorway, Laec followed Shade up a few steps. They hit a platform and then descended. The steps led to a natural tunnel encrusted with roots. Moisture seeped from everywhere and dripped from the ceiling. The humid tunnel did not last long and they soon ascended another stairway, this one made of roots. The stairs became a ladder, which took them up inside a fat tree, then dumped them out on a swinging bridge. There were bridges everywhere, swaying and creaking, linking many trees as far as could be seen in the poor light.

Shade took Laec to a large treehouse with a round front door. It was invisible from the ground, choked by foliage and knotted branches. The woman tapped a staccato rhythm on the door, then pushed inside.

Laec followed her into a round room lit with yellow mushrooms strategically placed in alcoves. Though Jess had not met them, and the images Beazle sent were grainy, she recognized the princesses immediately. There was an older fae female present who she did not know.

Princess Isabey's hair was done in a high updo like a crown, exposing sharply pointed ears. The gray cast to her skin confirmed her heritage. She and Serya shared dark eyes, dark hair, and small pointed noses, but that was the extent of their likeness. The fae female looked like an older sister. She sat on the end of a bed, a veil draped over her hair.

As Princess Serya, her dark hair a tumble of frizzy curls that swallowed her shoulders, got to her feet, Isabey moved close, offering an arm for support.

"Laec. Welcome. Shade tells us you are acquainted with Lady Çifta—that you helped her escape our brother," Serya said.

In an attempt to respect their royalty, Laec gave an awkward bow in the small space. The ceiling was a little low so he had to stoop.

"Yes, I am a friend of Lady Çifta's. I and the others mean to help you too. I hope you believe me."

Princess Isabey beamed and shot her sister a hopeful look.

Serya smiled knowingly. "You wouldn't be alive right now if we didn't believe you."

"We caught them just inside the inner ring," said

Shade. "Fixnix might have slain them if this one hadn't recognized me." At a look from Laec, he amended: "Tried to slay them."

The older fae woman lifted her veil. An oversized beetle with markings like eyes on his back, crawled over her shoulder and fell into her lap. He landed upside down, legs pedaling at the air. She gently turned him over and put him in the crook of her arm, his antennae twitching. Jessamine recognized him from her studies: a click beetle. The distinctive circular marks were defensive markings to make predators think twice before attacking him.

Beazle's attention homed in on the clumsy, overgrown bug.

I could live off him for a week.

She's flora fae, thought Jessamine, marking the woman's faded but ethereal loveliness. *Nearing the end of her magic. He's probably dying.*

"—the first to breach your magic," Princess Serya was saying to the elder fae.

Focus. I don't want to miss anything.

Beazle's senses sharpened on the conversation.

Setting the click beetle on the coverlet, the flora fae stood. "How did you find us?"

Jessamine could see one of her ears and was surprised how little point was left.

Laec withdrew the painting of Serya's seal from an inner pocket. "There is one among the Calyx who has magic that finds lost things." He handed the page to Serya. "Lady Çifta painted this from memory. We used Calyx magic to find it, and subsequently, you."

Shade and Isabey moved closer as she unfolded the drawing. Princess Serya looked from the drawing to her hand, where the original glimmered. "It's a good thing she does not work for our brother."

"Clever lady," murmured Shade.

Laec added: "She also made a portrait of you, Shade. Which was how I recognized you."

Jessamine was jolted out of the vision when someone shook her by the shoulder. Her head snapped up. Panther was leaning close. He whispered, "Are you alright?"

She whispered back, "I'm with Laec."

Panther looked startled, then impressed. "Sorry," he mouthed.

Jess let her face drop again and closed her eyes.

The flora fae was offering her hand to Laec, her manner had changed in the time Jess's concentration had been broken. She looked impressed. "It's not often we meet someone from Queen Elphame's court. My name is Calvatia, and this handsome fellow"—she pointed to her beetle—"is Jack."

Beazle felt Laec's body tense with surprise.

"Calvatia! My Uncle Ilishec gave me something to give you, and to bring back whatever you give me." He took a small sack from his belt and loosened the ties, pulling out a small snuffbox and a letter. The sack jingled like it contained coins. He handed the lot to Calvatia.

She brightened. "The gardener is your uncle?"

Laec nodded. "Whatever it is, it's of great importance. He is anxious for your response."

Exchanging a bemused look with the princesses, Calvatia lowered herself onto the bed. Concern spread across her features as she read the letter. Her hands trembled as she set the letter aside and picked up the box. Slowly, she opened the lid. A bit of fabric spilled out. She gave a little cry and snapped the lid closed, eyes wide with horror. Her complexion was ashen when she handed the box back to Laec. "You must burn this as soon as possible."

Laec took it. "Why?"

Calvatia put a hand protectively around Jack. His antennae were twitching madly. "It is not a danger at this moment, but in a matter of days it can do great harm. It must be burned. It is the only way."

The princesses and Shade looked curiously back and forth from Calvatia to Laec.

"May I look?" Laec asked.

She shuddered. "It is a horrible sight. Consider yourself warned."

Shade, Serya and Isabey crowded around Laec as he opened the box. Beazle crawled out from under Laec's cuff for a better look.

"You have a tiny bat on your hand!" cried Isabey, sounding delighted. "He is the most adorable creature I have ever seen."

Jess smiled as Beazle preened at these words.

"Careful or he'll get an inflated ego," Laec murmured. He tilted the box so that light illuminated the contents.

Jess felt herself suck in a breath as Beazle relayed the contents of the box to her.

It was Moony. He was dead. An inch-long growth

had emerged from the top of his little head, a pale stem with a softly rounded tip.

Princess Serya put a hand over her mouth. "Ugh!"

Isabey uttered an unladylike oath.

Jess's heart ached. Wisteria would be in pieces.

"What is that?" asked Shade, his lip curled with disgust.

"A parasitic fungus," said Calvatia with a shudder. She was covering her beetle with a hand. "Please close it. I can't bear to have that thing in the same room as Jack."

Laec closed the snuffbox. "I'll burn it as soon as I can."

Shade held out a hand. "I'll do it now."

Laec handed it over and Shade slipped out of the room.

Calvatia relaxed. "Tell the gardener I am sorry, but I have nothing for him. There's no cure for this parasite."

"How do you know?" Laec sounded as disappointed as Jess felt.

"I know about fungi," Calvatia told him. "I am connected to several species, a few with magical qualities. The bioluminescent mushrooms that light this room, and the forest, are my handiwork. Mine and Jack's." She looked sad as she scooped Jack onto her lap. "We are in the sunset of our magic. But for another year or two, we can serve those who live here, and keep enemies from our doorstep."

Laec gestured to the quaint lights. "We have bioluminescent mushrooms in Stavarjak, but none so pretty as yours. How do you know my uncle?"

Calvatia smiled. "I attended Discovery when I was twelve. Ilishec hadn't been the Honorable Gardener for very long. I know he wanted to offer us a place, but fungi are not desirable to the Solana monarchs. I had never felt appreciated for our abilities until we met Ilishec. We remained friends after our Discovery, and exchanged letters until we moved here, where there is no postal service. I told him that we had been offered safety and a home in the unnamed swamp at the heart of Syrgana. They would let us use our magic as much as we liked, we would be fed, and paid a little. We have been happy here."

Shade overheard the last bit as he came in and closed the door. "Its her magic that keeps people from finding this place."

Calvatia sat a little straighter. "When we were at our strongest, my magic had far-reaching effects. We could erase the memory of those who stumbled in by accident, and repel attempts to mark us on maps and signs. Those effects fade a little more every year, but we will put our efforts into maintaining the protective barrier we have grown around this place for as long as we can. We are a safe place for people in trouble, whatever the reason…"

"Nobility afraid for their lives, for example," Princess Serya said pointedly.

"Princesses, I have terrible news," said Laec. "You may wish to sit."

"If it is about our father's passing, we already know." Isabey was now stroking Beazle's head and Beazle was pressing against her fingertip, stretching his neck like a kitten.

Focus, Beaze.

I am focused. She is helping me focus.

If you were a cat, you'd be purring. That's not focusing, that's relaxing.

I am not a cat, I'm a bat. We're much smarter than cats. And shush. We're missing things.

"I'm very sorry for your loss," said Laec, awkwardly holding his hand up so that Isabey could continue to stroke Beazle. "King Agir and Queen Esha have a great desire to see you take your place as queen as quickly as possible."

Princess Serya didn't quite smile, but pleasure shone in her eyes. "That means a great deal. We have been talking about how best to return, but I must admit, I'm still not certain."

"Who is we?"

"Fixnix, Shade, Calvatia, and others. We left our home after there was an attempt on my life. If you think that I made the decision to leave in haste, I didn't. Shade, who is the only guard that we trusted, had been surveying the sentiment among the guards." Serya's lips twisted with displeasure. "The dominant feeling toward me is—at best—doubt that I have the strength to lead Rahamlar strong. At worst… well, let's just say many are not interested in serving a crippled queen. A cripple? Maybe they could live with. A queen? They've had before. Both at the same time?" She shook her head with a sharp bird-like movement.

Laec glowered. "Whatever the sentiment, Princess, we mean to install you."

"The citizens will come to love you. As I love you," said Isabey, sweetly. She scooped Beazle up and looked at Laec. "How is Lady Çifta?"

She smells like cinnamon, Beazle thought, soaking in the warmth of Isabey's palm.

You little flirt.

"She is anxious to see you returned to your rightful place—not only because she cares about you, but because she also needs your help. Her father has not released her from the betrothal to your brother. Are you aware that he imprisoned her for several weeks after you left?"

Princess Serya sighed and lowered herself into a chair. "We knew he was controlling her. We also knew that she escaped, though not how. Our brother was… is… furious. If Kazery does not revoke the betrothal, then Faraçek won't either."

Laec scowled. "Why would he insist on marrying a woman who does not want him?"

Serya leaned back in the chair, looking every bit as queenly as if she were on a throne. "You don't know my brother. He hates being made a fool of, outsmarted, or humiliated. If Kazery allows it, Faraçek will marry her and make her pay for the rest of her life."

"But when you become queen, you can rescue her from such a fate," Isabey said, sitting on a stool and cradling Beazle.

"Of course."

Laec crossed his arms with resolve, his voice hard. "So let's get you safely back to your home before Faraçek declares you deceased and has himself crowned."

Isabey looked up. "He cannot just have himself crowned. Our laws say that no coronation can take place until the current monarch—or in our case, the next-in-line—has been formally declared deceased. To do so, a body is required. In the event a body cannot be found, then sworn witnesses."

"Suppose Faraçek bribes the lawyers and ministers? Do you trust them to hold your birthright for you when it sounds as though many of the citizens are against you?"

A smug smile lifted the corners of Serya's lips. "That is why we took one additional step. We have an item that Faraçek covets. He will not be crowned without it."

"Which is?" Laec looked from princess to princess.

The women exchanged a look, then looked to Calvatia, who said enigmatically, "He is not duplicitous."

Isabey set Beazle on her knee then began to unpin her hair. Her locks fell away, revealing a circlet. Gently, she lifted it from her head.

Jess suppressed a shiver as Beazle sent her images of the crown. The design was simple, but there was something sinister about it. It was little more than a circlet, and did not glimmer. The metal was rusted and the band ran around the head in waves. At the front was the shape of a bird with its wings outstretched. Two glittering black stones represented the creature's eyes.

"This is an artifact that many believe lost. It has never been lost. It has been hidden away, its whereabouts known only to our family. It is Queen Toryan's crown."

Jess didn't know who Queen Toryan was, but Laec must. His eyes widened.

Serya read his reaction. "I see you have heard the stories of Queen Toryan."

"Only about Toryan's Massacre. This is not the crown that the monarch of Rahamlar wears, though. Is it?"

"You are right. We have another wrought of silver that our father wore. Toryan's Crown has been hidden because she was a villain, a deceitful unseelie queen who subverted our kingdom and ravaged the human and seelie populations. The crown cannot be destroyed, or even lost, as far as we know. There are stories of it being taken many miles out into the Valdivian and dropped overboard. Yet before the sailors returned to our rivers, it reappeared on the velvet pillow that had held it for centuries. It is said to be holding Toryan's power within it, keeping it for her unseelie heir. That is the reason the Rahamlar crown passes first to offspring with human blood before passing to any with unseelie blood—to keep unseelie off the throne."

Princess Serya gazed at the crown with unease. "It is Toryan that enchanted it. It is waiting for an heir that she would have deemed worthy. It certainly won't be me, as I am human, but it could be our brother."

Laec looked doubtful. "For hundreds of years it has been waiting, what makes you think that Faraçek will be the one to unlock its powers?"

The princesses exchanged a look.

Serya answered: "Our brother has a dreadful ability. He does not use it often because he never wanted people to know, but I caught him when we were little, and when she was older, I told Isabey. Faraçek sometimes used it to get his way. Our father and Ander never knew, and wouldn't believe us when we tried to warn them. I cannot tell you how he does it, or even the full extent of his magic, because he guards it closely, but no one should have such a power."

Isabey looked like a woman with a broken heart. "Faraçek does not have a good heart. We love him, he is our brother, but he cannot be trusted."

Serya nodded. "We know he wants this relic. With Ander gone"—she hesitated for a moment—"and we don't know if Faraçek had a hand in that, only I stand between him and the throne." She ran a hand across her brow in the manner of the heavily burdened.

Even though the images Beazle sent Jessamine were a bit fuzzy, she thought the queen-in-waiting looked exhausted.

Beazle flapped from Isabey's hand to Laec's head, looking down from that vantage point.

"What can you tell me about the prince's magic?" asked Laec.

A knock interrupted them and a hood poked his head in the door, his expression tight. "Shade, we have company. You'd better come."

Chapter Twenty-Seven

Jessamine

As Beazle's vision snuffed like a blown candle, Jess's senses rushed back to her.

Panther had a hand on her knee, gently shaking. "Jess?"

She sucked in a startled breath and shot to her feet. Her throat was dry and every nerve ending felt like a live wire. The feeling of danger in the air was as palpable as the humidity.

Better come back, Beaze.

We are.

She grabbed Panther's shoulder. "What's happened?"

The other Fahyli were clustered together, arguing with Fixnix, who had his sword drawn and looked angry enough to use it without thinking.

"You were followed!" He spat, his tone thick with accusation.

A group of hoods, hefting makeshift weapons, eyes

glimmering like jewels, stood ready to act. The Fahyli held their palms up to show they still had no weapons. Ferrugin and Tully were nowhere to be seen, still loyally obeying silent commands to not make the situation worse. Erasmus was in Kite's hand, which was unusual, his wings half flexed and his hooked beak open. He looked like he was panting, perhaps in an effort not to repeat his earlier performance.

While Jess had been with Beazle, Mae had come out of hiding. She crouched by Sy's ankle, her little bandit-face looking around, her paws snagged on Sy's trousers.

The crofter's tone was as calm as ever. "Not possible. Our animals would have told us."

Beazle zipped from the doorway, to Jessamine's relief, and to her shoulder. *Laec is coming.*

We need Calvatia and Shade, or we'll have bloodshed, thought Jessamine.

It's Serya they'll listen to, ventured Beazle.

Fixnix snarled. "How do we have invaders then? We should gut you where you stand."

Princess Serya emerged from the tree. "You will do no such thing."

She was followed by Calvatia, Isabey, Shade and finally Laec. They moved between the two groups.

Serya commanded: "Stand down. We need each other."

Fixnix's fist clenched around the handle of his scimitar. He looked as though he vehemently disagreed with the princess, but to his credit he didn't argue. The other hoods were tense, looking back and forth from Serya to Fixnix, unsure who to obey. Jess thought it must be confusing for them. Fixnix was their leader until a queen-in-waiting had come along, whom they technically didn't need to be loyal to since they were from another kingdom, but if they knew anything about Faraçek, they'd also know that supporting Serya was in their own best interests.

"They are friends." Calvatia added in a firm voice. Jack was perched precariously on her shoulder.

The fae woman's words seemed to have a more powerful effect on the hooded men and their intimidating leader than the princesses. Someone in the group asked, "The mushrooms tell you this?"

Calvatia moved into the middle of the group. "Yes, and my magic also tells me that more than one group has breached our defenses, one from the south and another from the west. We need to split up in order to defend both sides." She turned to the princesses. "It's no longer safe here. Go back to the caves and stay out of sight."

Isabey and Serya grasped hands, white-faced and nodding.

"Shade will take us. Will you come?" Serya asked.

Calvatia put a hand on Jack and shook her head. "Our place is here."

The crofter turned to Fixnix who still stood with his sword poised. "Will you take west or south?"

Fixnix seemed to take forever to answer. Jessamine held her breath hoping that the big churlish outlaw trusted Calvatia enough to combine forces, or they'd be in trouble.

"West," he grunted. "You take south."

Fixnix's hands flashed through the air in silent communication and a dozen hoods peeled away. Some moved toward the rafts, others melted into the shadows. Jess's body was vibrating. Fear? Excitement? She had a hard time telling the difference.

She could hear Panther's steady inhales and exhales as she was handed her knife and herded toward the rafts. Bargepole men immediately shoved out into the river. They crouched on the raft, water sloshing up through the cracks. Thick foliage, fat trunks, and lush grasses blocked almost all of the moonlight. For all their beauty and magic, the mushrooms were more attractive than helpful.

The crofter's silhouette loomed over Jess. His hand signals were difficult to read in the dark, but Beazle saw them and relayed to Jess: *He wants us to stay with Sy and Mae. We're supposed to watch out for each other.*

Then the crofter gave her a signal that she could understand. It both relieved and annoyed her: stay at the back. It was easy to understand why, but Jess was gnashing for an opportunity to prove herself. She had to defer to his judgment, just as she had to defer to Ilishec's. Chain of command was paramount for both Calyx and Fahyli.

The moment the raft struck the dock on the far side, they sprinted onto land with a whisper of footfalls. Jess held back, letting the experienced Fahyli draw ahead of her. The hoods evaporated into the forest like fog. Her heart in her throat, Jessamine felt her blade's heft in her hand. The group fanned out. Jess saw Laec slide behind a tree while Kite and Regalis moved with a sense of dark fatalism and confidence.

Beazle sent a snappy overhead view to Jessamine but she couldn't make sense of it.

Thanks, but don't bother, she thought. *Unless you have a clear shot of an enemy.*

Keeping Sy on her left, they ran between trees and over rugged terrain wretched with ankle-twisting roots. In the dips, puddles gathered, and an eerie blue mist hovered over them. They loped for what seemed like a very long time, seeing and hearing nothing out of the ordinary. The presence of mushrooms grew sparse. Larger breaks in the canopy let in more moonlight. Jess thought they had to be close to the place where her ears had popped—the magical barrier.

When the sound of combat struck up ahead, they sprinted, until Sy sent her a signal to get down. Jess caught a glimpse of Sy raising his sword, then of Kite and Regalis moving apart. Kite drew back an arrow, aiming at someone Jess couldn't see. Regalis dodged behind a tree. Kite fired then drew and fired another arrow immediately. There was the sickening sound of the first thudding into flesh, then the second. A rush of a dozen soldiers swarmed through the trees. Jess stayed crouched, her body tingled as she prepared to draw poison, until it became apparent that she wasn't needed.

Kite and Regalis moved with preternatural stealth and premonition, taking down foes with arrow and blade almost as soon as they materialized. They were liquid, they were light, they slipped into places where enemies appeared before Jess knew an enemy was there. A large winged creature screamed from above, a triumphant, haunting, terrifying sound. Ferrugin. Their familiars silently reporting where to be and when. All these veteran Fahyli had to do was trust their familiar, listen and respond with lethal force. They were chilling to watch. Time slowed down as she witnessed their magnificent and deadly display. She began to count as enemies fell: Kite and Regalis serenely dispatched thirteen soldiers.

Jess underwent an epiphany that had all the subtlety of a bolt of lightning. Her whole world changed color. Each well-trained fauna fae was worth a whole legion of human soldiers, maybe more, depending on the nature of the creature they were linked with and how honed their magical connection. Kite, Regalis and Panther had the sight and senses of nature's deadliest predators. They had trained for this. They were Fahyli and they were magic. Jess was filled by an almost violent sense of gratitude that she had a chance to see this. The Fahyli operated in the background of palace life, their activities mysterious, their roles esoteric. The Calyx had no idea, even the citizens of Solana had no idea—not a clue—about the abilities of the crofter's charges.

Jess, Beazle whispered into her mind. *Focus.*

Somewhere overhead, he wasn't missing any of this either. She could feel his cool detachment and drew from it to calm her racing pulse. He was not surprised the way Jess was. Why should he be? He also possessed keen senses, it could even be argued that his sonar was a step above eyesight. His challenge was getting Jess to listen to him, to trust him. Only then might they one day achieve a level of excellence approaching that of the experienced Fahyli.

I'm here, she returned.

They're leaving us behind.

Where is Sy? I lost him.

Far ahead now.

She swore under her breath. She couldn't stay crouched forever.

She left her hiding spot and jogged in the direction she'd last seen the Fahyli. She passed the carnage Kite and Regalis had left behind without looking too closely. When she came to a small clearing with three gashes marring the foliage, she paused, unsure where to go. She was about to send Beazle a request for an overhead view when he squeaked.

To your right! A big—

A huge soldier with a longsword materialized out of the forest. He'd seen her. His weapon was up, his eyes lit with malevolence, his lips peeled back from his teeth.

Jess did the only thing she had the presence of mind to do: dove out of his path.

As he swung, she felt the wind from his blade and winced, praying she did not next feel her skin and muscle separate. There was a ripping sound and a tug, but no pain. She rolled across the ground, dropping her knife. She grasped for her weapon, feeling only slimy leaves and roots. The soldier lumbered after her. He raised his sword again, another blow would fall any second.

Where was her blade?

Beazle was in her mind, saying something, but she was too panicked to listen. There was a dull impact close behind her, and a strange chirruping noise that was vaguely familiar.

Jess found her knife, grasped it and rose, spinning to face her attacker, trying to draw poison into her hand. She was muddled and panicked, not thinking clearly enough to decide what kind. Her magic stalled with a fizzling sensation. She cringed, inhaled so quickly that her throat burned, anticipating a blow.

The soldier was no longer there.

A choking sound, then a wet gurgle. Tully's huge black back arched over a pair of twitching legs. When the legs stopped moving, Tully released her grip on his throat and lifted her head. She looked up, licking unseelie blood off her lips. Her ears perked as she returned Jess's stare, as if to say, *Well? Aren't you going to say thank you?*

"Uh. Thanks," Jess choked out. "Thank you, Tully."

Tully blew a breath out of her impressive nostrils and slunk away.

Jess looked around for Panther but instead spotted Sy's profile as he slipped through the trees. She jogged to catch up to him, her blade gripped in her hand. She had choked, would have died had Tully not saved her. The crofter was right, she had to stay close to Sy.

Sy acknowledged her with a nod, then pointed, indicating the direction they would move in together.

Ahead, fifty steps, maybe sixty. There are three of them, Beazle telegraphed.

Sy signaled that he'd take two of them and she should take the one on the right. She signaled her agreement, her heart still banging around inside her like a caged monkey.

She paused behind a tree to listen. Beazle shared a snapshot. Another soldier, sword drawn. Her only chance was to not let him get close enough to use his weapon.

Jess saw Sy waiting behind his own tree. She'd seen Sy swordfight in mock battles many times, he was fast and skilled.

Focus! Beazle barked with the piercing effect of one of Ferrugin's screams.

She winced and peered around the trunk, watching the place where her potential murderer would emerge. A silhouette materialized. He turned his head as he passed behind a tree, backlighting the evidence of his unseelie heritage.

Summoning *atropa belladonna*, Jess sent Beazle an idea. She felt his agreement, then crouched low and waited.

And waited.

Her ears strained for his footfalls. He was as quiet as death. Almost. There came the faint whisper of leaves against fabric. Beazle sent her a flash: her enemy would pass in fifteen steps.

Now ten.

Every muscle was a coiled spring. Jess pooled the *atropa* in her palm. With her blade in one hand and her toxin in the other, she waited, her back plastered against the rough bark.

He came into view, his sword low. As his head swung away from Jess, she sprang. He heard her footfalls as she closed the distance between them. His eyes grew wide. His sword came up.

Jess leapt as Beazle swooped. Flinging the poison at

her enemy, she lifted her blade to parry his sword, bracing herself for an arm-shuddering impact. A thousand bats exploded into the air. He bellowed and swung, blade whistling wide as he staggered under a barrage of wings and teeth. Beazle's duplicates ripped and clawed. There was a flash of blood and he fell to the ground, covered in flapping, squeaking creatures.

When something plopped on her shoulder, she screamed and jumped sideways.

"I thought you'd be with them," she gasped when she realized it was just her bat.

He's finished. Beazle's thoughts managed to sound both wry and smug, before he took off again.

In groups by the dozen, the duplicate bats melted into shadowy black mists that blew away, leaving a corpse on the ground.

They had killed again.

Sy might be in trouble, Beazle thought, already somewhere overhead.

That was enough to get Jess moving. She sprinted toward the sound of blades clashing, men grunting.

She became tangled in brambles and had to ram her way through, heedless of scrapes and cuts. She emerged in a narrow meadow where another dead body lay—blood across his neck shining black under the moonlight. Sy was in a deadly dance with someone, back and forth across the clearing, swords flashing in the moonlight. Jess's body tingled, but she hesitated as it would be too easy hit Sy instead, and Beazle's duplicates would complicate Sy's vision. Jess crouched, blade ready and thighs quivering as she calculated and recalculated how she might help.

The combatants broke apart and a small shadow materialized. It ran up the back of the unseelie's leg, chittering and gnashing. When Mae reached his buttocks, she clamped down hard on one cheek. He gave a shriek of pain and faltered. Capitalizing, Sy ran him through.

There was a frozen tableau for a moment. Then one pulled his sword free. The other slumped to the ground.

Sy made sure the fae was dead, then beckoned, shoulders heaving. His eyes were wild with excitement. Jess bolted to catch up as he and Mae disappeared into the woods, expecting her to keep pace.

Sounds of combat came from all directions, and the susurrus of rushing water. Jess realized they were within hearing range of the whirlpool. They had traveled a long way in the dark without realizing where they were going.

Leaves and foliage slithered past as she pressed forward. In Sy's direction, a harsh but quiet exhalation of breath. Then the clang of metal on metal. She swerved toward him, breaking into a circular clearing. Sy was engaged in technical combat, an interplay of thrusts and parries, of rapid footwork over uneven ground. A fist connected, a grunt of pain. Sy danced back and the other moved forward.

The clouds broke, letting the moon grin its cold blue light down on them, highlighting Sy's opponent. Jess's blood turned to ice.

Ears like blades, long hair tied back in a warrior's

queue, broad shoulders, slender waist and hips, long lean legs. Prince Faraçek was here.

Behind you, Beazle barked.

Spinning and lifting her blade, Jess prepared as an unseelie soldier broke into the clearing, coming straight for her. Like water seeping from an underground spring, *atropa belladonna* pooled in her open-claw hand, as potent as she could make it.

He rushed her, lifting his blade—Jess was growing familiar with the sight—and she threw her poison as she dove to the side, narrowly avoiding the crushing blow. His blade snagged her tunic. A long ripping sound punctured the air. A sound of disgust. Jess's sleeve flapped open. A burst of pain just above her elbow made her scream. Rolling over and springing up again, she dodged another blow, and another, and another. His strikes became clumsy, but he was strong and she couldn't parry his blows with her small blade, she could only dodge. She prayed the poison would kick in before he delivered a fatal strike.

His swings became wild, then desperate, then utterly blind. Then he stopped and bent over. The tip of his sword hit the dirt as he vomited.

Now, Beazle urged her. *Finish him!*

Jess took a step forward, lifting her dagger. She froze.

Poison gave her a gift that a blade could not: distance. Could she slice across his throat, feel the sharp edge of her steel part skin and muscle? Could she watch his blood pour? She was paralyzed by the prospect.

Sy and Faraçek were still fighting in the clearing, but they sounded distant, detached. The soldier made a yurk, yurk sound as he tried to control his heaving. He attempted to straighten, wiping his mouth, then staggered sideways. He tried to lift his blade, then bent over to throw up again. He bent over too quickly and lost his balance, pitching forward onto his face. He dropped his sword. He groaned and mewled, almost childlike.

What are you waiting for?

What could she say? Beazle would not understand that Jessamine felt mired. She didn't want to take a life in such a primal, brutal way.

There is nothing that is not primal about poison, Beazle thought, proving that perhaps he did understand something of her feelings.

The soldier went silent, then—after curling in on himself like a baby—still.

Jess stared down at him, wondering if she would ever get over the shock of her way of killing, her way of violence, as Beazle so astutely pointed out.

Not without sympathy, Beazle sent: *You're thinking too much. It could get us killed.*

The sound of Sy and the prince still clashing drew her back to the present. She loped toward them. Mae was a little plump body running around in Faraçek's shadow, snapping at his heels and snarling, like a small but incredibly vicious dog. Without looking down or breaking his barrage of elegant thrusts, Faraçek kicked back a booted heel—like a dancer—straight into Mae. She gave a cry that Sy echoed. Jess cried out too as Mae flew into the air.

Sy hesitated for a split second, and—just as Sy had done earlier to his unseelie enemy—Faraçek capitalized with a cold and heartless delivery: a thrust of the needle-sharp end of his rapier straight into Sy's chest. Mae screamed again as Sy took the blow.

Still yards away, Jess—in shock—stumbled on a tussock and sprawled face first. Her jaw struck the ground hard, her teeth clicking together. Ignoring the pain, she scrambled to her knees, hoping that what she had seen was an illusion born of shifting moonlight.

It had not been an illusion. Faraçek's blade emerged from Sy's back.

Oh no. Beazle's mournful thought came out like a sigh.

Faraçek put his boot against Sy's stomach and withdrew his sword with a gentle slide. Sy slumped to the ground. The prince took a fighting stance for a half second, as though expecting Sy to spring up. Then, he put the handle of his rapier to his chest and bowed to Sy, bringing the performance to a perfect close.

The prince and Jessamine locked eyes across the grassy glade. He weighed her, and found her unworthy. He wiped his blade on Sy's leggings, turned his back on Jess and melted into the trees.

Jessamine staggered to her feet. Stumbling and falling again, she closed the distance on her knees, her vision blurry. She put her hands on his warm body, amazed to find him still breathing. A wet spot bloomed on Sy's leather just beneath his left collarbone. It was a small flower of blood, so minuscule yet so devastating. Tears streamed down her face.

"Sy. I'm here." She took his hand. His fingers gave

a gentle squeeze. A little drop of blood at the corner of his mouth trickled toward his ear. He rolled his head toward her.

He struggled to talk. "Br…br—"

"Don't talk, Sy. I'll get help, I'll—"

"No." He licked his lips, it seemed to take such effort. "Bri… bring…"

She brought her ear close to his mouth. "Bring?"

He took a breath. The rattle of it was a dagger in Jess's heart.

"M-m-m…"

He wants Mae, Beazle shoved into her mind.

Jess cursed her own stupidity and bolted to her feet, casting about on the shadowy ground where she'd last seen the racoon. She found the little curled-up ball of fur and, as gently as she could, scooped up Mae and cradled her. Jess set the racoon beside Sy.

Mae uncurled. With a sad chittering exhale, she pulled herself onto Sy's stomach. Moving like she was ancient, Mae crawled up Sy's body to his chin, and draped herself across his neck. When Sy tried to lift his hand, Jess helped. Sobbing—not caring if a soldier found her and finished her—Jessamine curled Sy's hand around his familiar. His fingers caressed Mae's fur. The ghost of a smile touched his lips.

He doesn't want you to be sad, Beazle told Jess.

A fresh wave of sobs shook Jess. *How do you know that?*

Mae told me. They are together. In life and in death, beginning or end, as long as they are together, all is well. As well as can ever be.

Tears poured down Jess's face.

She wanted to fetch help, but she knew Faraçek's thrust had been true, and she would not leave Sy and Mae to draw their last breaths alone.

Beazle landed on her shoulder and crawled toward her neck so she could feel his soft, warm body thrumming with life.

Sy's breaths became shallow and labored. The hand cradling Mae relaxed by degrees, losing strength as the moments passed. Finally, his hand fell away. Jess caught it and placed it on Mae's body, pressing palm against fur, wishing for strength to return to his fingers.

It did not. She and Beazle were alone in the clearing. Sy and Mae were gone.

Chapter Twenty-Eight

Laec

The night insects chirruped, sounding as dense as ants in an anthill as Laec wove his way through the trees, keeping the crofter and Digit to his left. Laec had suggested—as they came off the rafts and climbed the slimy, reedy banks—that they fetch the horses. Ian had grunted that it would take too long. Laec tried to read the crofter's face but the shadows made it impossible.

"Wishing for Kashmir?" Laec asked, thinking of the crofter's bear after hearing a cry from Ferrugin.

"No. Too risky." The crofter sensed Laec didn't understand and added: "She's only ever duplicated once, and she hates doing it because she's lazy. Under these circumstances, she's more of a liability than anything else."

Laec ruminated about this as they slipped through the forest. All the other familiars he'd come

to know seemed to abhor being separated from their Fahyli while on duty. He wondered if Kashmir agreed with Ian's opinion. She was an impressive creature, and it would be a chance to use her dominating presence to help her kin. Laec's own blood was infused with adrenaline, eager for a break from the safety and pampered lifestyle of palace routine.

He glanced at Digit, but the slight male had no weapon in his hand, and the one at his hip wasn't much larger than the one Jessamine had been given. Digit's tiny hummingbird familiar zipped and hummed, dodging branches and keeping close to her fae. Doubt flickered through Laec as he saw Ania stop on Digit's head for a rest. She peeped.

Ian must have noticed Laec's concern. With a smug curl to his lip, he said, "Worried? Don't be. They're more dangerous than any of us, except maybe Jess."

Another jolt of surprise. He shook his head, mystified. The bear stays at home but the hummingbird—that can't duplicate—is more dangerous than the rest? Surely the crofter was kidding, only this wasn't a great time for jokes. Shrugging it off, Laec pressed on.

The first invaders to rush them gave Laec an opportunity to confirm that Ian had been telling the truth, and the witnessing of it left him feeling numb with shock.

How Digit managed to get in front of Laec and Ian was mysterious enough, the lad moved like a ghost. But when three armed unseelie appeared, fangs bared and blades ready to taste blood, it seemed like it was over before it even began. Digit put his hands up as though to push the unseelie when they got close enough. He never touched them, but one after the other, they went rigid. Two of them clutched their chests, the other made a strangled sound, and all of them collapsed. They were still twitching as Digit passed them, hardly slowing down.

Laec stopped by the bodies, his jaw sagging and his eyes bulging as he took in their dying spasms. Their faces were locked in grimaces of pain. But one by one they relaxed, their limbs went limp, their expressions eased, their eyes drifted mostly closed. They were dead. No blood spilled, no puking or staggering around. A chill enveloped Laec's body. He didn't know how much time passed as he gaped at the sneaky death Digit and Ania had meted out, but when he looked up again, wanting an explanation, Ian and Digit were gone and Laec didn't know which way they'd headed. He listened until he heard twigs snapping, then followed at a jog.

In Stavarjak, Laec's magical abilities gave him physical advantages. He could make himself almost weightless and "fold" short distances to cross them, resulting in a teleportation-like effect—only a hundred yards, but doing it repeatedly meant covering ground much faster than most adversaries. He also had a rune-marked sword that gave him faster reflexes. Here, Laec had no enchanted steel and no more dominance over an opponent than any human would. He had to rely solely on his training. The thought thrilled him. He couldn't deny that it was good to feel his pulse racing, and to hold well-balanced steel in his hand. That admitted, if Laec found himself bested, he'd wish for his magic the way a marooned sailor wishes for rain.

Had he gained a little thickness through the middle over the course of the Midwinter? Had his reflexes lost some of their sharpness? Had his technique suffered after all the feasting? Before Laec caught up to Digit and Ian, his answer came: a dismaying yes to all three. Laec crossed swords with a squat but muscular unseelie. The clash was short and brutal, leaving Laec bruised and bleeding from a slash on his right calf, but the unseelie without a head.

Panting, he ripped off the edge of his tunic and bound his leg, thankful that the cut was not too deep. While doing that, Laec considered how strange it was that this unseelie, and the three that Digit had felled, had not hesitated before launching an attack. The only conclusion Laec could reach was that the soldiers were under orders to slaughter anyone they found in the unnamed woods. Therefore, Captain Yorin—which also meant Faraçek—knew the princesses had hidden here. Still, it was bold. They'd been given permission to search Solana's territory for Serya and Isabey, but they had certainly not been given permission to kill citizens. Did they believe that these people were outcasts so Agir and Esha wouldn't care? If so they'd made a grievous error; and if not, then this was a provocation to a degree that launched wars.

A terrified scream jerked Laec upright and lifted his hackles. A woman's scream. Kite never screamed. Jessamine might, but it hadn't sounded like her. Dread filled Laec's mind with a throbbing ache as he sprinted toward the sound, hoping that he was wrong about who it *had* sounded like. Isabey and Serya were supposed to have gone into hiding with Shade.

Another scream, much closer now. His heartbeat filled his ears with thunder. A twig sliced his cheek.

He exploded into a clearing. Princess Isabey thrashed and kicked, fighting a soldier who held her crushed in his arms. It appeared he was trying to haul her off somewhere—not kill her—but she was not having it. Another bloodcurdling shriek gave Laec the split second he needed to calculate an action. She saw Laec, her eyes stretched wide in a face gleaming with sweat. He lifted his sword. With a violent jerk that involved her whole body, Isabey writhed out of the soldier's grip and dropped to the ground. The soldier had no time to reach for his weapon and Laec dispatched him quickly and mercifully. As the soldier collapsed, Laec helped Isabey up. Someone was coming, they could hear at least three more bodies crashing through the bush.

Laec and Isabey ran.

When they were sure they'd escaped, they slowed. Laec realized that it was rockier and steeper here and that he had no idea where "here" was. Digit and the crofter could be a half-mile away by now. Isabey was panting but calmer. She had a bruise forming on her cheek but seemed otherwise unharmed.

"What…" He tried not to seethe at her, she was royalty, after all. "What are you doing out here? You're supposed to be in hiding with Serya and Shade."

One hand on her stomach, she nodded, still catching her breath. She raked a stray lock of hair from her forehead. Laec realized that the relic-crown had been messily reinstalled in her hair. He hoped the circlet didn't fall out.

"We were on our way," she said on an exhale. "But we were attacked, and in the confusion we got separated. It was so dark, I couldn't tell who was friend and who was foe."

"Was Serya hurt?"

"I don't know, I don't even know if she and Shade are still together." Her face crumpled. "Serya has a poor sense of direction. She'll never find the caves by herself, especially the one that connects to the underground passage. They all look so similar."

Laec eyed her warily. "What passage?"

"It links up to the big one that connects the fortress with Solana Palace, there's an entrance through our dungeons. It's partly underwater so you'd never find it if you didn't know it was there. It's how we escaped Rahamlar without anyone realizing it. Shade knew about it, bless him."

It clicked into place, and he wondered why it didn't occur to him earlier. Of course that was how the princesses had gotten out from under their brother. "I didn't realize there was another passage branching off the big one. I've been down there. I don't remember seeing it."

She was breathing more calmly now but her face dripped with sweat. "It's a narrow horizontal crack that you have to squeeze through. Hard to spot. And there isn't just that one connecting to Syrgana, there's a whole network. I don't know how far they go. Probably, no one does anymore."

This illuminated the situation like a little firework for Laec. "But you remember how to find it from here?"

She nodded. "I know how to get to the first landmark. After that it only gets easier, but I won't go without Serya. Help me find her?"

He ignored the pain in his calf and forced himself to think about a less risky scenario, because the idea of the two of them going on a woman-hunt together was daunting. Not only would he have to protect her, she was in a long dress that had already snagged every thistle and shrub on their sprint, slowing them down. "How about this… one can move faster and hide more easily than two. I'll make sure you get to the entrance safely. You wait there, hidden, while I find Serya, and hopefully Shade. I'll bring them to you and—"

But she was already shaking her head, looking mulish. "I will not go without her, I say."

Laec tried to persuade her to see how foolish this was, but only saw that she'd gotten her way for most of her life, and that she had authority and expectations that he would respect and follow her orders, even though he was not her subject. After wasting ten minutes, they set off together into the night, away from safety and with Laec grinding his teeth with annoyance.

Chapter Twenty-Nine

Jessamine

The distant sound of fighting seeped into Jess's awareness. She straightened. Her other companions were still living, still fighting, still in danger. She had to move. Brushing away tears, she kissed Sy's still warm cheek—his face peaceful in death—and stroked Mae's soft fur. The racoon had died with her nose tucked under Sy's chin.

"We will come back for you," Jess murmured. "We will carry you home and bury you in the shadow of the West Keep."

A change came over Jessamine, subtle, like torn flesh scarring over. Her heart had torn for Greta, torn for Julian, torn for Marion, and now it was torn for Sy and Mae.

"I will repay." Jess's skin tingled with poison. Her jaw was clenched and aching. Rubbing at the hinges beneath her ears, she flexed her mouth open and closed. The taste in her mouth turned acrid. "I *will* repay."

There was a sense of dismay from Beazle but Jess couldn't find the energy to focus there. She put a hand against her furry little companion and got to her feet, turning toward the sound of the whirlpool. Her eyes were dry and hot now. Her mind felt even drier, even hotter.

She began to run.

Beazle shot into the sky, keeping pace.

She began to sweat.

She let go of the tight control she had been trained to keep over her poisons, letting her skin grow moist.

There are many ahead. Beazle sent her a visual flash. *Bank right. Be careful.*

Jess was no longer thinking. She was a throbbing, breathing, running, collection of raw nerve endings and toxic magic, a paroxysm of enchanted rage.

The first soldier she saw—with those wicked-looking ears—became her target. Soundlessly, she charged him. He barely had time to lift his sword, let alone register that a slip of a fae woman had slid beneath his defenses. His eyes stretched with shock as she flew straight at him, wrapping her arms around his neck. She heard his sword fall to the ground. Involuntarily, he closed his arms around her, too shocked to do anything else.

Jess pressed the side of her face against his, squeezing him tight. Then she put her hands on either side of his face and looked into his eyes. His look transformed, and she knew he could see his death in her face. Jess planted a lethal kiss on his lips, pushing saliva into his mouth, then backed off. She did not wait to watch him collapse.

No one but Beazle witnessed what she had done.

The sound of rushing water grew loud, shushing past Jess's ears.

She burst through the trees not far from a group of unseelie arguing among themselves, but only one of them noticed her. He looked curious and surprised, not registering her as a threat. He calmly alerted at his comrades. They stopped arguing to study her. A few of the soldiers laughed. Why should they fear some skinny female, all alone out here in the woods?

Retreat, Beazle squeaked telepathically. *There are too many!*

Jess had no such intention. She could feel Beazle's concern for her, like a little fist embedded in her mind.

Some distance beyond these soldiers were another two. One was excessively graceful. Jess's heart lurched. Faraçek.

"No friends?" One of the closer soldiers snarled, drawing a wicked-looking curved blade. He stalked her, signaling to his fellows to stay back, perhaps wanting an opportunity to show off.

Jess watched him come, her mouth filling with poison saliva, her skin glowing with it. Keeping her eyes locked with his, slowly, deliberately, she showed him her knife, holding it between her thumb and index finger. She waggled it teasingly, swinging it back and forth. The soldier cocked his head, confused. With deliberate slowness, she sheathed it at her hip. Then she put her hands up, her palms out. Droplets of perspiration ran down the sides of her face. Uncertainty flickered across his face, followed by pleasure. He thought she was surrendering.

He sheathed his own blade and closed the distance, confident and in control. He produced a strip of leather with which to bind her.

Jess's mouth was now completely full, the mixture of nightshade she'd conjured tasting unbearably bitter.

He loomed over her, massive shoulders blocking out the others. He reached for her hands, then paused to sniff the air. A realization crossed his face, as easy to read as the pages of a child's primer. He expelled a single word on a harsh breath. "You!"

An unexpected pleasure rush through her. He knew who she was.

She spat half the dose into her hand and delivered a smack across his face with a juicy, wet *splat*. His head jerked to the side and he gave a cry of disgust. Before he had the chance to recover, she spat a second time, straight at his eyes. He backpedaled, crying out.

The others—who had gone back to their argument—now raised the alarm.

As her opponent dropped, already beginning to convulse, the others rushed her, blades ready. She backed up, summoning more poison. As they closed the distance something remarkable happened: fear filled their eyes. She made a show of spitting into each of her hands then held them up as she sank into a half-crouch, preparing to spring.

They skidded to a halt just beyond her. None went to the dying soldier.

One of them ground out a few words in a language Jess did not understand. They exchanged looks of deepening disquiet. They began to argue, one of them—seemingly a superior—appeared to give a command that the other two should arrest Jess, or kill her, she wasn't sure. He sheathed his sword and stalked away, as though utterly confident in their ability to do this. The other two exchanged unhappy words, gesticulating toward Jess. The scenario might have bordered on funny if Jess wasn't so aggrieved. She did not care if these fae tried to kill her. She was Calyx, she was Fahyli, she was lethal. She would make the prince pay or die trying.

Sasha's beautiful face flicked into her mind. Their moment in the glade, stolen kisses. Her gut tightened. No, she did care. She wanted to live. Thinking of their time in the glade, an idea came to her.

She lifted her hands gracefully, stealing from Ilishec's choreography. Mystic *atropa belladonna* spun from her fingertips: little berry clusters with delicate leaves and tiny bell-shaped flowers. How could something so pretty be so dangerous?

One soldier grabbed the other and they stared at her chromatypes. The corners of her mouth lifted in a joyless smile. Mystic blooms filled the air and began to drift on the breeze. The soldiers watched them as though hypnotized. Emboldened, Jess moved toward them, spinning out chromatypes as she walked, moving as elegantly as she ever had in the ballrooms of Solana. The soldiers shuffled backward.

Someone shouted angrily but—remarkably—no one

came to assist them. Why should they? Two burly unseelie against *her*? She wasn't even armed.

Jess banked around the men, herding them as she conjured her poison. They kept back, fearful of her, but more fearful of calling for help.

"How humiliating." Jess circled them, corralling them toward her first cluster of prettily drifting poison. "You fear me, a little nothing of a fae creature. You don't know what to do. How sad. Let me help you decide."

As the soldiers backed away, there was another angry bark. She did not have long. The paralysis of terror that she had cast over these soldiers would break, and soon.

Another is coming. Behind you, Beazle whispered. *Shall I?*

"Please," Jess replied aloud as the soldiers backed into her trap.

Her blossoms began to burst against their bodies as more poured from her fingers. Her skin tingled as sweat trickled across her body, drawn to her hands by magic.

A dull pop-pop-pop sound ricocheted in Jess's mind as thousands of bats materialized.

Her victims, already dead but not yet realizing it, screamed. Mystic blossoms popped against their faces and drifted around them like deadly jellyfish. Jess turned to see Beazle's duplicates close in around the soldier coming up behind her. Hardly visible behind a storm of wings and claws and sharp teeth, he screamed and slashed with his blade. Duplicates vanished under his steel in puffs of black mist but there were too many. He too collapsed. Jess passed him without looking down. Already the last of the duplicates were disintegrating and blowing away on the breeze.

Jess strode toward Prince Faraçek and the soldier at his side, both watching her with hatred, blades ready.

"Do you know me?" Jess came to a stop. "Faraçek," she sneered, drawing out his name.

They knew what she and Beazle had done to their companions, she saw it in their eyes.

With trickery and a bit of flora magic, she had disarmed and dispatched three soldiers, all without lifting her blade. The prince couldn't ignore her, not this time. He stared, his face hard and cold. His companion had bared teeth, a noxious malevolence lighting his eyes. Faraçek looked annoyed, and curious.

"What devilry do you have, child?"

In response, Jess hooked her fingers under the cuff of her sleeve, the one already torn and tattered. With a yank, she pulled it away with a loud rip, leaving one slick arm bare. She held the rag up so he could see it for what it was, a sweat-soaked sleeve.

Faraçek's eyes widened. "You're the one. You stole my bride out from under my men. You humiliated me and ruined my plans."

"Yes. It was me," she replied.

Jess, Beazle whispered, worried, perhaps as much for her sanity as for her safety. *What are you doing?*

I will repay, she responded silently.

He did not agree with what she was doing, she could feel that, but he was with her. He would always be with her, to the end of everything, just as Mae had been with Sy.

"What are you going to do about it?" she asked.

Beazle gave a deep mental sigh. *Must you provoke him? I cannot keep duplicating endlessly. I need to rest. Magic has a price. Yours too. You seem to have forgotten that in your quest for vengeance.*

Faraçek gave a nasty laugh. "Sheath your sword, Rax. You are not needed."

"But Sire," the soldier shot his prince a shocked look. "She—"

Without taking his eyes from Jess, Faraçek said, "Find the captain. Tell him we've lost three men here, perhaps more. And that I have dealt with the culprit. That is an order."

Reluctantly, the soldier sheathed his blade and departed.

Faraçek moved toward Jess, but leisurely, his thin blade held low. He stopped to consider her. Unlike his men, he was utterly unafraid.

The prince lifted his blade a little, gesturing to it, conversationally. "This is called a rapier, brat. Did you know that?"

Jess stared at him in mute rebellion, her mouth tasting terrible and poison drying on her skin.

"I always liked these blades. They are much lighter than the broadsword, more flexible. I like that they don't make a mess." He took a fighting stance and made a few lighting fast jabs into an imaginary opponent. "One tiny well-placed hole, that's all it takes. No hacking. No slashing. No spilling of viscera. I like things, neat, you know? Like me."

I will duplicate, Beazle informed Jess, questing for approval. *I think I can muster the energy, I just need a little more time. I need to hunt first.*

Concern darkened the doorway of Jess's mind. *Are you sure?*

Honestly?

Of course, honestly.

I am not sure. I'm still new at this. But I think I can… maybe. I could make enough to fluster him, do a little damage. While he is distracted, you do your bit.

Faraçek was still talking, casually, as though discussing his art with an old friend. "…since I was four. Not this blade of course. This one I have handled since I was fourteen, since I could fit it. I know this pommel, knuckle guard, and these fine sweepings like they are an extension of my own arm."

Jess gave Beazle her agreement, her stomach in knots, her body reeking of fragrant poison. Fear slipped through her bravado like a mouse through a crack at the bottom of a door. He was somewhere in the darkness, her little friend and bodyguard. She wondered how far away he was.

Like a flash of lightning he sent her an overhead view of herself and Faraçek, taken from behind and to her left. He was not far but Beazle's attention was on stalking buggy prey.

She felt incredibly alone.

Faraçek lifted the slender blade and made small circles in the air, punctuating his storytelling. "It was a kindness I delivered to your friend, with this blade. I would give my rapier a name if I were the sentimental type, like my brother was, but I am not. I do not have emotional relationships with inanimate objects, it serves me, and well. Nothing more. You'll see what I mean shortly. You should feel honored that I spend this much time with you, but you did something extraordinary when you came into my kingdom and took my betrothed. I suppose there is some part of me that should be impressed. Perhaps if I weren't so irritated. No one does such things to Prince Faraçek. It might have taken time, but I would have found you. Maybe not this year, maybe not next, but I am patient and I never forget. Down the road, when you had stopped looking over your shoulder, I would have come out of the shadows. But incredibly, here you are, before me. A wisp of a fae wench barely into womanhood." He paused and took a breath. "I would like to know before I kill you, since you did not do this thing alone, who was it that helped you, girl?"

Beaze?

I am coming. It is difficult to rush my kind of hunting, you know. Prey does not just fly into my open mouth.

Faraçek neared. Jess did not step back. She revealed nothing to Faraçek, none of her fear, none of her expectation that a thousand bats would burst between them at any moment.

Casually, Faraçek hefted his rapier. "I can kill you fast or I can kill you slow, little fae. Tell me who it was who helped you?"

Jess flicked her fingers and a single mystic nightshade blossom no larger than the end of her thumb materialized in the air. She tried to summon saliva but she was too dry.

Dread pooled in her belly. What if she couldn't produce enough poison to do the job? What if she could conjure only a small handful then missed when she threw it? What if she couldn't get close enough, with all the bats in the way? She would need to use her blade. She reached for the knife at her hip, barely conscious that she was doing so.

Faraçek's gaze flicked to her hand, his dark slashes of eyebrows arched. "Really? This is your answer?"

It was too late to change her mind, he was advancing. Jess took a few steps back. She needed to think, and Beazle needed time. She drew her knife and held it in the way she'd been taught.

Faraçek chuckled at the sight of her weapon. "They sent you to fight us with that? My girl, I believe your superiors hate you."

I am coming!

The prince advanced, a deadly look in his glittering eyes.

Jess backpedaled, desperately seeking moisture in her mouth, in her palms—a well gone dry.

A succession of dull popping sounds and a cauldron of bats exploded between them, not so many as before, and with none of the larger more terrifying beasts, but they had the desired effect. Now it was Faraçek backpedaling, his black eyes lifted into the storm of wings, his form obscured by them.

Moonlight flashed off Faraçek's sword as he twitched it this way and that, destroying duplicates left and right, even as bats clawed at his body and head.

Where are you? Jess's thoughts scrambled after Beazle.

What do you mean? I am fighting! They only fight because I fight!

Faraçek's blade dispatched more bats even as he ripped one from the side of his head. His reflexes were deadly.

As she lifted her dagger, working up the courage to rush forward and finish the job, terror that the rapier would find Beazle overwhelmed her. She silently screamed, *Get out of there!*

But—

Faraçek spun his back to the bats and knelt to the ground. Just as quickly, he spun back his chest inflated. He blew a long exhale, ignoring the duplicate chomping on his ear.

The entire remaining cauldron vaporized simultaneously, blowing away in a gust of black smoke.

"Beazle!" Jess screamed.

She strained for sight of him. Was he dead? Surely the mystic bats would only have vanished like that if he had been killed, but she was more certain that she would have felt it if Beazle had died. She and Beazle were connected in spirit and soul. She'd felt nothing, which gave her hope.

She searched the ground desperately.

Beazle? Answer me! Where are you? Please!

If she had felt the point of Faraçek's rapier slip between her ribs in the moment, would she have even noticed? She had dropped her dagger. She was dried out. She had no defense, and the pain that was tearing her heart in two had taken all the fight out of her.

When Faraçek grabbed her by the collar, making sure not to touch her skin, she was certain of receiving her own neat little hole. But as he lifted her off the ground and held her out like a bad puppy, his other hand held the rapier down and away.

"Beazle," Jess sobbed.

"You're pathetic," Faraçek said. "Repellant. Running you through is too good for you. But I'll give you one last chance to tell me who helped you. Tell me and I'll run you through the heart. It will be over in a moment. Do not tell me, and you will discover my way of delivering a slow death."

Faraçek's words barely penetrated her mind. Could she even recall who had helped her? What name did he have? Was he even a he? Nothing mattered if she had lost her bat.

Beazle, Jess thought, her heart utterly smashed. *Beazle, love. Tell me you are alive. Whisper something.*

"I won't ask again," the prince promised.

Jess kicked at him half-heartedly, sobbing.

Prince Faraçek took in a deep breath, then blew it straight into her face.

Chapter Thirty

Laec

Keeping Isabey behind him, Laec squinted at the figures through heavy mist, straining to hear voices over the thunder of the water. His eyes were burning with tiredness, his body felt sore. Dawn was a dim promise beyond the trees, casting a grayish light through the forest.

"It's Serya. Oh Laec!" Isabey clutched at his sleeve. "He has Serya."

"Stay here," Laec told her. "Don't go any closer."

He moved around the whirlpool until the mist thinned enough for him to see the figures on the bridge. A chill seized Laec's body. It was as Isabey feared.

He and Isabey had followed the sounds of conflict until they'd heard the thunder of the gorge and Laec realized where they were. They could hear voices and snuck closer, listening for evidence of Serya or Shade. Laec had dispatched two unseelie soldiers, but most of the time they managed to stay hidden in the trees and thick foliage. At times Laec thought he recognized voices of Fahyli, but they never met them. He even mimicked the sound of a hawk's scream in the hopes that Ferrugin might spot them, tolerating Isabey's doubtful expression as he did so.

There was no sign of Shade—Laec really hoped he was alive—but Serya was still very much alive, standing on the bridge between two male figures. He and Isabey had found her, but she was irretrievable, at least without the help of all the Fahyli.

At the far end of the bridge, waiting for commands, were more unseelie soldiers, at least eight, but it was difficult to see if there were more in the shadows. Prince Faraçek's figure cut sharp angles out of the mist on one side of Serya. Captain Yorin stood on her other side, one arm around her. Protectively, or possessively? It was difficult to tell with the mist obscuring the details. Laec's eyelashes dripped water onto his cheeks and moisture ran down his face like tears, his hair lay sodden against his shoulders.

Faraçek repeated himself, and this time Laec understood.

"Bring me the crown, Isabey!" The prince's dark eyes were focused on his sister, and Laec's heart fell when he realized she'd moved to where he could see her. The prince's voice was powerful, confident that his sister would do as he demanded.

Laec put a hand out, signaling she should stay back. To his dismay the youngest member of Rahamlar's royal family moved to the gorge's edge.

"Isabey," he warned. "Don't."

She hardly seemed to hear him. Her face was etched with worry. Her gaze never wavered from where her siblings stood on the bridge. "I have to. He'll hurt her if I don't. I couldn't bear that, not when I could prevent it."

Laec touched her arm. She seemed so fragile, so tender and young. "Do you really believe he'll let her go if you give him what he wants?"

Her lower lip quivered. "I'll make him. I'll bargain. Serya's freedom for Toryan's Crown."

"Princess… don't do this."

But how could he tell her what to do? That was her sister on the bridge. It was the fate of her kingdom in her slender hands. He was merely a foreigner offering protection. Queen Elphame's command was to be her eyes and ears, not to interfere. Still…it chafed. His queen had seen darkness. Had that darkness something to do with Faraçek? Yet, Laec had no right to prevent the princess from making her own choice.

Isabey's big fae eyes left her brother and sister for a moment to settle on Laec's face. "I cannot thank you enough for what you did for Lady Çifta, and the protection you've given me this night. My brother won't hurt me, I'm not a threat to him. He cannot legally be crowned anyway, not with Serya alive and so many people watching."

"They're *his* men," Laec hissed.

"Then stay, and be my witness."

His stomach clenched. "I'm not going anywhere. But you can't trust him, Isabey."

"They are my family. I must go to them. Thank you. I am sorry if this night has cost you friends." She kissed his cheek, then took a few steps closer to the bridge, calling, "Our sister for the crown, brother. Let Serya go and you may have Toryan's relic."

Laec closed his eyes. Helpless.

Serya's eyes widened in disbelief. She shook her head, her mouth dropping open to rebuke the trade. Yorin clamped a hand over her mouth and said something into her ear.

Faraçek turned toward the end of the bridge as Isabey approached, his sharp features soft in the hazy air, almost tender.

"It was never yours to take, little Isabey. You do understand that all of this is your fault? The two of you? Yes?"

His words seemed to bounce off her. "Will you promise to let her go?"

Faraçek looked hungry, his eyes raking his sister's frame, searching for the cursed object. "If you produce the relic, I will have Yorin release her. Yes. I swear it."

Isabey pushed her hood back, revealing her updo, mussed from the exertions of the night. Damp curls spilled down her back. She took the remaining pins out, one by one.

Faraçek's expression changed as he realized where she'd been hiding Toryan's Crown. He laughed and said something to Yorin. Both looked exultant with their victory so near.

"Stop there, sister. Let me see it," Faraçek called. While he said this, he gave someone a signal. Laec tensed. Yorin couldn't see it, not the way he was standing with Serya between them. It had to be for one of the soldiers at the other end of the bridge.

Isabey stopped and lifted the crown. She held it up with both hands, letting Faraçek get a good look.

Movement from the far side of the bridge made Laec's hair stand on end. Two armed unseelie soldiers emerged from the wood. One led a saddled horse onto the bridge and approached the prince and Yorin. The horse tossed its head and whinnied, nervous about the raging water far below. The other soldier crossed the bridge fully, closing the distance to Isabey.

"Give him the crown, Isabey. I'll give the order to release Serya when I have the relic in my hands."

Isabey passed the circlet to the soldier and waited while he made the trek back to the middle of the bridge. With a shallow bow, he put the circlet into Faraçek's possession. The prince inspected the crown, saying something to Yorin. The captain removed his hand from Princess Serya's mouth. Serya looked livid, and glared at her brother. Laec thought he also read a secret satisfaction in her expression. The rightful heir had made no promises of any kind.

Yorin gave Serya a little nudge. She limped toward her waiting sister.

"One final thing," Faraçek called. "I am addressing you, Serya."

Serya froze.

"You promised!" Isabey yelled, taking a few steps forward.

"I have fulfilled my promise," Faraçek replied, "I

commanded Yorin to release her. I only require one final thing before I let you both go."

Serya did not turn around. Her eyes were on Isabey, filled with a horrible knowing.

"Sister, you must abdicate. Here. Now. In front of me and my captain."

For a long time, Serya did not react. Then, slowly and clumsily, she turned and looked at her brother. In doing so she shifted, and Laec got a clear view of Captain Yorin—and the short spear he held in his hand.

Serya said something, but it was lost in the angry churn of the whirlpool.

Faraçek cupped his hands to his mouth. "What? I cannot hear you?"

Serya inhaled, her shoulders expanding. She bellowed, anger making her voice harsh. "You know I cannot."

Faraçek glanced at Yorin with an expression that was as much like a shrug as the action itself. He said something, and turned his back on his sisters, stepping toward the waiting horse.

Captain Yorin hefted the spear.

Isabey screamed.

Laec dashed forward.

The captain threw as Laec barreled into Isabey, knocking her out of the path of Yorin's weapon. He looked up to see the spear's head emerge from Serya's back. There was very little blood. Serya staggered, then flailed for something solid. She struck the railing at mid-thigh.

Isabey cried out again, deafening Laec. She thrashed

away from him, scrambling toward her sister. He grasped at Isabey's garments, but they ripped from his hand.

Serya lost her balance, the spear perfectly lanced through her torso. She flipped over the railing and fell, swallowed by the mist. She never made a sound.

Screaming for Serya, Isabey ran to the place she'd last seen her sister. Faraçek's horse cut in front of her. Isabey pummeled at Faraçek's legs, wailing, almost bowed with grief, yet somehow strong with righteous anger.

Faraçek leaned over and grabbed a handful of Isabey's cloak. He lifted her into the air like a wayward pup.

On his feet, Laec sprinted for the bridge.

"Halt!" Yorin barked, hefting another short spear. "Or I'll pierce you where you stand."

"If you harm me, you'll have Queen Elphame to answer to," Laec yelled, but he did stop.

Something flickered in Yorin's eyes. Fear? It was impossible to read but the captain said no more. He kept the spear hefted, which was enough to keep Laec's feet glued to the spot.

Faraçek hoisted his little sister higher. He looked at her for a little while, Then nudged his mount closer to the bridge's railing where he tossed her over. Isabey's scream was swallowed by the thunder of the gorge as she fell. That done, the prince turned his horse and cantered away, casual as afternoon tea. Captain Yorin waited for Faraçek to reach the far side of the bridge and withdraw into the woods before lowering his spear.

"You'd best go back where you belong, Stavarjak," Captain Yorin called. "You chose the wrong side once.

Respect for your queen stayed my hand, but I cannot promise that if I see you again, her renown will save you a second time."

His teeth gritted, Laec could not think of anything to say. If Yorin knew that he had freed Çifta, he'd have a spear in his throat right now. Elphame or no Elphame.

When the captain loped across the bridge, Laec bolted for the railing.

CHAPTER THIRTY-ONE

JESSAMINE

SHE DID NOT know where she was, she did not know how she got here, but it didn't matter. Even her name did not matter. Had it ever? She had to get to the highest point possible, that was all that mattered. When she reached the highest point, something wonderful would happen. She craned her neck, turning in place, her feet in deep grass. She was surrounded by trees. That was good. Trees were tall, and she could climb. These trees, however, were more thick than tall. She could do better. The moon hung low behind the trees, soon it would drop from view entirely.

She pressed toward the tallest trees she could see. The forest swallowed her as she slipped between fat trunks. She touched the rough bark, looking upward, her head always tilted back. She tripped and recovered as she went from tree to tree. Dissatisfaction burned in her chest. Not tall

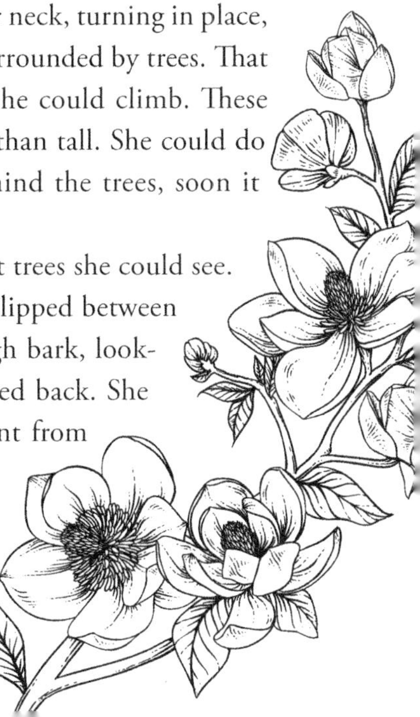

enough. The wonderful thing would not happen unless she was high. Very high. Above the canopy. She needed to see for miles around, although it was not the view that was important. Just the height was critical. More than anything she had ever dealt with in her past… if she had a past. She must, because she was alive and not born yesterday.

But her past was not important.

Her mouth was horribly dry. Her eyes were dry and getting drier. As she ascended, the air grew cool. The wind picked up, it licked her bare arm and lifted her hair, whipping it against her face. She ignored the chill making her shiver.

Up, and up she went. These trees were taller, she reckoned. She did not have much time. There was urgency. She had to choose one before the sun came fully up.

Her legs were burning now, not just her lungs. Fatigue chewed at her like a predator gnaws a corpse. It was getting harder to lift her feet. She stumbled and fell. Her hands stung. Her elbow throbbed.

Keeping her head up was getting harder too. Her neck was aching, her temples ached. She tripped over a tussock and landed in the grass, panting. She had to get up. Rolling onto her back, she looked up at the canopy. It did look far away. Very far, in fact.

She was tired. This would have to do.

Her body burning with fatigue, she rolled onto her knees and drew herself to standing. It was very hard. She reached for the nearest tree to steady herself. She missed, unable to judge the distance. She fell to her knees again, but she would not give up. Crawling forward, she found the tree and hauled herself to her feet. The nearest bough was small, but at eye level. With the help of a well positioned boulder, she drew herself up into the tree.

The world closed in. All that mattered was the next bough. Using her remaining strength, she climbed. The distance between her and the earth widened as the minutes ticked by. She was in the heart of the boughs now. They were fat and frequent. She felt a burgeoning hysterical elation as she drew closer to the boughs at the top. Soon, very soon. She could taste victory. She wondered how the wind would smell. Wind was important. Wind had a vital role to play.

Up and up she went. Her hands scratched and bleeding. Her body bruised as she bumped against knots and the points of broken branches. Rough bark scraped her face. Something wet and warm trickled up her arm.

The boughs became thinner. That was good. She was closing in on the highest point. The branches bounced under her weight. Branches were slender, and increasingly flexible. The foliage was thinning, no longer preventing the wind from buffeting her.

Her foot slipped. She locked her hands around a branch no thicker than a broom handle. Sucking in air, she gazed at the sky through half-lidded eyes. Her feet dangled. She lifted them, seeking a foundation without looking down. A tear leaked from the corner of her eye, trickling back into her hairline. A breeze licked it away, like a cat.

The branch took her weight. It was difficult to unlock

her grip to reach for the next branch. She bounced up and down on the bough as she pulled herself up. She gripped two more branches overhead. One of them snapped off in her hand. Her upper body swung dangerously outward, arm flailing. She was so close. She could do this. Desperately, she grabbed at anything, always looking up. A gust of wind ripped at her as she clung to her perch.

Jessamine.

Sliding over toward the narrow trunk, she wrapped her arms around it, panting. She coughed. Her throat was so dry. Had someone spoken?

Remember who you are. Remember.

Who she was. Why did that matter? She resisted the voice. It was deep, it was calm, even primeval. It was very soothing, but she would not let it distract her from her goal. She reached for the next branch, no thicker than her finger. It flexed easily, but it would take her weight. Sure it would. Her mission was vital, these boughs would not fail her. She pulled herself upward.

Jessamine, you will die if you go any further.

Die? Well, that was the point actually. She *would* die. Death was the desired outcome. The voice was not telling her anything she didn't already know.

You will fall.

She shook her head, no. When she reached the highest point, she would not fall. She would fly. The voice was lying. She pressed upward, her arms shaking, her hands slipping, her body bouncing up and down on the flexible narrow limb.

Jessamine, listen. Beazle is alive. You must stop. If you

go any further, you will not only kill yourself, you will kill him too.

She gasped as the name sliced through her brain like a beam of light through fog. She shook herself against this voice. Trying to deceive her, trying to distract her, trying to thwart her plans.

I know it's hard, but you can resist this magic. You have been convinced of something that is not true. Look at me. I am beneath you.

She clung to the tree. She shook her head frantically. She was not to look down. There was nothing down. There was only up.

Look at me. I am right here.

Her neck creaked. Her chin dropped for the first time in what seemed like a lifetime. An ache throbbed deeply in her neck. Straightening it felt good. Looking down would feel even better. But down was… bad. Clenching her eyes shut, she tilted her chin down to her chest. The stretch in the back of her neck was glorious. She took a deep breath and luxuriated in the feeling.

I am here. Just below you. I love you, child of Solana.

She leaned out enough to look past her own body, straining into the darkness. There was something there, a source of light, close to the trunk, several feet down.

Take a step down, child.

Even as she shook her head, she lowered herself to the branch below her. Just a little fatter, just a little bit more stable. There was a glow, but she could not yet see its source.

And another, my darling.

She shook her head again, but still she stepped down. She did not sway so much now. Her arms did not burn so much to hold her in place. She looked down, leaning out, just a little. Her eyes stretched wide as she saw the source of light, glowing beneath her feet like a tiny sun.

There was a lion in the tree, a beautiful majestic male lion.

He was perched impossibly in a crook, looking up at her with kind eyes. *Come down, Jessamine. You can do it. Already the magic is losing its grip on your mind.*

She dropped down another level, and other. Stretching her legs, she reached her booted toes for the bough the lion was perched on. She lowered herself, never losing eye contact with him. She came to be seated, her feet dangling, gripping the branch above her.

What is your name, child?

He had already said it. He knew it. He should give it to her, because she couldn't remember. She shook her head. She didn't know.

He licked his chops with a big tongue and she realized she could see the trunk behind him, and the leaves and branches beyond that. He was enormous, far too big to be sitting in this tree. Yet he looked comfortable, unconcerned.

Say it. Say your name. Come back to us.

Her mind was so sluggish, so slow. She thought and thought—a most taxing thing—but when it came surging to her lips, it brought tears to her eyes.

"Jessamine F-Fontana," she whispered. Then again, louder now: "Jessamine Fontana."

The lion lowered his head a little and his mouth opened. He was smiling.

Very good. Now Jessamine, you will start to feel better. You must climb down, dear one. Beazle is waiting for you.

"Beazle," she cried, her voice a throaty rasp.

Everything came rushing in on her at once, a dust storm of memories.

She began to hyperventilate. Then sobs took over. She moaned as she looked around. What was she doing up here? This was so dangerous! Where was she?

The prince's breath. It had smelled like mulch and wet soil and rotting leaves and… and magic. After, there was nothing but a driving force to climb, and climb, and climb… to her death.

The lion gazed at her with those ancient eyes, out of an ancient scarred face. His huge thick, bushy mane was threaded with bright filaments of light.

You're alive. You will not die up here. Breathe. You are not too late. Follow me.

The lion vanished, leaving her in darkness. Jessamine cried out, but a light appeared below, drawing her gaze down. He was still with her.

Shaking, she began the journey back to the safety of the earth. His kind voice guided her, encouraged her, comforted her.

I am here.

"Don't leave me," she whispered. "Please don't leave me."

Even when you cannot see me, I am with you. You are never without me.

He vanished, taking his light with him, to reappear on a lower bough, waiting for her. She made her tremulous way to him many times over before her feet finally touched the blessed ground. She collapsed on her back, safe. Her body ached and her skin stung in a million places.

You cannot stop here. You must come.

She rolled over and lifted her head. He stood a short distance away, his huge glowing body rippling with muscle. His mane stood out around his face, a corona of glorious light.

Come, child.

She got to her feet and staggered after him.

He stalked through the bush, silently, slowly. He waited for her, looking back, talking to her with incredible sweetness. He led her to a brook of cold water, where she collapsed, putting her face in the water. She drank her fill. She splashed her face and her bare arm, washing the itch and burn away. She sat back on her haunches and looked up at the sky where colors had begun to appear. She looked around.

The lion was gone.

She covered a sob with her hand. She was so sad, but so grateful. She was filled with such love, such relief, even a strange kind of joy. Her sob turned to weepy laughter. She threw her head back, her arms out, exposing her heart to the night.

"Come back!"

I am always with the children of Solana. I will never leave you.

Beazle needed her.

Renewed and amazed, Jess got to her feet. Water soaked into her boots and she looked down at the brook. This little stream would flow downhill, join larger ones and eventually flow into the river, the river that led to the whirlpool.

"Thank you," she said.

Jessamine began to jog, keeping the brook beside her.

Chapter Thirty-Two

Jessamine

By the time Jess returned to the place where Beazle had fallen, the sun was cresting the tops of the trees, casting light like beams of hope to the forest floor. She could sense her bat's fatigue and confusion as she drew near.

Beaze?

Jess! I'm here. My wing is caught.

He sent her a flash of his perspective. There was a distinct V-shaped trunk on his left. It took her some time to locate the tree, but after another helpful snapshot, she was on her knees in a tangle of undergrowth, parting thorny brambles. A thorn had pierced the tip of his right wing.

Oh Beaze. Jess felt a hitch in her chest as she saw how his little wing had been pulled taut. *Are you in a lot of pain?*

Not much. He was filled with joy upon seeing her, and his

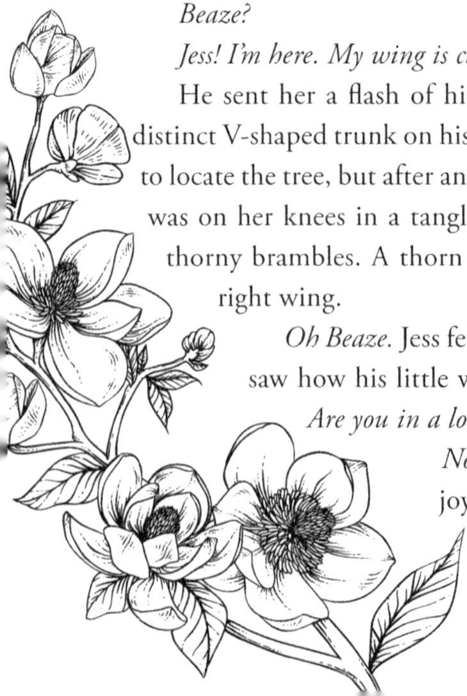

elation flowered inside her too, like the opening of a new daffodil. She laughed through her tears. Gently, she released his wing from its cruel pin. He flexed and his little body shuddered as he tucked it into his side.

Can you fly?

Maybe tomorrow, he told her optimistically.

So brave, she thought as she lifted him to her cheek. *You have the heart of a lion. I love you so much.*

He gave a dry squeak and licked his lips with his tiny pink tongue. *I knew you were alive. I knew you'd come for me. But what happened? I can't remember.*

He stunned you. All your duplicates vanished. I looked for you desperately but I couldn't find you. That was how he stunned me too, I was so terrified that I'd lost you, Beaze, I wasn't thinking about anything but you when he grabbed me. I'll tell you more about it after. We need to find the others. She got to her feet, her legs were burning with exhaustion. *Where are we?*

Head for the whirlpool. Maybe we can also find a drink.

Good idea. Oh you're so smart.

Carrying Beazle, Jess followed the sound of the crashing water in the gorge. She lifted Beazle to her shoulder. He crawled into the cradle of her collarbone.

You missed me a lot, huh?

I thought you might be dead, Beaze. I couldn't feel you and you didn't answer when I called. It's the most frightened I've ever been.

Except for maybe "waking up" high in the treetops and not recalling how she got there or why. She longed to tell him about the lion, but not while they were so tired and a little lost.

Did it really happen? Beazle thought as a memory struck him out of nowhere. *Are Sy and Mae really gone, or did I dream that?*

Her mind felt full of cobwebs, but she knew she had not imagined it.

They're really gone, Beaze. The prince killed them.

Beazle was quiet. Jess could feel his sadness.

They walked until every step Jess took felt like a monumental effort. Her legs were shaking, there was a knot of hunger in her stomach.

I need to sit down, just for a little bit.

Beazle was dozing.

Jessamine settled onto her knees in a pretty little glade, then slid sideways to one hip. Butterflies and bees went about their business, dancing prettily in the morning light. Birds tweeted glorious songs. Her eyes drifted closed. She let her head hang, wondering if it would be a bad idea to go to sleep, just for a few minutes. A throb behind her eyes threatened to blossom into a full blown headache. She rubbed her temples in slow circles, pausing when she realized that the birds had stopped singing.

She looked around, suddenly wary.

Putting a protective hand on Beazle, she struggled to her feet. The feeling of being watched was overpowering. The glade had gone deathly silent. A branch broke behind her. She turned to see a pair of glowing green eyes in the underbrush.

"Hello?" she rasped.

Tully's sleek muscular body emerged from the foliage.

"Tully!" Jess couldn't stop her cry of relief. "You have no idea how happy we are to see you."

Silent as a shadow, the big cat approached and stopped beside Jessamine. Her back nearly reached Jess's waist. Tully leaned against Jess's leg, almost making her fall over. The cat made a chuffing sound, and swung her head to look back at Jess. She bumped her ribs against Jessamine's leg again. Jess fought to remain on her feet.

"What is it, Tully? Where is Panther?"

Get on, Beazle thought sleepily. *She'll take us to the others.*

Jess's eyes widened. "Seriously?"

Beazle's answer held a smirk. *Wait too long and she'll change her mind. She's not a horse.*

"Well who am I to turn down the opportunity to ride a panther," murmured Jess, her heart skipping a beat as she lifted a leg over the cat's back. Settling her weight gingerly onto Panther's familiar, she expected the cat to groan or struggle to walk. She needn't have worried. Tully gave Jess a moment to latch on to the thick ruff at the back of her neck before starting a long-strided lope.

Jess had to lay her chest right down along Tully's back or she would be ripped off by passing branches. Tully did not take the open sunlit pathways that a person would choose. Her way was straight through the foliage-choked dark places beneath and between close growing shrubs. Jess tucked her face against the thick, soft fur along Tully's shoulder. Riding a cat was like clinging to a log in a river. Tully's muscles flexed and oozed, skin sliding over smooth muscle. Jess was certain that before long she would simply tilt, then slide gracelessly to the ground. But somehow, despite every muscle quivering, she managed to cling like a burr.

The air grew humid and the sound of rushing water grew loud. When Tully broke out of the underbrush, Jess unclenched her fingers and made an effort to sit up while Tully was still in motion. The cat stopped, allowing Jess to get off.

"Thank you, Tully," Jess managed, stretching a cramp out of her hip.

"Jessamine!" Panther ran over, face dirty and hair damp. He looked wild-eyed but relieved to see her. He and Tully shared a silent communication, then the panther moved away. Panther swallowed Jess up in a hug.

"What happened to you? Now we're only missing Sy and Mae."

Over Panther's shoulder, Jess caught a glimpse of Kite and Regalis standing at the edge of a crowd of hoods. Digit was there too, standing beside the crofter, who had an arm around Digit's shoulder. Jess didn't have time to contemplate the strangeness of seeing Ian with his arm around one of the Fahyli. She looked into Panther's eyes, moisture lining her lower lids. She tried to speak and coughed instead. She gestured to Panther's water pouch.

He fumbled for it and handed it to her as he removed the lid. Jess moved the collar of her shirt away from her neck. She lifted the water pouch but her hand was shaking. Panther steadied her hand, helping her pour a little water into the hollow above her collarbone for Beazle.

"What happened to you?" Panther asked.

"It's a long story," she husked. "Sy and Mae are dead, Pan. I saw it happen. Killed by the prince."

Panther's expression grew heavy. "I feared that. The worst has happened."

Jess realized that no one else had come over, though she was sure that Kite had noticed them. The group stood where the bridge over the whirlpool struck land. It looked like a discussion was taking place.

"What's happening?"

"Come on." Panther led her toward the group, an arm slung around her shoulders. "They've spotted Isabey in the gorge. She's clinging to an overhang."

Before Jess could absorb this news, the sound of Ferrugin's scream startled her. She looked up, finding Regalis's familiar wheeling over the gorge.

The hawk splintered into a dozen duplicates, each bigger than the last. The largest had a terrifying wingspan. Jess staggered with surprise as the huge duplicate banked then pinned its wings and dove straight down. Ferrugin looked like a tiny sparrowhawk beside her monstrous duplicate as she dove shoulder to shoulder with it. They disappeared into the mist, lost from sight. The other duplicates circled high overhead on updrafts, screaming.

A moment later the duplicate exploded from the gorge, pumping enormous wet wings. It shook its head, water spraying in all directions. A figure was clutched in one talon. Banking in circles to control its descent, the hawk deposited its cargo on the ground. As the group closed in, Ferrugin's duplicates vanished—puffs of black shadow drifted away on the breeze. She settled on the ground beside Regalis, tucking her wings.

Pather told Jess: "Isabey was dropped over by her brother. I overheard Laec telling the crofter. She's lucky she fell in close to the edge. She landed on an outcrop."

Jess's stomach turned over. "Where's Serya and Shade?"

Panther tightened his arm around her. "Jess you need to sit, you're trembling all over."

But Jess couldn't sit, she drew close enough to see Kite's look of relief. When Regalis saw Jess, he picked his way out of the crowd to fold her in a hug.

"Tully found you? Or did you finally find us?"

Jess hugged him back, thankful for his solidity, his strength. He smelled of sweat and leather and salt. "Tully rescued us."

A flash of red hair, and a frustrated bark gave away Laec's whereabouts. "Give her some air, people! Step back, I say!"

When the crowd moved back Jess got a view of Isabey. She lay cradled in Laec's arms. Laec gently ran his free hand over Isabey's limbs and ribs, checking for broken bones. Her oversized fae eyes fluttered open. She looked up at him, glassy and in pain. Laec's voice was gentle as he brushed Isabey's tangled hair away from her face, keeping her upper body supported against his chest.

"Easy Princess. Don't try to move. You'll be sore for a few days, but you're alive. Aye, you're alive."

"Serya," she choked, and her face crumpled.

"I know, Princess. I know. I'm so sorry." Laec held her as she sobbed brokenly.

Jess shot Panther a questioning look. He just shook his head, his expression sad. Serya was gone. Jess was desperate to know what happened, but it wasn't the right moment to ask.

Those watching backed away like there was a bad smell, uncomfortable with Isabey's grief. Silence lay over them like a heavy blanket. Regalis put his arm around Kite, who dropped her face, either hiding tears or unable to witness Isabey's mourning. It was bad enough to hear it.

Panther stood with Jessamine, an arm still around her.

After long moments of silence, Fixnix drew together his men. They talked quietly among themselves. Jessamine wondered what Princess Serya had meant to them.

The crofter and Digit approached the Fahyli. Ian nodded at Jessamine. "Good to see you alive and in one piece. Erasmus found you?"

Jess started to shake her head no, but of course Erasmus had found her, Tully had only fetched her. "I guess. Yes." She looked at Kite. "Thank you." Then to Panther, "Thank you."

Panther squeezed and released her, saying to the crofter: "Sy and Mae didn't make it. Jessamine was there when Faraçek killed them."

A lance of guilt went through her heart. "I'm sorry… we couldn't stop it."

"We know, Jess." murmured Regalis.

Kite's eyes were bright with unshed tears.

Ian looked sad but unsurprised. "I figured we had lost them."

Digit added, "They'd been gone too long."

The crofter addressed Jessamine: "Can you take us to where they fell? If you can't recall, we can send Erasmus, eventually he'll see them."

Kite turned her face up to the sky as Erasmus gave a throaty scream. A tear streaked over her cheekbone, which she brushed away. "He's already found them. They're not far."

"I remember," murmured Jess.

Would Sy and Mae ever be far from her mind again? How did one forget such things?

Sy and Mae were wrapped in fabric delivered by Fixnix's hooded men, along with the horses, well rested after their night in stables. The hoods had six of their own wrapped in fabric, lying along a grassy knoll and ready for burial. The only one still missing was Shade. Given that Serya had been captured, it was assumed he'd been killed, but no body had yet been found. Fixnix told the crofter they'd keep looking and would send word if they discovered him. Taking the dead home meant borrowing a wagon from the villagers, who seemed forlorn now that the queen-in-waiting they'd been protecting was dead. Maybe they hadn't known her long enough to love her, but Serya would have rewarded them well had she fulfilled her destiny to rule Rahamlar.

Princess Isabey watched as Sy and Mae were loaded, holding Grex by his bridle as Laec secured his saddle. People avoided talking to or even looking at Isabey, except for Calvatia, who held her for a long time while murmuring soft words.

In a quiet corner, Laec had told Jess what had happened to Serya. Jess could only shake her head. She knew Faraçek was ruthless, but she still couldn't grasp how the prince could kill his kin. Laec told her simply that Serya had been in his way. Jess thought about what Sasha had said about his queen, that the citizens of Silverfall were afraid of her, and even the weather echoed her hostile unseelie nature. So some unseelie were bent toward darkness, but the willingness to murder family for power defined a new low, even for an unseelie. Faraçek was evil.

Jess overheard the crofter asking Isabey what her wishes were, and she elected to retreat to the safety of Solana until she could decide what to do next. She would ride in front of Laec. As she settled in the saddle and Laec mounted behind her, Jess drew her mount near to Grex.

Struggling to say it in a way that didn't sound stiff or overly formal, Jess said, "I'm sorry for your loss, Princess Isabey,"

Isabey gazed at her with watery, red eyes, taking a long time to register that someone had spoken to her. "Th-thank you… Miss…"

"Jessamine, and you have already met Beazle," she gestured to where the bat sat in her collarbone, resting his wing.

"Jessamine and Beazle," Isabey repeated, dazedly. "You're Fahyli?"

"Yes, Princess."

Isabey nodded and looked away. A tear ran down one cheek. Laec clucked at Grex and they began to move. The goodbyes said to Fixnix and his hoods were perfunctory and distant. It seemed some of the villagers appreciated that the Fahyli had tried to help the princesses, while others blamed them for leading the Rahamlarin prince into their bubble of security. Nothing could be done about bad feelings. The villagers were relieved that the Fahyli were leaving and taking Isabey with them. Jess guessed they might not accept royal outcasts in the future.

When they reached the bridge, the crofter halted the party.

Isabey dismounted and—out of respect—so did the Fahyli. Isabey began to pick some sad dead wildflowers. When Jess realized what she was doing, she used her magic to conjure fresh honeysuckle, *ergeron* and moonflowers. Isabey harvested them and made a bouquet. If she knew where they'd come from, she didn't acknowledge it, but Jessamine didn't want acknowledgment. She wouldn't be sad if the young princess never turned those haunted eyes upon her again.

"What will she do now?" Jess asked Laec as she watched Isabey carry her bouquet to the bridge, the last place she'd seen her sister alive.

"I don't think she knows," murmured Laec as he sat on the ground and took off one boot to examine the cut along his calf. He wrapped a piece of silk around the wound with expert fingers. Tugging his legging over the bandage, he gingerly pulled his boot back on. As he was leaning forward, a small letter fell out of his pocket.

Jess picked it up and saw that it was addressed to Ilishec. "What's this?"

Laec got up and took the letter, tucking it inside his jacket. "It's from Calvatia. I'm just the messenger."

"Ah." Jess stroked Grex while they waited for Isabey to finish her goodbye.

"One thing is certain," Laec murmured as he straightened a twist in his stallion's bridle, "Queen Esha and King Agir do not want Faraçek on the throne. Isabey is extremely valuable: the youngest sibling, who always thought she'd be safe from the burden of the crown. The crofter says they'll arrange a search party to see if they can find Serya's body. It's proof she was murdered, but finding her won't be easy. She could be anywhere along the Tadylat or the Tamyrat by now."

Or stuck at the bottom of the whirlpool, thought Jess with a pang.

Isabey dropped the bouquet over the railing. A few more moments of silence and she returned to Laec. She thanked the crofter for stopping before she climbed into Grex's saddle. Grieved she might be, but she was still a princess.

She had to be aware that Faraçek's actions eliminated him from Rahamlar's succession. But if justice was going to be served in her kingdom, it would be up to her to enforce it. Jess could not imagine the weight of such responsibility. Isabey had lost her father to illness, one sibling to an untimely death, another to murder, and the other—while still alive, essentially also lost to her—to betrayal, all within a few months. Suddenly Jess's problems felt insignificant. Whatever life delivered, it would never compare to the challenges Isabey now faced.

Digit came over to Jess as she was preparing to mount and pulled her into an unexpected hug. "You okay? Sorry I haven't checked in. I know you had a rough night." He said quietly in her ear, "I'm glad they weren't alone, in the end."

She could only nod. She scanned Digit's face when they separated. She remembered Ian with his arm around him. Jess had thought the young Fahyli was probably pretty upset and emotional, everyone was, but looking at him now, he seemed strong and stable. His eyes were clear. "How about you?"

Digit stepped back as Ania zipped up to him out of nowhere, making an orbit around his head. "I'm alright. The crofter wants to know if you still want to stop in Nasyk on our way back?"

Jess was surprised that Ian would even give her the option after everything that had happened.

She looked around. How tired they all looked, how badly they must wish they were home already. How much must they want to give Sy and Mae a proper goodbye. There were Fahyli back in Solana City who still didn't know that they'd lost friends, and family in Tryske that didn't yet know they'd lost a son.

"No. Thank you so much, but it's not that important," she replied. "I'll visit on my own when I have time."

Jess was beginning to think there would be no answers there anyway. They'd be buried in Marion's casket forever. What she wanted more than anything was to feel Sasha's arms around her, to lay her head on his shoulder and savor doing nothing but appreciating being alive. She might even tell him about the lion, which she was beginning to credit to her own imagination.

Digit looked relieved. He went back to join Ian at the head of the group, Ania winging along beside his head. Jess noticed that Laec's perceptive eyes stayed on the young Fahyli all the way to the front.

Without any further words, the group crossed the bridge and began the journey home.

Chapter Thirty-Three

Çifta

Çifta turned the portrait of Vanda toward the flora fae so she could view it. Now that the Decennial was over, the Calyx were starting to request paintings. Vanda's eyes widened as Çifta lay the likeness down beside the one that had been done six months previously.

"You're still changing." Çifta canted her head, eying the differences. "Look at the length of your neck, and the distance from outer corner of your brow to the outer corner of your eye. See the extra tilt that wasn't there before?"

Vanda nodded. "I see it. Wow. And my hair. Is that red truly accurate?" She fingered a lock of her updo, trying to pull it in front of her face where she could see it.

"It is. Such a beautiful color, especially with your lilac eyes." Çifta shook her head with appreciation. "One would guess that you had reached your peak months ago, but one would be wrong."

"Thank you, Lady Çifta. Your talent is remarkable. Do you have time tomorrow to do Dianthus? When I show her your style…" Vanda lowered her voice so the other artists would not overhear. "I know she'll want you."

"I draw what I see." Çifta smiled. "That's the promise we make when we take the artist's role. No affectation, no impressionism, no additions or deletions. But if that is what she wishes. I have time. Will you take this to the archives, or shall I?" Çifta started putting away her paints and gathering her brushes for cleaning.

Auvo entered the tower. When he saw Çifta, he rolled his eyes like a man who had come to the end of a long frustrating journey, and arrowed for her.

"Oh, I'll do it." Vanda grinned. "I'd like to look at it a moment longer, if you don't mind."

Çifta grinned, turning toward Auvo, her hands full of artist's supplies.

"I've been looking for you everywhere but the tower. These are your off-hours, Çifta. What are you doing here?"

"I just love it."

"Well, don't burn yourself out. This career is a marathon, not a sprint." He adjusted his glasses importantly as he switched subjects. "I thought you'd like to know that the party of Fahyli has just returned, the one with the redhead from Stavarjak."

Çifta forced a calm outward appearance. "I don't know who you mean."

Auvo gave her a weary look. "Darling, no need to pretend. We all know you're lovesick for him."

Çifta mustered a sound of indignance, even as she dumped her brushes into the nearest sink and yanked on the tap. Sending droplets of water flying everywhere, she scrubbed the bristles. "I am no such thing. We are just friends."

Auvo snatched the brushes with exaggerated annoyance softened by amusement. "I'd prefer not to have my fine Tryskian horsehair brushes ruined. I'll do this. You go. Be warned, the courtyard is absolute mayhem. The Silverfae are leaving today and the groups have converged at the same time. You're lucky your man has such vivid hair or you'd have trouble spotting him."

"Thanks, Auvo." Çifta let his comment about "her man" pass. The thought of Laec as hers made her feel deliciously warm, but perhaps the possibility of any forbidden relationship did such things to a body. She rinsed her hands, hurriedly patting them dry, then headed for the door at a fast walk. The moment she was through it, she began to jog, holding her skirts up.

It wasn't only the courtyard bustling; every hall, stair and corridor had twice the usual traffic. Çifta begged to be excused and forgiven at least a dozen times as she plowed her way through the palace, barely maintaining her ladylike demeanor. Rather than going directly down the steps, she went to the balcony overlooking the courtyard from the second floor to get a view before joining the melee.

Auvo had not been exaggerating. A tangle of horses, stableboys, Fahyli, humans and fae of all kinds, some with silver-white hair, filled the courtyard with tumult. Closer to the palace steps a sea of servants, carriages, humans and fae clogged the courtyard—the Silverfae party preparing for departure. People bellowed orders or chatted with friends. Servants hauled trunks between them. Horses whinnied, either eager for the stables and rest, or to get on the road.

Near the front gate, there was a flash of red hair as Laec leaned over the side of his stallion. Her heart thrummed like a hummingbird. She raked Laec's form from head to foot, looking for injury. He appeared unharmed. She was disconcerted by the rush of relief that ran through her. He straightened, having helped a woman who had been riding with him down to the cobbles. Çifta craned for a glimpse of her but she was hidden by a couple of Fahyli.

Jessamine sat on a mare not far from Laec, looking tired and sad as she waited for enough room to dismount. Her horse was trapped against the side of a wagon by other horses.

"Laec!" Çifta called, hoping he'd hear her over the din. Çifta couldn't wait to talk to Laec and learn the fruits of their assignment, if there were fruits. She didn't know the details of the mission, but she was sure that finding the princesses had been the goal. Oh how she hoped there were fruits.

Laec didn't hear her, but someone on the steps directly below did. A richly dressed Silverfae noble looked up with disapproval, followed by a sharper analysis, likely judging her for unladylike behavior.

She headed for the stairs, joining the thick flow of

activity going up and down. Tightening her shawl about her shoulders, she stepped out the palace doors. The chilly wind took her breath away. It was the coldest since her arrival and felt properly wintry. Bracing herself for the effort it would take to cross the courtyard without getting kicked, stepped on, or backed over—and with a little shiver—she thrust herself into the sea of busywork. As she reached the cobbles she felt the disapproval of the Silverfae noble. She did not meet his eyes.

"Hey!" he called as she pushed into the crowd. "Lady!"

Pretending he was speaking to someone else, she pushed ahead, leaving him behind. A large man carrying a trunk on his shoulder crushed Çifta's foot. She squeezed her eyes shut and moaned in pain. He muttered a half-hearted apology and was swallowed by the crowd. She skirted a pair of saddled horses and dodged a crew of stableboys carrying sweaty tack. A raptor's scream made her jump. One of the horses tossed its head, buffeting her shoulder.

"Careful, Lady!" someone admonished.

Halfway across the courtyard, Çifta came face-to-face with Princess Isabey.

They halted, eyes wide. Isabey took a moment to register that she knew the woman in front of her. The princess's eyes were glassy and red, but she brightened as recognition sank in.

"Lady Çifta!" Isabey—bookended by the big Fahyli leader and another tall male with long hair—grabbed her by both shoulders. "You look splendid. Oh, I'm so glad to see you!"

Çifta had no time to curtsy or even start a proper greeting before Isabey yanked her forward and crushed her in a back-breaking hug.

"Oh! Oh, Princess," Çifta murmured as she felt Isabey's body shaking. Something was terribly wrong. Isabey was crying into her neck. Çifta looked up at the crofter, alarmed. The Fahyli waited quietly for the young princess to collect herself, their expressions heavy and sad.

"Darling." Çifta held the young woman close, thoughts of etiquette as far away as her former life.

From the sound of Isabey's sobs, it seemed that her heart had been smashed into a million pieces. It struck Çifta like a cold splash of water and her heart felt suddenly hollow. Whatever had happened, had to do with Serya. What else could make Isabey fall apart like this?

Çifta looked at the Fahyli, still holding Isabey and unable to contain her need to know. "What's happened? Where is Princess Serya?"

They exchanged a look but didn't answer. Isabey's trembling diminished and she sniffed. She released Çifta and withdrew, the most miserable look Çifta had ever seen on her face.

The princess's voice quavered. "It was Faraçek… I cannot believe it, Çifta. He… m-murdered her." A fresh wave of tears came. "He k-killed my sister, and t-took Toryan's C-crown."

Çifta was not surprised, somehow. She already believed Faraçek was capable of sororicide, and worse. She tried to block out horrible images of how Faraçek might have done the deed, but ideas flew at her like a flock of screaming starlings. Çifta didn't know what Toryan's Crown was, but it clearly wasn't good that it was in the possession of the prince.

Deep down, there was a tiny sliver of… not quite pleasure, but something close enough to it to flush her with shame. Esha and Agir would be displeased to learn of what Faraçek had done. So would other rulers. The unseelie prince had pushed his relationships with other monarchs from tenuous ally to despised enemy. This would surely—and finally—relieve Çifta of her father's pigheaded commitment. She could not prevent these thoughts, but cursed herself for being selfish. Poor Isabey, poor Serya. They did not deserve this.

Çifta took Isabey by her forearms, the same way they had grasped one another in what seemed like a lifetime ago in the Rahamlar courtyard. "Princess, if it is the final thing that I do on this earth, I will see you on Rahamlar's throne."

Isabey looked startled. The crofter and Fahyli nodded in agreement.

"You are not alone, Princess," said the crofter. "There are many who will promise the same. I know the loss of your sister can hardly be borne, but you will heal in time. Do not despair."

"Th-thank you," murmured Isabey, wiping at her eyes. She looked unable to process the meaning behind such words. What lay ahead of her. "I am so tired."

Çifta released her. "I'll find you later. Rest now, Princess."

When they moved on, Çifta went up on tiptoe to

locate Laec again. The press in the courtyard eased a little as the wagon was moved away, but now the Silverfae group was filling in the gaps as more of them emerged from the palace. Çifta caught a flash of red as Laec moved toward the stables, leading Grex. If she wasn't mistaken, Laec was walking with a limp. Beside him, leading her own mare was Jessamine.

She surged toward them, her way a little easier now. As she closed the distance, a striking Silverfae male with long white hair and powerful shoulders approached Jessamine from behind. He caught up to her and touched her shoulder. When she turned, Jessamine's expression could not be described: she grasped the man's forearm, hard, almost desperately. Çifta tried to avert her eyes, embarrassed at what was so obviously lover's passion, but the sight was too compelling.

"Sasha," Jessamine choked out his name, then in a hushed voice: "Are you really leaving today? It is exactly what I feared."

"I meant what I promised," he returned solemnly. His pale eyes—much like Çifta's own—were full of Jessamine and only Jessamine.

Laec had continued walking, either pretending not to see their exchange or too lost in his own thoughts to notice.

Skirting Jess's horse, Çifta came up along Grex and grasped Laec's sleeve.

Laec turned weary eyes, then melted in a smile. He did exactly what her heart had been yearning for since she'd seen him last: pulled her into a hug and buried his nose in her hair. He smelled of leather and trees and sweat and fresh air. Her chest hitched. She would die without the scent of him in her life every day.

They shouldn't be holding each other this way, it was far too intimate, but Grex offered them a little privacy, and she was beyond caring anyway. She could never get away with such behavior in the courtyards of Boskaya—but in Solana? Perhaps no one would tell her father, perhaps they would have that much discretion.

"Princess Serya is dead." Laec looked down at her.

Her fingers tangled in the fabric of his tunic. "I saw Isabey before they took her inside. Poor thing. My heart is broken for her."

He nodded. "Let me see to Grex and bathe. Meet me in an hour, at the alcoves near the library? I'll tell you everything."

"Of course. But are you alright? I thought you were limping."

"Just a scratch. I'm fine. I promise."

She watched Laec lead Grex away, admiring everything about the pair. Even exhausted, they moved with grace and confidence. When they disappeared through a stable door, Çifta turned toward the palace. Jessamine and Sasha were still talking in hushed tones, their expressions fraught with some intimate conflict. Çifta wondered if they had the same kind of relationship that she had with Laec, and pitied them. She looked away, heading for the steps.

Sasha looked at her briefly as she neared, then turned back to Jessamine. But his gaze flashed back to Çifta as though caught by a hook, widening with something like horror. So strong was it, that Çifta halted, returning his stare.

He recognized her, obviously, but she was sure she'd not seen him before. She was about to ask if they knew each other, when Jess spoke.

"Sasha, what is it?"

She followed his gaze, seeing Çifta for the first time. "Oh, hello. I'm sorry I didn't realize you were here… let me introduce you. Sasha, this is Lady Çifta, one of my friends. You've not met because Çifta did not attend the Midwinter dances…"

Sasha's icy eyes were locked on her own, his expression eerie, even haunted. "Daughter of winter—" he whispered hoarsely.

Goosebumps sprang out on her body. Laec's long ago assertion that her mother had to be Silverfae came rushing back to her, frothing like a wave. "What did you say?" she gasped.

"Lady!" someone bellowed from across the courtyard.

As though she'd fallen into a dream that made no sense, Çifta looked to see the Silverfae noble she had passed earlier. Everyone in the courtyard stopped, frozen in mid-activity. Even the horses and familiars seemed locked in a tableau. Hundreds of eyes turned to the Silverfae, his hand going for the sword at his hip. Çifta could not process what she was seeing. There had to be a mistake. Who were these Silverfae who thought they knew her? Why was one of them bearing down upon her, eyes bristling with murder.

Sasha turned to see his kin, expression overwrought. "Prince Ruskin! No!"

Çifta blinked. Prince?

"Wait," she said to no one, her pulse going jagged. "What's happening?" Çifta was unable to tear her eyes from the beautifully dressed Silverfae—apparently a prince—coming straight for her, his sword flashing. That was a real blade he wielded, not a toy.

She took a step back, but didn't really believe he would attack her. There had to be some kind of mistake. Someone would step in, fix this. Surely.

But no one was. They were all too frozen in shock.

"Who are you, sir?" she yelled, infusing her voice with authority, trying to get attention, and some bloody aid! "Please stop!"

Sasha turned to Çifta and hissed, "Run!"

Chapter Thirty-Four

Jessamine

JESS FELT LIKE her mind had stopped working. How to interpret what she was seeing? Prince Ruskin was bearing down, his frozen glare fixed on Lady Çifta, his curved sword reflecting the morning sunlight. There wasn't a soul in the courtyard who had not stopped to watch in fascination as Ruskin ate up the cobblestones between himself and Çifta with long, determined strides. Jess grabbed Sasha by the sleeve but his attention was on Çifta. She heard him tell Çifta to run.

Sasha's plea shocked Jess to the soles of her boots. Run? Surely someone should interfere?

He's going to kill her, Beazle observed sleepily.

He cannot, Jess returned. *In front of everyone? He'll be hanged!*

Not likely. He is a prince.

That's not... no. He can't just... he wouldn't!

"Prince Ruskin," Jess

called, hoping her words penetrated, reminded him that he was a guest here, and had an audience. "Have you met my friend, Lady Çifta of Boskaya?"

Surely the prince would realize he'd mistaken her for someone else. Surely, he would come to his senses. Surely a conversation was in order before he used that blade for anything. Failing that, Sasha would step in.

Çifta took a step back, then another, her expression telegraphing disbelief, the hope that this was a prank. She did not truly believe she was in any real danger.

"Your Grace, please don't," Sasha begged.

Horror and shock rushed in on Jess. How could Sasha not act? How could *she* not act? Even if she could use poison without risking those around her, she was forbidden from violence toward nobility of any kind, domestic or foreign, upon pain of death. What to do?

It was as if Sasha hadn't spoken to the prince at all.

Ruskin was steps away. Çifta put her palms out. The prince lifted his sword.

A single blow from that thing would cleave her in two.

As Ruskin lifted his blade, Sasha stepped closer to Çifta, his long-fingered hands forming stiff claws.

There was a flash of light, and a series of cracking sounds.

Jess was blasted by a powerful gust of freezing cold air. Ice pellets raked her cheeks. She hid her face and fought to maintain her footing, stumbling against her mare's shoulder. The mare whinnied and shied sideways but kept steady enough to keep Jess from falling.

A heavy silence came over the courtyard.

She opened her eyes, cringing.

Where Lady Çifta had been, stood a jagged block of ice. Ruskin's sword was stuck in one corner of it, more than half buried. Ruskin stared at it, confounded. Then the prince gave a scream of rage unlike anything Jessamine had ever heard. Though Sasha was armed, he did not reach for his sword.

"What have you done?" Prince Ruskin yanked at his sword, trying to dislodge it from the ice. "Traitor! You bastard deceiver! I'll have your life! Sorcerer's whelp! Dog! Traitor!"

The commotion had drawn a larger audience; bodies gathered at windows. Someone gave an order to fetch Captain Bradburn and Ian Peneçek. No one moved to step between Ruskin and Sasha. No one wanted to interfere between a Silverfall prince and his subject. The other Silverfae watched the unfolding drama with as much wide-eyed surprise and terror as everyone else.

"My prince." Sasha held his palms up in surrender, his tone was placating, as though trying to calm a rabid animal. "You can't know for certain that she is the one you seek!"

Still yanking on the sword, now with a booted foot braced on the ice, Prince Ruskin seethed and roared. Spittle flew from his lips. He looked insane with rage.

"I sentence you to death for your interference. Here and now! You will breathe your last today. Your end will come at my hand. You should have been killed when your father betrayed us!" He tugged fruitlessly on his sword. "Blast this demon's work!"

Ruskin gave up on the sword and—fists curled, eyes hot with malice—went for Sasha. Sasha ducked the first and second blows, then danced sideways, moving like a liquid, drawing Ruskin away from Jess. Ruskin pursued, landing clumsy blows on Sasha's shoulder and chest.

"Be still, I command it!" Ruskin screamed, whaling punches and kicks as he followed Sasha across the courtyard. People moved out of the way like a flock of frightened turkeys as the white prince delivered retribution. Sasha lifted his forearms to cover his head. The sound of his punches and Sasha's grunts filled the courtyard.

Jess screamed, "Stop it!"

Others joined in after her, including Silverfae.

"Stop, please. Your Highness!"

"My prince! Do not do this!"

Sasha took blow after blow. When Ruskin stopped for a breath, Sasha lifted his head. Silver blood poured from a split lip. One eye was already swollen.

Unable to bear it, Jess ran for Sasha, unsheathing her dagger. Strong arms snaked around her waist. She was yanked back against a solid chest.

"You cannot!" Regalis hissed in her ear. "You *must* not interfere. You risk your life!"

"Let me go!" Jess kicked back at him.

Regalis locked her foot between his calves, hobbling her. "This has nothing to do with us, Jess. You are Fahyli! Behave like one!"

As Ruskin beat Sasha, Jess heard a choking sound from nearby.

Laec stood beside the block of ice, palms against it,

peering at the shape inside like a boy at a window. He moved to the lodged blade, running a hand over it as if to prove to himself it was real. His huge fae eyes were like hollows in his face. He looked blankly over at Ruskin and Sasha, not really registering the violence, then ran his hands over the ice again.

Still struggling, Jess called, "Laec! Do something!"

But he only had eyes for Çifta.

Ruskin's blows had not ceased. Sasha was on his knees, his arms over his head.

"Please, let me go Regalis," she begged, tears pouring down her face.

A long, keening, high-pitched howl filled the air and the entire courtyard went still. All the hair on Jess's body went painfully stiff.

Prince Ruskin stopped punching to look around. Sasha kept his head covered. When further blows didn't come, one huge white-irised eye peeked out.

A growling, snapping white streak exploded into the courtyard. A terrifyingly massive wolf skidded into a turn, hindquarters swinging, claws raking the stones. She stopped, ribs heaving, looking at Ruskin. She lowered her head, snapping her jaws, eyes filled with hate. Saliva dripped from her mouth.

Everyone in the courtyard inhaled. Jess's stomach roiled with a dizzying combination of gratitude and dread. *She frightens the horses.* Rialta.

Ruskin's eyes widened as the wolf charged. Whirling, he grabbed for the sword at Sasha's hip. There was a ripping sound as he yanked it free, tearing the scabbard from the belt.

Sasha lifted his battered face. "Rialta, no!"

Ruskin unsheathed Sasha's blade, hefted it and, a split second after the wolf leapt, brought the blade to bear with frightful force. Jessamine wasn't the only one who screamed when the sword bit into Rialta's shoulder, but the direwolf didn't even yelp. As bright red blood stained her beautiful white fur, she snaked her nose under Ruskin's arm. Closing her immense jaw over his throat, she bore him to the ground.

Sasha scrambled forward, trying to push Rialta off Ruskin. To stop her though, he would have to hurt her, and he was unable to harm his own already wounded familiar. Blood pooled on the cobblestones, red blending with silver. Ruskin thrashed and kicked at Rialta's belly. Her rear claws scored the cobblestones as she drove forward, her jaw working.

Ruskin's cries were abruptly cut off.

The conflict felt like it had gone on for days, yet mere seconds had passed. Her mind whirled as Jess fought to clear her vision of her tears. Regalis loosened his grip and released her trapped foot.

Sasha's bloody blade lay on the cobblestones beyond the prince's hand.

Prince Ruskin was still for several long moments before Rialta relaxed her jaw. When she backed away, the snarling nightmare of a direwolf was gone. She had the look of a shamed dog. She licked her bloody lips, then tried to lick Sasha's face, whining. With a hand on Rialta's neck, Sasha knelt at Ruskin's head, his own head bowed in defeat. Rialta was visibly trembling now, pressing her forehead into Sasha's chest and whining. The sound was pitiful. Slowly, like in a dream, Sasha wrapped his arms around his wolf, burying his bruised face in her ruff. Blood poured from her wound.

The sight electrified Jessamine. Ripping a long swatch from her tunic, she ran toward them. Rialta heard her coming and turned her huge head with a snarl that froze Jess in place. A soft murmur from Sasha and the wolf swallowed her growl with another whine. She sniffed at her wound, then tried with modest success to lick her injury. Moving slowly, Jess held the fabric toward the wound, suggesting she use it to stanch the flow of blood. But when Rialta's lip curled, she drew back. Turning to Sasha, she wiped away some of the blood from his nose and mouth, amazed by its pearly appearance. He lifted his gaze to hers, finally. His eyes were filled with misery.

"I didn't want this." His voice was tremulous. "I only wanted to protect her."

Unable to bear his suffering, Jessamine wrapped her arms around him.

Out of the corner of her eye, she caught sight of Laec, his palms and the side of his face pressed against the big block of ice. Inside it, the shape of a woman could barely be seen.

Chapter Thirty-Five

Laec

THE AIR OUTSIDE the Lion's Den stank of stress and fear—coming from the press of bodies and a sea of upset faces. People were arguing over the true version of events, a few of the Silverfae were weeping. Laec pushed and shoved his way through the cluster of upset Silverfae and Solanan citizens to get to the doors, where four soldiers stood guard, stoic and solid.

"Let me in please, I have relevant information," Laec said to the nearest soldier, lifting his voice so he'd be heard over the din. "I'm expected."

"By whom?" the guard asked, flicking his gaze over Laec's face.

"The gardener."

Laec reached into his tunic and pulled out the letter from Calvatia, holding it so the guard could read Ilishec's name in Calvatia's scrawl. The letter was neither relevant to the proceedings inside the room, nor was Laec expected, but the guard didn't know that. When the guard lifted a hand to take the letter, Laec pulled it back.

"I must deliver it personally."

The guard gave a surly nod and turned to his neighbor to relay Laec's request. The neighbor knocked on the judas window, and when it slid open spoke to someone on the other side. Laec was made to wait for several long minutes. Finally the guard shuffled over and the door was opened just wide enough for Laec to slip inside. The crowd surged forward and the guards had to cross their spears and push back to keep others from following Laec.

Inside the Lion's Den was another crowd, standing in loose groups around the low dais—the two marble stools empty and waiting. Captain Bradburn and the crofter stood on either side of the dais, faces impassive. A few Silverfae had been allowed into the room—a little cluster of white heads among a sea of dark ones—those who had shown themselves capable of keeping their emotions under control. Their faces were fraught, a few were mutinous.

The air was thick with tautly held emotions and stank of both blood and sweat.

Keeping close to the rear wall, Laec strained to look over the heads of Silverfae, Fahyli and others. He spotted Ilishec to the left of the dais beside the crofter. As he shuffled his way over, Laec spotted Sasha kneeling on the floor, his head hanging, glossy white hair hiding his face. Rialta, a bandage wrapped around her great shoulders, lay at his side, her jaw and neck flat on the floor, ears nailed to her skull. Guarding—or protecting, depending on one's point of view—Sasha and Rialta were two mastiffs, and Tully. Panther and other Fahyli were not far away. Jessamine stood between Digit and Regalis. Her eyes looked huge and tormented, and the muscles in her jaw were flexing like she was grinding her teeth. Beazle wasn't visible.

Laec nudged his uncle in the arm and held out the letter. With a start, the gardener turned glazed eyes on his nephew. He stared at the letter for a long moment before registering what he was seeing. He looked up. "Calvatia?"

Laec nodded.

Ilishec took the letter and opened it as the guards let one of the Silverfae entourage into the room, a mature female with a thick white braid hanging over one shoulder. Her face was pale and set, her brow dewy with moisture. Her white-pupiled eyes were red-rimmed and glassy, but focused. She wore an empty scabbard—only Fahyli and Solanan guards were allowed to wear arms in the Lion's Den.

The gardener scanned the letter, and Laec heard him take a sharp sip of air. His head jerked back like he'd been slapped.

"Everything alright?" Laec asked.

"No. Not remotely." Ilishec refolded the letter and shoved it in a pocket. "I'll fill you in after."

There was a murmur of discontent from the crowd outside the room, followed by thumps of bodies against paneling, and a few louder protests and pleas.

Someone yelled, "They're killers, Highness!"

Another cried, "Our prince! Murdered on Solanan ground, Sire! Murdered!"

The door opened, and Captain Bradburn announced: "His Royal Highness, King Agir." Everyone genuflected as the king entered at a brisk pace, surrounded by a cordon of soldiers.

The mood in the room shifted, a feeling that now something would be done, sense would be made of the horror and chaos that had occurred. Now, justice would prevail. People whispered and jostled as they made a semi-circle around the dais.

From the look on King Agir's face, he'd been told—in broad strokes at least—what had happened in the courtyard. Agir stepped up on the dais, and sat without ceremony or drama. He shifted to move his cape from beneath his hip, giving Bradburn a nod.

Captain Bradburn gestured to the Silverfae woman waiting patiently at the front of the crowd. She stepped forward and bowed, unusual for a female, but she was wearing trousers and a tailored jacket.

"Sire, good King Agir," she said, her voice clear and steady. "My name is Rayven Sabran of Silverfall. I am second cousin to Prince Ruskin and have been chosen by the Silverfall entourage to present our petition."

"You have my ear, Miss Sabran," said Agir. "What is your request?"

"Thank you, Sire. Prince Ruskin was killed in the front courtyard of your palace only three hours ago, by two of our own citizens. The citizens you now hold in your custody"—she gestured but did not look at them—"Sasha and Rialta Drazek. We deeply regret these events, and offer our sincere apologies to you, Sire, to your wife the queen, and to the citizens of Solana. Our entreaty is simple. This is a matter of Silverfall concern, and we ask that you transfer custody of these criminals to us, and allow us to rid your kingdom of the expense and nuisance of dealing with them. Prince Ruskin was Queen Sylifke's only child. We must return to Silverfall with Prince Ruskin's body and her son's killers, to be tried by our judges in our courts."

A murmur of discontent swept the room, but the Silverfae were nodding their agreement.

"Silence, please," said King Agir, and the room hushed immediately. "Miss Sabran, were you present when these events took place?"

Rayven lifted her chin. "I was in the courtyard, Sire. Yes."

"And did you see everything that happened?"

"I—" She paused and swallowed. "Not everything, Sire. I was half inside the foyer when I heard a lot of shouting, and the crowd was thick. I ran outside but I could not tell what was going on, and at first I didn't realize it involved our prince. When I arrived at his side he was already dead, and it was obvious who had ended his life. I daresay one look at them is enough to condemn them, let alone the testimony of hundreds of witnesses."

"Be that as it may, Miss Sabran, we are not accustomed to condemning people after one look, and testimonies can vary." King Agir looked grim. "I have personally experienced this in the last few hours. I was told by another witness, one who was in the courtyard when the conflict began, that Prince Ruskin had been about to kill one of our visitors, and that Sasha stepped between them and foiled him with Silverfae magic. After that, Prince Ruskin took to beating Sasha, who did not defend himself against his prince, but took blow after blow. It was the wolf who used lethal force."

"Regardless of the details, Sire," said Rayven confidently, "the Silverfall heir is dead, and it is clear who the killer was."

The king was unmoved. "It is not the purpose of this gathering to determine what should be done with Sasha and Rialta. It is the purpose of this gathering to determine who should take responsibility for what must happen next."

"Yes, Sire. It was not a Solanan citizen who died, and it was not a Solanan citizen who did the killing. Therefore we humbly propose—"

"But it happened on Solanan soil," interrupted the king. "Before Solanan witnesses. On my very own courtyard stones. This is my jurisdiction, Miss Sabran. We have laws in place, even for such unusual matters. I require time to confer with my lawyers and ministers."

"Sire, we do not have time." Rayven's tone took on an edge. "We are expected back in Silverfall. Can you not make your decision swiftly, so that we may leave at once?"

"You may leave at once," replied Agir. "I will send a letter when I have made my decision."

The room went quiet, so quiet that Laec heard Rayven swallow.

"Forgive me, Sire. This is not… but I… this is urgent, Your Grace. If we return to Queen Sylifke with Prince Ruskin's body, but without them…"

"Queen Sylifke understands jurisdictional sovereignty, does she not?"

"Of course, Sire, but—"

"Then she will be content to wait, as I would be content to wait if the situation were reversed." King Agir's voice was strong but not unkind. "I am very sorry about what has occurred, and I intend to understand these events as much as they can be understood. Can you shed light on why your prince tried to murder a foreign lady in my yard? A lady who may or may not survive what has become of her, but who would most certainly not have survived your prince's sword? Can you explain this to me?"

"I…" Rayven shifted uncomfortably. "No, I can't, Sire. If Prince Ruskin could speak, I know he would have adequate reason… I mean, he could explain himself."

The king lifted a finger. "But he cannot speak. And you cannot speak for him. And given that you were elected to represent your entourage, I can only assume that you know more about this matter than any other Silverfae here today. Yet you can explain nothing." King Agir looked at those watching. "Can anyone else explain anything to me?"

"If I may speak, Sire."

King Agir's gaze sharpened on the long-haired Fahyli. "Regalis. Were you there?"

"Yes, Sire. If the Silverfae can make a petition, then perhaps you will allow your own citizens a petition about this matter as well."

There were murmurs of agreement from the crowd at this.

"Speak."

Regalis took half a step forward. "I cannot explain why Prince Ruskin attacked Lady Çifta, but I can say with confidence that when Ruskin turned on Sasha, Sasha did not fight back, he did not raise a hand to his prince, and he did not defend himself, as his wounds may attest."

"It's true," someone said from a corner of the room. "I saw it. It was as the Fahyli has said. I'll second his petition."

"The lad did nothing but try to save the girl," someone else called.

"He set his familiar on the prince," snapped Rayven, color rising in her pale cheeks. "Everyone in Silverfall knows that Rialta and Sasha are as good as one entity. He did not fight back with his own body, he fought back *through her*! *Of course* he would not raise his own hand against Prince Ruskin. He knows that Rialta—here in a foreign kingdom—could potentially be excused because she is an animal, with nothing more than a beast's intellect and instincts. He could claim that she became enraged when her fae was beaten, that she attacked the prince of her own accord. But we in Silverfall know better."

Regalis directed his opinion calmly to the king. "Respectfully, Sasha was heard prevailing upon Rialta to stop. It was heard by many present. And those of us with familiars could never be misled into believing that a familiar is nothing more than an animal—"

"With a beast's intellect…" Kite snarled, her eyes flashing with fire.

"Kite," warned the crofter, and the Fahyli averted her gaze to the floor.

"It was a ruse," cried Rayven. "He's got you all deluded. He is a deceiver, with a deceiver's blood. You don't know him like we know him. He is a Drazek, the son of Elvio the betrayer."

"If he is so untrustworthy," said the king, "why was he part of your entourage?"

Rayven's jaw opened but nothing came out. The king's brows rose as he waited for her response.

Finally, she spoke, flushing with embarrassment. "I-I was not party to the rationale behind that decision, Sire. But, please, you must see that they should be returned to Silverfall to be dealt with!"

"I must see nothing," interjected the king. "And be careful with your demands, for you are in my court, subject to my rules, Miss Sabran."

Sasha had kept his face down during the exchange, but he now lifted his head a little. One eye was swollen shut, but the other flicked to Rayven, then it rolled up and he swayed forward, as though drunk. Rialta whined and lifted her nose to touch his face.

"Have care," the crofter said to the Fahyli.

Rialta shuffled in front of her fae, cushioning Sasha he drooped forward. He landed on her neck, limp and unconscious. Jessamine tried to bolt for him, but Laec saw Regalis restrain her as Panther and Kite went swiftly to Sasha's side.

Realization came to Laec: Jess had feelings for Sasha that went far beyond friendship. He almost groaned aloud, and chastised himself for not noticing sooner. She'd been with Sasha when Laec had found them hiding behind a potted plant—just the two of them, leaning as close as if they were lovers—and she'd been the first to get to Sasha after Ruskin was killed. Laec had been so shocked to find Çifta encased in ice that he hadn't registered anyone else's suffering, but now some of the details of the moment came back to him.

He glanced at Ilishec but the gardener seemed too preoccupied by his own thoughts to notice Jess's wretchedness. Whatever had been in Calvatia's letter, it disturbed Ilishec even more than what was happening in the Lion's Den.

"Is he conscious?" King Agir asked, his tone sharp.

"No, Sire," replied Panther, bent over Sasha's form. "Out cold."

"Damn it, Bradburn!" the king snapped, showing the first signs of strained temper. "What are they even doing here? They're not in any shape for this. This is not a trial. Take them to the infirmary. We don't do things this way in Solana. We are not barbarians."

There was a flurry of activity as Sasha and Rialta were taken from the room—Sasha on a stretched out piece of tapestry, and Rialta limping heavily, braced by Tully and the mastiffs. They were so surrounded that they could hardly be seen. One of the Silverfae hissed as the group passed. Out in the hall there was yelling and thudding as people were moved out of the way, then the doors were shut once more.

King Agir gave a long weary sigh and rubbed his forehead. "Miss Sabran, your petition is denied. You can see for yourself that they are not in any shape to travel, which makes my decision easy. Even if they were, I feel too pressed and this is no small matter. You say you cannot delay, so I suggest you go. Before you prepare the prince for travel, I am sure you will not protest my coroners documenting the wounds on his body for our records. I will send a letter with the reasons for my decision for you to deliver into Queen Sylifke's hands."

"Sire, you do not understand." Rayven's expression edged toward panic. "Queen Sylifke, she will be…"

"Devastated? Angry? Aggrieved? I would expect nothing less. She, and all of Silverfall, have our sympathies. You are all dismissed."

The king rose, everyone genuflected and held their positions until the king was out of the room. As Laec straightened, he noticed Rayven was the only one not shuffling toward the door. She stared at the floor, her throat moving as she swallowed. She seemed unable to believe the outcome.

As news of the king's decision reached the Silverfae outside the room, voices murmured in protest. Inside, the Silverfae clustered together in an unhappy group, whispering and muttering among themselves.

Laec approached Rayven. He'd never had a good feeling about Ruskin, but even a selfish royal didn't deserve the death he'd been dealt. "I'm sorry for your loss, Miss Sabran."

Rayven looked up at him with tormented eyes. "Not as sorry as we Silverfae shall be when we arrive home."

Laec didn't know what to say to that. An awkward

beat of silence passed. "I do have to ask you something." He took a breath. "Will she live?"

Rayven looked blank. "Who?"

"Lady Çifta, the woman locked in the ice. Will she survive?"

"Oh." She turned and moved slowly toward her kinsmen. "I never got a look at her. Does she have Silverfae blood?"

Laec hesitated. Çifta had denied it, but she did possess those striking Silverfae eyes, and Laec felt certain that Sasha believed Çifta had Silverfae blood or he wouldn't have frozen her in the first place. "I believe so. Half, anyway."

"Then it's not probable. I'm sorry but Sasha may have frozen her for nothing." Rayven's tone was monotone, indifferent. She had bigger concerns.

Laec felt like she'd thrust a blade straight into his gut. He caught her arm. "But there's a chance?"

"The odds for full-blooded Silverfae to survive the ice are about half. Why do you think so few of us choose it? What odds do you think that leaves a half-blood? Excuse me. I must go." She pulled out of his grasp and strode away. But just as abruptly, she rounded back on him with suddenly ravenous eyes. "Do *you* know why Prince Ruskin wanted to kill this woman? You were her friend, right?"

Laec looked at her, sadness welling up in his heart. "I wish I did. How will we explain this to her father?"

With a single jerk of her chin, she left the room.

Laec stood for a minute, thinking. He was glad that Sasha and Rialta had some level of sanctuary here, at least for now. He felt sure that Sasha knew something, and had he not fainted a critical piece of information may have been shared.

Laec looked around for Ilishec, but he'd slipped out, so Laec headed to the gardens. The upset crowd had dispersed, but every servant Laec passed had a wrinkled brow and downturned lips. There was no one in Solana palace who had not either seen what had happened, or heard about it from someone who was there. *What a way to wrap up the Decennial,* Laec thought. This Midwinter Festival would go down in history, but for all the wrong reasons.

Laec found Ilishec in his workshop giving orders to a group of under-gardeners and a few Calyx. This group looked even worse off than the Solanan servants. Each held what looked like empty glass boxes under their arms. There was a trunk on the floor filled with more of the same boxes.

"...for pride's sake," the gardener was begging, "please be careful! We don't want them any more frightened than they're already bound to be. I don't want a single feather or wing damaged."

Laec stood aside as the group left the workshop. He went to the trunk and picked up one of the glass boxes. It had holes drilled in one side and a simple hook and nail clasp to keep it closed.

"What's going on, uncle?"

Ilishec took a kerchief from his back pocket and wiped his waxy brow. "It's a nasty business, Laec. Nasty. We have to quarantine the familiars."

Laec's eyes widened. "All of them?"

"Just the insects." He tried to shove the kerchief into his breast pocket but it fell to the floor. He didn't notice. He handed Laec Calvatia's letter with a trembling hand.

"Read it for yourself."

Putting down the box, Laec took the letter into the light and read aloud.

"My dearest Ilishec, I am sorry that the events that reconnected us were not happier, for I have very disturbing news. Based on what you explained in your letter about Moony, he was exposed to a dangerous fungal parasite called *cordyceps*. This parasite takes time to infect an insect's brain, but it is deadly and there is no cure. Any insect who was around Moony in the days before he began to behave strangely must be quarantined. This is critical and urgent. If none of the other insects are showing signs of illness, they may yet be in the clear, but it is better to be safe. Quarantine them for a week. If they appear healthy after that, they may be freed. But you must find the source and destroy it, or it will surely kill again."

Laec looked at Ilishec with horror.

Ilishec nodded and took a gulp of water from a cup sitting near a stack of open books. "I know. And that's not the worst of it. I've already discovered the source and its worse than you could possibly imagine."

Laec raised a brow.

"It's Prince Faraçek. He's flora fae, Laec," Ilishec ground out.

Laec felt as though his blood had turned to ice. He thought he'd misheard, and shook his head. "What?"

"He has no familiar, so no one ever guessed. He has

no familiar because he is the enemy of insects. He is lethal to them. I've been reading…" Ilishec tapped frantically on the open pages of one of the books. "*Cordyceps*, infects an insect's mind and takes over its body. It forces them to climb as high as they can while they are still alive. When they've reached the highest place, they die. After that, spores grow out of the body. When they're mature, they burst into the air and spread, infecting any insect that is nearby. Then the cycle begins again."

Laec's skin was crawling. He rubbed his arms. "But humans and fae are immune?"

"They're immune to *cordyceps* in the wild, yes. It's only deadly to insects. However, based on what Lady Çifta told us, I believe Faraçek's magic gives him some level of mind-control over larger entities, the same way Jessamine's magic helps her find lost items. Lady Çifta said that Faraçek somehow made her unable to fight back, hardly able even to think, and she even believes he might have been able to force her to marry him, had she not been rescued. How else could he have exerted such power over her but through his flora magic?"

"Oh, this is bad." Laec sat on the workshop table, rubbing his temples. But then he straightened as though electrocuted, eyes nearly popping out. The thought rose in his mind like a sea monster from deep waters: *Toryan's Crown.* What if the legend was true? What if it really was waiting for Toryan's heir? For someone who was as evil as she was? The ugly little circlet was in Faraçek's hands. What if it magnified his powers?

Queen Elphame's premonition came thundering back

to him: *I have foreseen trouble for Solana. I cannot see the shape of this threat, but it is dark and it is persistent.*

"What?" Ilishec was alarmed by the look on Laec's face. "What is it?"

With great effort, Laec wrestled his features into some semblance of his usual calm arrogance. Ilishec had enough on his mind, Laec wouldn't burden him by reminding him of Elphame's vague forebodings of doom. Nothing was certain.

"It's alright, uncle. Not to worry." He put a hand on Ilishec's shoulder. "I'm overdue to write a report to my queen. Let me get that out of the way, then I'll come back and help with the quarantine."

Ilishec looked relieved. "Thank you, lad. If you're sure. I haven't yet spoken to all the Calyx, and I'm dreading it. We're going to have to comb every inch of the gardens for infected insects."

"Of course. I'll be back soon and will be at your service." Laec squeezed his uncle's shoulder and left the workshop.

Epilogue

Laec

Your Royal Highness Queen Elphame,

Forgive me for the lengthy time between reports. It has not been without excellent reasons, as you will see.

The present state of affairs in Solana are as follows:

- *Prince Faraçek is a flora fae with a connection to cordyceps, a fungus that is deadly to insects. Lady Çifta believes he used this magic on her, so we have evidence that it is dangerous to other beings as well—mind control being of particular concern.*
- *Although not legal according to Rahamlar's laws, I believe Faraçek plans to crown himself with Toryan's circlet, which is said to have been waiting for an heir to bequeath its powers upon.*
- *Faraçek believes that Princess Isabey is dead, but she is sequestered here at Solana Palace.*

- Princess Isabey is the legal heir—Faraçek being guilty of sororicide—and the Rahamlar royal that Agir and Esha would much rather have on the throne, but the young lady's intentions are unclear as she is grieving for her sister. Enforcing her right could trigger a war. Will she find the courage and strength to interfere with her brother's plan?
- Prince Ruskin of Silverfall is dead, killed by a familiar (a direwolf named Rialta) of one of his own citizens (Sasha Drazek). He was Queen Sylifke's only child.
- Sasha and Rialta have been given sanctuary in Solana but await trial.
- The vendetta Ruskin had against Çifta makes no sense to anyone. At this point we believe it to be a case of mistaken identity. When Sasha is recovered, perhaps he will disabuse us of this notion.
- Prince Ruskin's entourage of Silverfae have left, in a state of extreme upset, taking the prince's body with them. We do not know how Queen Sylifke will react when she is told what befell her son.
- To protect her from Ruskin's sword, Sasha froze Lady Çifta in ice. We are hopeful that she remains alive, and will survive its thaw, thanks to her possible Silverfae heritage, but it is not certain.
- Lady Çifta's father, Kazery Unya, is due back in Solana soon. He is not yet aware of his daughter's predicament.

So, my queen, the darkness you foresaw for Solana appears to be taking shape. The kingdom is in a state of shock and your cousin Esha could use your advice, should you wish to offer any. I await additional commands. If there are none, I shall continue to be your eyes and ears.

Your loyal servant,

Laec Fairijak

The epic fable continues with

A DAUGHTER OF WINTER

The Scented Court

BOOK 3

Printed in Great Britain
by Amazon

57557622R10255